Between Faith and Criticism

Evangelicals, Scholarship, and the Bible

Mark A. Noll

 APOLLOS

APOLLOS (an imprint of Inter-Varsity Press),
38 De Montfort Street, Leicester LEI 7GP, England.

First edition published 1986 by Harper & Row, USA.
Second edition published 1991 by Baker Book House, USA.

First published in Great Britain in 1991.

Acknowledgment is made for the following: Excerpts from "Fundamentalist
Renascence" by Arnold W. Hearn. Copyright 1958 Christian Century Foundation.
Reprinted by permission from the 30.4.85 issue of *The Christian Century.* Excerpts
from "Evangelical Disagreements about the Bible" by R. T. France, reprinted from
the *Churchman* 97 (1982): 236–68. Used by permission.

British Library Cataloguing in Publication Data
A catalogue record for this book is available from the British Library.

ISBN 0-85111-425-3

Typeset and printed in the United States of America.

To Bob and Jo Ann Harvey,
Servants of the Word of God

Contents

Tables

Acknowledgments

Many individuals and organizations generously assisted in the writing of this book. I am pleased to acknowledge their often indispensable assistance, while at the same time exonerating them from all blame. A number of comments on an earlier essay that first tried out some of the themes in this book sharpened my grasp of the subject. For these I am grateful to Carl Armerding, Don Carson, the late Peter Craigie, Stan Gundry, David Hubbard, Alan Johnson, Robert Johnston, John Piper, Moises Silva, and David Wells. Several gracious individuals—Gerry Hawthorne, George Marsden, Craig Noll, John Stackhouse, Bernard Stonehouse, Grant Wacker, and David Wells—kindly took time from their pressing schedules to critique portions of this book, or the whole of it. In several cases this help was only the latest manifestation of longstanding and deeply appreciated concern for my work. I am especially indebted to David Bebbington, David Livingstone, Ian Rennie, and David Wright, who read Chapter 4 and rescued it from many misperceptions about matters in Britain. I can only regret that the restricted purposes of this book prevented me from following out many of the excellent suggestions I received to the full extent they deserved.

I would like to thank Wheaton College librarians Dan Bowell, Jonathan Lauer, and Paul Snezek who provided space to write, books from inter-library loan, and access to a word processor. Others at Wheaton also lent a helping hand: student assistants Steve Graham, Greg Clark, and Ron Frank; secretary Mrs. Beatrice Horn; Tom Kay, chairman of the history department; and administrators Ward Kriegbaum, Bill Henning, and Patricia Ward.

It is a special pleasure to acknowledge the financial assistance of the Wheaton College Alumni Association for support to carry out the survey of evangelical scholars described in the Appendix. With this assistance, the director of the Alumni Association, Mr. Lee Pfund, continued a long history of encouragement. Colleagues

Lyman Kellstedt, Alvaro Nieves, and John Hayward helped make sense of that survey.

The William B. Eerdmans Company graciously allowed me to examine its records in order to understand something about the distribution of evangelical books. I am also in debt to Eerdmans for the use of several paragraphs from essays in books that they had published ("Evangelicals and the Study of the Bible," in *Evangelicalism and Modern America,* edited by George Marsden [1984], and "Introduction: Christian Colleges, Christian Worldviews, and an Invitation to Research," in William C. Ringenberg's *The Christian College: A History of Protestant Higher Education in America* [1984]).

In recent years, fellow teachers and the coordinators of adult education at Bethel Presbyterian Church in Wheaton have increased my appreciation for the rewards of serious attention to Scripture. For that assistance it is a privilege to thank David Benner, Robert Harvey, Paul Heidebrecht, Arthur Holmes, Carolyn Nystrom, Lee Ryken, and Robert Warburton.

Families come last in acknowledgments, though they deserve better. In this instance I would like to thank Mary Constance and David Luther Noll for nicely complementing the nature of this project by listening—more often than not attentively—to nightly Bible stories. Maggie Packer Noll provided spiritual support and splendid household management during the writing of this book, a period of more than usual domestic upset. Robert Francis Noll had not yet appeared in the world when work on this project began, and his sole interest to date in the life of the mind has been to chew thoughtfully on the volumes that come within his grasp. But by so doing, he has already responded to the appeal of this book.

1. Introduction

All Scripture is given by inspiration of God, and is profitable for doctrine, for reproof, for correction, for instruction in righteousness.

2 TIMOTHY 3:16

This book is a historical essay on evangelical interaction with critical Bible scholarship in America over roughly the last century. As a history, the book is meant to be useful both to those who do, and to those who do not, think of themselves as evangelicals. As an essay, it is not exhaustive, comprehensive, or entirely impartial. It will sometimes rely on secondary accounts, where a full-blown monograph would pay stricter attention to the relevant primary sources. I am a church historian and not a professional student of the Scriptures. As such I will no doubt displease evangelical Bible scholars by misconstruing various aspects of their work. In compensation, I may be able to communicate some features of that work to Bible scholars who are not evangelicals and to evangelicals who are not Bible scholars.

The eminent British historian Christopher Hill once began a book on the Puritans by saying that the problem of defining these Englishmen was a "dragon in the path of every student of that period."[1] No less fearsome a dragon awaits the historian of modern evangelicalism. The term "evangelical" is a plastic one. Efforts to define it narrowly can lead to both strife among historians and battle among theologians. But it is nonetheless the place to begin.

DEFINITIONS

Although other ways of using the word "evangelical" have their place, this book employs a descriptive, historical definition. Admittedly, normative, prescriptive definitions are useful for other purposes, and so it is worth looking briefly at them. Such definitions help pollsters categorize aggregate data for the purpose of making general statements about the American population. They provide a means for theologians to sharpen confessional boundaries or

facilitate ecumencial advance. And they are handy, shorthand
designations for communicating within denominational or confessional constituencies. But for a subject like the study of the Bible,
this form of definition is not as helpful.

The rapidly accumulating polling data on evangelicals might
conceivably be useful for describing the context within which Bible
scholarship proceeds, but it provides little help for more academic
work. The difficulty may be illustrated from a major Gallup Poll
conducted for *Christianity Today* in the late 1970s. Using a fairly
sophisticated measure to define "evangelicals" (including an experience of New Birth, belief in biblical inerrancy, and traditional
opinions on major doctrines), Gallup found that 15 percent of
such evangelicals did not read the Bible even weekly; 40 percent
of them could not identify Nicodemus as the man to whom Jesus
said, "You must be born again"; and 50 percent of them could not
name even five of the Ten Commandments.[2] Polling data can play
a secondary role in describing what evangelicals more generally
feel about the Bible and how they put it to use. But they cannot
be the first place to turn for an examination of scholarly activity.

The use of a normative, theological definition might seem to
pose fewer problems. Much literature can be found to define evangelical by three or four central convictions. A recent effort by a
scholar engaged in professional study of the Bible is typical. "I
define an 'evangelical' as one who (1) holds a high view of canonical Scripture as the inspired word of God, (2) believes that God can
act and has acted in history, (3) affirms the Lordship of Christ and
the centrality of his salvific work, and (4) believes in the importance of a personal experience of grace."[3]

This kind of definition is a good beginning for theological reflection or for efforts at self-definition over against other Christian
approaches. And it is certainly part of the picture for a study of
evangelical Bible scholars. But it is not entirely helpful for the sort
of enterprise this book examines. For one, the definition fails to
do justice to the history of the term. Lutherans, the original "evangelicals," might not feel entirely comfortable with what such a
definition includes or excludes. Heirs of the evangelical movement
in England, as well as prominent participants in the "Evangelical
United Front" of nineteenth-century America, might desire different emphases in their definition of the term. For another, this

approach can easily lead to time-consuming strife over categories. Will one person's "high view" of Scripture be high enough for others who also use such a variable to define "evangelical"? Is the "centrality of Christ's salvific work" a hermeneutical principle as well as a more general confession? Must one hold all of these beliefs to qualify as an evangelical, or only some? Finally and most seriously, this definition designates an amorphous group with few common institutions, scholarly networks, or shared values. Christians from many disparate communions can identify themselves by these convictions: Catholics and Protestants, high church and low, independent and denominational, charismatic and Reformed, dispensational and anti-dispensational, mainline and fundamentalist, and many more.[4]

The advantage in defining "evangelical" through theological affirmations is to gain a measure of conceptual clarity. The cost is to lose a specific field for research. In order to obtain a definable subject, this book turns from theological definition to the history of interlocking institutions, personal networks, and common traditions. The risk in this procedure is to offend those who, by every theological and historical measure, have an equal right to the term "evangelical" as the subjects of this study. This is a regrettable offense. But if those so offended can remember that I am using a descriptive, rather than a prescriptive definition, it may ease the pain.

Who then are the "evangelicals" of this book? They are the less separatistic and more educationally ambitious descendants of the fundamentalists of the early twentieth century along with their allies in the older churches of British origin (Presbyterian, Baptist, Methodist, and, to a lesser extent, Congregationalist and Episcopalian) and the newer American denominations (Holiness, Pentecostal, and Restorationist).[5] Historically considered, these "evangelicals" have been those most willing to be defined by the activities of the best-known evangelists—Charles G. Finney, Dwight L. Moody, Billy Sunday, and Billy Graham.

This ascription comes close to identifying "evangelical" with the conservative Presbyterians and Baptists of the north who fought the advances of "modernism" at the turn of the century; with the remnants of those conservative forces in Presbyterian and fundamentalist splinter groups during the 1920s and 1930s (Westminster and Faith seminaries, for example); with the "neo-evangelical-ism" of Harold John Ockenga, E. J. Carnell, and Carl Henry of the 1940s and 1950s; and with the institutions that first embodied this "neo-evangelicalism" (Fuller Seminary, *Christianity Today*, Wheaton College, the National Association of Evangelicals, the Youth for Christ movement, the Billy Graham Evangelistic Association). Along with these pioneers, it also includes more recently founded institutions that carry on the same emphases today (Gordon-Conwell Seminary, Trinity Evangelical Divinity School, Denver Conservative Baptist Seminary). But this would be too narrow, even for the interlocking organizations that are the focus of the book.

In reality, the stream that flows from late nineteenth-century northern conservatives to recent "neo-evangelicalism" has always been fed by a number of tributaries. Or, to change the figure, the membranes separating this tradition from others have always been porous, the boundaries always blurred. From the first Presbyterian and Baptist disagreements over Scripture in the 1880s, theological conservatives in those communions were joined by some Congregationalists, Methodists, Disciples, and Episcopalians in efforts to preserve evangelical or confessional distinctives. Some organizations from these latter communions (for instance, several Wesleyan institutions like Asbury College and Seminary) continue to play significant roles in the ongoing story of the "evangelicals." During the twentieth century the "evangelicals" involved in the fundamentalist-modernist controversy and then in the emergence of a "neo-evangelicalism" retained ties with Holiness churches and, later, with Pentecostal bodies. In addition, while formal institutional cooperation between "evangelicals" and European confessional groups have never been close, contacts with individual Mennonites, Lutherans, and especially the Dutch Reformed have been numerous since the 1920s. After World War II, moreover, the mostly northern, white "evangelicals" had more contact with the Southern Baptists, and even with America's black churches, than before. Moreover, the lines dividing the "evangelicals" from their closest associates to the theological right and left have been thin to the point of transparency. This is especially true for connections between "evangelicals" and the dispensational "moderate fundamentalists" represented by Moody Bible Institute, Dallas Theological Seminary, and, more recently, the programs of Jerry Falwell. And it is no less the case for relationships with theological conservatives in the northern and southern Presbyterian churches. Finally, connections with Canadian and especially British "evangelicals," in both the Church of England and the dissenting denominations, have been extensive and of special importance for Bible scholars.

The way in which these various denominations and theological elements contribute to an identifiable, cohesive entity will become clearer as we examine the contribution of "evangelical" seminaries, colleges, commentary series, professional societies, youth ministries, colloquia, festschriften, periodicals, and journals to the study of the Bible. The pieces making up "evangelicalism" never fit together exactly, overall organizational discipline is practically nonexistent, and channels of communication can be a puzzle to insiders as well as to outsiders. But it is nonetheless beyond question that something like an "evangelical denomination" exists. George Marsden recently coined this phrase to describe the complex, but integrated, "evangelical" phenomenon. As he put it, this

meaning of "evangelical" refers to a consciously organized community or movement. Since mid-century there have been something like "card-carrying" evangelicals. These people, like their nineteenth-century forebears, have some sense of belonging to a complicated fellowship and infrastructure of transdenominational evangelical organizations. . . . Typically, those who have the strongest sense of being "evangelicals" are persons with directly fundamentalist background, although persons from other traditions—Pentecostal, holiness, Reformed, Anabaptist, and others—often are deeply involved as well. Sometimes the people, groups, and organizations that make up "evangelicalism" in this sense are rivals; but even in rivalry they manifest the connectedness of a family grouping that is quite concerned about its immediate relatives.[6]

This family grouping defines the "evangelicals" of this book. From here on the quotation marks will be dropped. It should be remembered, nonetheless, that this is a historical, social definition which leaves legitimate questions about ownership of the term for other occasions.

THEMES AND THESES

Several arguments weave their way through the history, evaluations, and interpretations which follow. It would be well to spell these out at the start. Some are conclusions from research, others a result of authorial perspective.

THE WORD OF GOD

When examining the evangelical study of Scripture, everything hinges upon a recognition that the evangelical community considers the Bible the very Word of God. Further, most evangelicals emphasize that the Bible is the Word of God in a cognitive, propositional, factual sense. Whatever else one may say about the Word of God (and many evangelicals are willing to recognize the supremacy of Christ as Word or to organize community life around the Word of proclamation), the Word of God always involves the truth-telling Bible. Although evangelicals typically give some attention to the human character of the Bible, they believe that Scripture itself teaches that where the Bible speaks, God speaks. Benjamin B. Warfield, a scholar whose views continue to shape evangelical convictions about the Bible, wrote in 1899 about two kinds of texts which undergird this conviction: "In one of these classes of passages the Scriptures are spoken of as if they were God; in the other, God is spoken of as if He were the Scriptures: in the two together, God and the Scriptures are brought into such conjunction as to show that in point of directness of authority no distinction was made between them."[7] This conviction remains a theoretical foundation of evangelical life as well as evangelical scholarship.

This should not imply that twentieth-century evangelicals ignore the questions about transcendent objectivity that Europeans began to formulate in the eighteenth century and Britons in the nineteenth. Yet for all the seriousness with which at least some study Kant, Schleiermacher, Marx, Dilthey, Durkheim, Freud, Heidegger, and related voices, the conviction remains: When we read the Bible, we read the Word of God.

It would be fatal in a study of evangelical biblical scholarship ever to forget this central conviction. Many evangelicals now share with their academic peers the conviction that professional writing benefits from a fiction of religious neutrality. These same ones display great openness to certain kinds of scholarship provided by nonevangelicals and even non-Christians. Conceding all this, however, the supreme reality remains that to be an evangelical student of the Scriptures is to believe that the object of research is also a definitive revelation from God.

Two Communities

Since this is the case, a history of evangelical biblical scholarship must heed both the professional community in which scholars willingly adopt a mien of intellectual neutrality, and the community of belief, in which the same scholars embrace a childlike faith. Evangelical students of Scripture live in both communities at the same time. The often hostile interaction of the two communities over the last century has constituted the decisive context for our subject.

The story of these clashing communities is, however, really two stories. Of most interest to outsiders is the record of traditional Bible-believers first competing in the intellectual marketplace as full partners in the academic discussion of Scripture (roughly 1880 to 1900); then retreating from that world to the fortress of faith (roughly 1900 to 1935); then slowly realizing the values of some participation in that wider world (1935 to 1950), finding the strategies to put themselves back in the professional picture once again (1940 to 1975), and finally confronting new spiritual and intellectual dilemmas because of success in those ventures (1960 to the present). This part of the story is largely an account of technical arguments, of conflicting assumptions about the Bible, of academic professionalization, and of the effort to gain the respect of the scholarly world without forfeiting the blessing of the church. The first story, in other words, concerns mostly the connected history of late nineteenth-century American Protestant conservatism, the fundamentalist movement, and the emergence of a new evangelicalism out of fundamentalism.

The second involves the interplay of cultures, first British-American and second immigrant-American. It is a story of greatest interest to insiders. The chapters that follow trace in some detail how American evangelicals drew upon scholars and faith traditions from both Great Britain and immigrant communities with roots in the Continent. American evangelicals have always benefited from British models, techniques, and mentors. From the early example of Lightfoot, Westcott, and Hort through the time of C. H. Dodd, to the contemporary influence of F. F. Bruce and I. H. Marshall, British Bible scholars have offered American evangelicals a fund of cautious, generally conservative, yet professionally responsible scholarship. More recently, American evangelicals have also received assistance from Lutheran and, even more, Dutch Reformed communities, which have contributed insights from European conservatives to the evangelical enterprise.

These British and immigrant contributions have been a boon to American evangelicals. But they have not left an entirely settled situation. The appropriation of European academic work has created tension not so much for the evangelicals as scholars as for the scholars as Americans. This tension may not seem worthy of notice by nonevangelicals, but it has been important within the movement. Relationships with Great Britain illustrate the tensions. The British scholarship has often arisen out of a pluralistic academic environment, but American evangelicals put it to use in one of dogmatic particularism. Britons lay a somewhat greater emphasis on the empirical data of the Bible, their American colleagues and pupils on the theological meaning of Scripture. The church context in Great Britain is both more stable and more sedate in comparison with the tangled and vibrant ecclesiastical history brought on in America by fundamentalist-modernist battles and subsequent developments. Under the influence of British models, American evangelicals are drawn to a study of the Bible which attempts to find an appropriate place for believing criticism in the church. Within the dynamics of American evangelical life, scholars are prone to employ criticism more for its apologetic value. The strains which result define a major part of the inner history of the recent evangelical study of Scripture.

PROFESSIONALIZATION

Evangelical scholars, by using British and other kinds of resources, have made great strides over the last fifty years in achieving academic respectability. The fact of this professionalization and the speed with which it has been obtained are signal matters in themselves. But they also point to other, even more significant issues.

There can be no doubt, first, that experiences in the academy have led some evangelicals away from their traditional religious moorings to other forms of Christianity or none. It is also beyond doubt that a more professional study of the Scriptures has led some evangelicals in the other direction, to a firmer, more nuanced, more profound understanding of Christian faith. Both of these developments create problems for the evangelical community. On the one hand, scholarship looms again, as it did for many at the start of the twentieth century, as intrinsically threatening. On the other hand, scholarship appears not so much dangerous as unsettling, since it calls into question cherished interpretations, conventions, or readings of the evangelical tradition itself.

The result is an irony by no means unique to the evangelical community. As the sons, and later daughters, of a minority sub-community go to the universities, and eventually to the best universities, the community swells with pride. But when a few of the scholars return to repudiate the community values or to propose even their modest restructuring, confusion, antagonism, and consternation result. The emergence of a class of learned evangelical Bible scholars is a remarkable development of the last half century. The effects of that emergence in the evangelical community have been no less worthy of attention.

EVANGELICAL CONVICTIONS

Finally, it remains to make clear that I write this book as an evangelical who feels that evangelical convictions about Scripture are not only defensible as religious sentiments but are viable in a free market of ideas. The book is not an apologetic for evangelical views on the Bible. As it unfolds, however, it will be necessary to examine some of the charges leveled against both the intellectual integrity and the academic persuasiveness of evangelical views, and to describe evangelical responses. I hope that this is done with reasonable objectivity. My own conviction is that, while these attacks are warranted in regard to many particulars, they do not undermine foundational evangelical beliefs about the Bible, nor do they jeopardize common patterns of evangelical scholarship.

Evangelicals suffer from having paid scant attention to what might be called a theology of criticism, or a self-conscious perspective on academic method. One of the collateral arguments of the book is that the resources for such a theology are latent in the evangelical tradition and that if these resources were developed more self-consciously, it would be possible to engage in a biblical scholarship at once more open to the contributions of criticism and more faithful to the Bible's divine character.

Finally, this book is not a history of the doctrine of inspiration among evangelicals, however much evangelical notions of authority impinge on the tale. Other works, cited at the appropriate points, have done that job. In addition, this book does not pretend to offer a comprehensive picture of evangelical Bible study. I concentrate upon evangelical interaction with critical scholarship, and pay only slight attention to an important related topic, but one that is largely unexplored, namely, the so-called devotional literature, the immense amount of evangelical writing on the Scriptures that does not concern itself with the academic world or its conventions.

2. Response to Criticism: 1880–1900

We rest in the joyful and unshaken certainty that we possess a Bible written
by the hands of men indeed, but also graven with the finger of God.

A. A. HODGE AND B. B. WARFIELD, "Inspiration," 1881

A distinctly evangelical approach to the study of Scripture, involving a self-conscious stance toward biblical criticism, did not
emerge in America until the last third of the nineteenth century.
Before then, American Protestants shared generally the belief that
the Bible recorded the infallible words of God. The Scripture's
truthfulness was axiomatic. Moreover, American Bible-readers
generally assumed that, with the possible exception of a few passages in the book of Genesis, this truthfulness should be taken in
commonsensical terms—events described as historical were historical, statements about matters of fact were matters of fact. The
Americans who held these views developed a lush variety of interpretations from the infallible Scriptures. And they were never
reluctant to champion their interpretations against other, sometimes antithetical, readings of the same inerrant volume. In spite
of interconfessional strife, however, the overwhelming majority of
American Christians shared beliefs in Scripture as the Word of
God and in commonsensical methods for interpreting it.[1]

Growing respect for biblical criticism from the Continent
brought an end to this American consensus. In 1870 most Americans, including most academics, agreed on *what* it meant for the
Bible to be the Word of God. By 1900, Christians contended with
each other as to *how* the Bible was the Word of God. And the
academic world at large had asked *if* it was.

By the end of the century, in other words, the evangelical approach to Scripture was only one among many in the academic
sphere. To be sure, the bulk of America's Christians still took it for
granted, however much popularizers of the new criticism promoted alternative opinions. Evangelicals' views, moreover, still

appeared viable in the marketplace, even though serious questions were being raised about their adequacy for believers and their usefulness for scholars.

This chapter outlines the emergence of self-conscious evangelical positions on criticism, a process which drew earlier amorphous convictions into sharper focus. The next chapter considers the relatively rapid decline of this evangelical position in the academic world during the first third of the twentieth century. Before we then continue the story with a chapter on the return of evangelicals to the professional study of Scripture after roughly 1935, we pause to sketch an account of evangelical scholarship in Britain from 1860 to 1937, which differed from contemporary American work in subtle ways even as it contributed to the continuing story on this side of the Atlantic.

AN ALTERED LANDSCAPE

The division of American thinking on the Bible which occurred during the last third of the nineteenth century came in response to new information, new institutions, and new methods. New knowledge was the most impressive yet least significant reason for the division. The discoveries of inscriptions and documents dating from the biblical era, the awareness that the Old Testament Hebrews and the New Testament Christians shared more with their surrounding cultures than had previously been thought, the advance of research in philology, archaeology, and non-Christian world religions, not to speak of successful efforts at determining the original text of the biblical documents themselves, provided many challenges to old views of Scripture and many opportunities to formulate new ones.[2]

Yet new discoveries in themselves were less important than the new contexts in which they were studied. Institutionally, the rise of critical Bible scholarship in the United States corresponds with the professionalization of academic life and the rise of the university. The founding of the Society of Biblical Literature in 1880 was only the most manifest sign that the movement to professionalize the academic world at large was affecting the study of Scripture. When Johns Hopkins University opened its doors in 1876 as a graduate school for specialized study on the Germanic model and when Charles Eliot transformed Harvard into a research university shortly thereafter, a new conception of academic life, which would swiftly dominate all others, had made its appearance.[3] Leaders of the new academy self-consciously set themselves apart from the pious and intellectually parochial mentors who had traditionally directed higher education in America. The grail of science beckoned invitingly. To attain it, the sacrifice of uncritical deference was a small price to pay. As Andrew D. White put it in his vision for Cornell, his university would "afford an asylum for Science—where truth shall be sought for truth's sake, where it shall not be the main purpose of the Faculty to stretch or cut sciences exactly to fit 'Revealed Religion.' "[4] Received dogma was suspect in every field, not least for the Bible.

Most important, however, the new universities embodied a new attitude toward history. The Germans seemed to have demonstrated conclusively that facts were always relative to historical context, each stage of history was always the product of what had gone before, minds were always a function of cultures, and divinity (where it existed) was always immanent in human experience. This was "the belief," as a recent historian has phrased it, "that culture is the product of its own history, that ideas, values, and institutions of every sort are wholly conditioned by the historical setting in which they exist."[5] Historical consciousness of this sort had revolutionary implications when applied to Scripture. The Bible might retain its status as a revered document, but only because it was a unique expression of religious experience. The Bible might remain a book in which to hear the voice of God, but those who accepted the new views thought they were hearing it within history rather than from the outside.

Once before, Americans had faced a similar critical challenge. During and immediately after the War for American Independence, views of free-thinking *philosophes* found a hearing in America. Some in consequence began to regard the Scriptures as merely a singular human book rather than a divine revelation. These, however, were mostly limited to New England and to the religious bodies furthest removed from the kind of evangelicalism that dominated American religious life. Thus the transcendentalist Theodore Parker (1810–1860) accepted many of the then radical conclusions about the human origin of Scripture, and he popularized German views about the mythological character of biblical stories. More typical in this first wave of Bible scholars were Harvard professors like Andrews Norton (1786–1853), who also read biblical criticism from the continent, but only to buttress his Unitarian views of the Bible's divine character and its recital of supernatural events. Moses Stuart (1780–1852) of Andover Seminary was the rare theological conservative who also appropriated the current scholarship from Europe. But he did so from the conviction that such research made it possible to discern more accurately the actual messages of the Bible, which to him was still very much a supernatural revelation.[6]

Along with continental criticism some new information concerning the world of Scripture had come to the attention of Americans during this period. But institutions and perspectives were lacking to provide criticism with a congenial home. The reverse was rather the situation. Careful apologists like Yale's Timothy Dwight (1752–1817) and Princeton's Samuel Stanhope Smith (1750–1819) enlisted the new facts on the side of orthodoxy. Energetic ecclesiastical leaders created the seminary (Andover 1807, Princeton 1812, Yale 1822) as centers of advanced study designed to de-fang criticism and to absorb the new facts into orthodoxy. The seminaries tied scholarship securely to the church and succeeded in preserving lay confidence in the nation's theological elite. They were America's only major graduate schools for the first two-thirds of the nineteenth century. Leaders at these institutions were able to champion inductive science as a way of reinforcing dogma. They knew about G. E. Lessing, J. G. von Herder, and Immanuel Kant, and even more about F. D. E. Schleiermacher and Samuel Taylor Coleridge; yet for them historical investigation cast no shadow between the facts of induction and the dogmas of orthodoxy.[7]

But by the end of the century everything had changed. Now new information seemed to drive a wedge between faith and scholarship. The new learning secularized the academy, confused the pulpit, and alienated at least large numbers in the pew. The new professional scholars championed a method which they still called induction; but this was a science that relativized traditional dogma, rather than confirmed it.

Before these broad and deep changes occurred at the end of the century, virtually all Americans concerned about the issue had evangelical views on the nature of the Bible and how it should be studied.[8] Under the impact of new ideas a significant number of scholars, uneasy with either criticism itself or its contemporary application, mobilized to resist the spirit of the age. The result was a self-consciously evangelical approach to the study of Scripture.

PRESBYTERIAN DEBATE: 1881–1883

From their first entrance upon questions of criticism, evangelicals carried a twin commitment to inductive research and to an infallible Bible. Both were traditional in America, though neither was entirely specific. From the end of the eighteenth century, evangelicals with other Americans had hailed the inductive methods of Francis Bacon as the royal road to truth.[9] The historic Protestant allegiance to Scripture had become even more intense in the century after the Revolution, perhaps in large part because of the absence of an establishment or any other strong inter-Protestant institutions. It was the Bible alone, and the Bible studied as the scientist studies nature, which sustained evangelicals throughout the nineteenth century when they were the overwhelmingly dominant force in American religion. Now at the end of the century these historic commitments marked out a path for an evangelical scholarship that would have to compete in, rather than set the rules for, the marketplace of ideas.

A remarkable exchange of essays in the *Presbyterian Review* from April 1881 to April 1883 not only defined positions which are still basic to evangelicals but also differentiated such views from efforts to appropriate historical consciousness within an evangelical faith.[10] At this stage the term "evangelical" again is ambiguous. Two groups participated in the exchange, one opposing the results of the new scholarship, one giving qualified approval. In the context of the 1880s both were evangelical.[11] Yet it was the more conservative party which established the precedents for what would become, in the twentieth century, the evangelicalism defined in Chapter 1.

The exchange arose from the feeling that, since a great deal of publicity was being given to the new views from Europe, particularly concerning the Old Testament, it was the responsibility of the church to examine them seriously. American Presbyterians had taken special interest in the affair of William Robertson Smith, an Old Testament professor at the Free Church of Scotland college at Aberdeen. In essays, books, and, most visibly, widely read contributions to the *Encyclopedia Britannica* (ninth edition), Smith popularized German critical conclusions about the Hebrew Scriptures. A long and complicated series of judicial procedures in the Free Church from 1876 to 1881 led to Smith's acquittal on charges of heresy, but also to his removal from his professorial charge. Smith succeeded in defending his position that the new criticism was compatible with evangelical faith, but he could not quite convince the Free Church that such a conjunction should form the basis of instruction for the rising generation.[12] The editors of the *Presbyterian Review*, A. A. Hodge of Princeton Seminary and Charles A. Briggs of Union Seminary, represented contrasting views on these developments among the northern Presbyterians. The *Review* itself was an experiment to test whether American Presbyterians with differing theological inclinations could work together.[13] Hodge and Briggs agreed in 1881, as the latter subsequently put it,

that the great attention given to these topics in the Old World, the prolonged conflict in Scotland over the "Robertson Smith case," the large number of publications presenting these subjects in crude and dangerous forms, and the increasing attention given to them in the religious journals and at ministerial gatherings, rendered such a series of articles indispensable to a theological Review that proposed to discuss the living topics of the time.[14]

The group more kindly disposed to the results of the new criticism was headed by Briggs, then at New York's Union Seminary. He penned two essays defending the propriety, within limits, of critical approaches to Scripture. Henry Preserved Smith of Lane Theological Seminary in Cincinnati and Samuel I. Curtiss, who taught at the Congregational Theological Seminary in Chicago, joined Briggs by providing cautiously favorable reports on the pentateuchal criticism of, respectively, Julius Wellhausen and Franz Delitzsch.[15] For this group, as for the other, the new criticism posed both doctrinal and methodological problems. Briggs, Smith, and Curtiss insisted that a careful appropriation of the new criticism would result in a clearer understanding of "the incarnation of the divine revelation in human forms of thought," and a greater appreciation for the "sublime harmony" of the Bible.[16] Moreover, their approval of criticism was predicated upon the continued belief in the supernatural. A proper criticism, that is, could not reject "accounts of miracles *a priori.*"[17] The results of cautious criticism did not overthrow the historic faith in Scripture, for as Briggs elaborated at great length, "theories of text and author, date, style, and integrity of writings" can never by themselves establish or undercut confidence in the Scriptures. This is true even if criticism reveals minor errors in the biblical record: "The doctrine of Inspiration as stated in the symbols of faith will maintain its integrity in spite of any circumstantial errors that may be admitted or proved in the Scriptures, so long as these errors do not directly or indirectly disturb the infallibility of its matters, of faith or of the historic events and institutions with which they are inseparably united."[18]

Briggs, Preserved Smith, and Curtiss justified their acceptance of criticism not only as compatible with an evangelical doctrine of Scripture, but as demanded by the facts. They were committed to "the principles of Scientific Induction."[19] And since Old Testament studies had "been greatly enlarged by the advance in linguistic and historical science which marks our century," it was only proper to take this new evidence into account.[20] On several Old Testament issues the scholarly consensus was especially striking: The Pentateuch was the product of several hands and times, some development did occur in the nature of Israel's faith, the Old Testament writings as we possess them reveal the work of editors who did their work long after the traditional dates assigned to the books. Even Franz Delitzsch, who was usually regarded as conservative, believed in multiple sources for the Pentateuch and insisted on saying no more than that Hebrew history began with Moses.[21] To these Presbyterian intellectuals the situation, as Briggs described it, was clear: "It is significant that the great majority of professional Biblical scholars in the various Universities and Theological Halls of the world, embracing those of the greatest learning, industry, and piety, demand a revision of traditional theories of the Bible on account of a large induction of new facts from the Bible and history."[22]

CONSERVATIVE COUNTERARGUMENT

These confident assertions—that new scholarship justified the overthrow of some traditional conclusions about the Bible and that the new conclusions were compatible with traditional Christian faith—set the stage for a contrasting evangelical view. The Presbyterian conservatives could not have disagreed more. Their conception of a proper criticism and their beliefs about the relationship between criticism and dogma set them on a course far different from that of the first group. In this exchange, the conservatives also published two largely doctrinal essays and two assessments of European biblical critics. One of the dogmatic essays came from A. A. Hodge, his father's successor in the chair of systematic theology at Princeton Seminary, in conjunction with B. B. Warfield of Western Seminary in Allegheny, Pennsylvania, who soon succeeded Hodge at Princeton. The other was by Francis L. Patton, who had only shortly before assumed a chair at Princeton Seminary as Professor of the Relation of Philosophy and Science to the Christian Religion. The two exercises in criticism were an attack on William Robertson Smith by Princeton Seminary's William Henry Green, and on the Dutch scholar Abraham Kuenen, by Willis J. Beecher, professor of Hebrew at Auburn Theological Seminary in New York.[23] These essays deserve close attention, for they sketched positions and suggested questions which have remained foundational for the evangelical study of Scripture since their day.

While the conservatives made no effort to hide their traditionalism, they nonetheless professed a willingness to be swayed by new facts concerning the Scriptures. As Hodge and Warfield put it at the start of the exchange,

The writers of this article are sincerely convinced of the perfect soundess of the great Catholic doctrine of Biblical Inspiration, i.e., that the Scriptures not only contain, but ARE, THE WORD OF GOD, and hence that all their elements and all their affirmations are absolutely errorless, and binding the faith and obedience of men. Nevertheless we admit that the question between ourselves and the advocates of [modern criticism], is one of fact, to be decided only by an exhaustive and impartial examination of all the sources of evidence, i.e., the claims and the phenomena of the Scriptures themselves."[24]

The only major difference from the Briggs group was the determination to give inductive study of biblical "claims" even more weight than inductive study of Scripture's "phenomena." Beecher could admit that conservatives "have not adequately used the materials which recent research has provided." And Hodge and Warfield could speak of "the critical examination of all the most intimate phenomena of the text of Scripture" as "an obvious duty." Yet it was a significant indication of evangelical priorities that, at the outset of their work, Hodge and Warfield chose to postpone that duty in favor of doctrinal affirmation.[25]

The conservatives were not, in general, greatly impressed with claims to new knowledge about the Bible. They were as ready as Timothy Dwight and Stanhope Smith of an earlier generation to incorporate new facts into old views. Thus Green foreswore an examination of W. Robertson Smith's "presumptions" and chose rather the way of induction: "We shall concern ourselves simply with duly certified facts." Beecher insisted that in order to carry out a genuinely critical study, the critic must follow the facts wherever they led: "It is conceivable," he wrote, "that a man may find his critical results to be better founded than his dogmatic opinions concerning inspiration, and may be compelled to give up the latter in favor of the former."[26] In theory, the results of criticism could not be predetermined.

At the same time, however, these scholars conceded that their view of the church's traditional understanding of Scripture made it very difficult to accept the new critical conclusions. Hodge and Warfield once again stated it most clearly: "The historical faith of the Church has always been, that all the affirmations of Scripture of all kinds, whether of spiritual doctrine or duty, or of physical or historical fact, or of psychological or philosophical principle, are without any error when the *ipsissima verba* of the original autographs are ascertained and interpreted in their natural and intended sense."[27]

Charles Briggs responded to this claim about history with a long series of citations to demonstrate that many figures in the church's past, as well as the Presbyterian's own Westminster Confession, affirmed the Bible's truthfulness in religious substance but not in minute detail.[28] But this would not wash for the conservatives.

Francis Patton answered Briggs citation for citation to prove that the church's historic belief was in the accuracy of the Bible in part as well as in whole.[29] Unlike Briggs and his associates, Patton and his colleagues acknowledged that allegiance to traditional views remained a determinative influence as they approached the task of criticism.

As the conservatives engaged in their study of Scripture, moreover, they paused to criticize the uncritical attitudes of the critics. The principal problem in their view was the large role assigned to presuppositions. According to Patton, it was "naturalistic postulates" that led scholars to discredit the Mosaic authorship of the Pentateuch. Green thought that W. Robertson Smith accepted evolutionary ideas about Israel's religion mostly because "the development theory is all the rage."[30] But it was Beecher's attack on Kuenen which asserted most directly that unfounded personal convictions fatally compromised the new scholarship and made it "not primarily critical." Beecher admired Kuenen's industry, but not his point of view: "The vast mass of detailed proofs by which our author would invalidate the testimony of the Bible narrative, is so utterly valueless for that purpose, that one is led to ask how it could possibly seem to him worth while thus laboriously to advance them. And when we ask this question, we find the answer to it in certain assumptions which underlie his whole argument." These assumptions were that all religion reflects an evolutionary development from the primitive to the complex (so that the patriarchs could not have possessed as strong a consciousness of God as the prophets) and that supernatural events are not possible. Beecher continued, "Without these assumptions, his charges against the body of the Old Testament Scriptures amount to nothing. . . . No dogmatist could be narrower than is Dr. Kuenen in some of the assertions he makes in this matter."[31] The end result of such criticism was clear. Green put it most colorfully: "Kuenen and Wellhausen have shown us by what clever tricks of legerdemain they can construct castles in the air and produce histories which have positively no basis whatever but their own exuberant fancy."[32]

The conservatives did more than merely attack anti-supernaturalistic, evolutionary presuppositions, however. They also put forth a view of criticism fundamentally different from that held by the new critics, whether evangelical or not. Contrasting conceptions of criticism presented by Preserved Smith and Willis Beecher in this early exchange encapsulated the growing divide in American Protestantism over new biblical scholarship. To Briggs and his allies, proper critical method meant an analysis of the organic relationship between text and context. They took for granted a developmental scheme of history. Thus, for Preserved Smith, the essential "axioms of criticism" expressed the conclusions to which most of Western scholarship had been heading since Herder and Kant:

(1) Differences of style imply differences of author.
(2) The historical circumstances in which an author writes are apt to be reflected with more or less definiteness in his work.
(3) The ethical and religious conceptions of his time will also influence his work.[33]

For Smith, Briggs, and their party, criticism of this nature did not necessarily subvert the supernatural character of Christianity, but rather made it possible for the church to absorb the new light which God through academic progress was now shedding on his written word. These scholars were making peace with historical consciousness.

For Beecher and his allies a very different conception of criticism prevailed. To them proper critical method meant stripping away everything that stood in the way of ascertaining the factuality of the text. And they took for granted an older, more static model of scientific inquiry. Beecher's "canons of criticism" were thus very different from Smith's "axioms."

(1) We must avoid groundless assumptions. . . .
(2) Reputable human testimony has a presumption in its favor. . . .
(3) Mere hypothesis proves nothing. . . . But without some element of positive evidence, a hypothesis or a hundred hypotheses fail of themselves. . . . Any author is uncritical if he indulges in assertions which are based on mere hypotheses. . . .
(4) We must go as near as possible to the original sources to obtain evidence [e.g., a statement from Chronicles is closer

to its evidence than a statement by a critic from the late nineteenth century]. . . .

(5) All the laws of deductive reasoning are fundamental canons of critical procedure.[34]

For Beecher, Warfield, and their party, criticism that did not follow these canons undermined the ability to understand the facts of the Bible and the capacity to be led by those facts to reconfirm the church's historic confidence in Scripture. Historical consciousness, as exemplified by the new critical conclusions, sounded a death knell for the faith.

The conservatives came to the conclusion that neither the vaunted new facts nor any of the new historical consciousness justified either the ascription of error to any part of Scripture or any serious modifications of traditional views on authorship, composition, and origin of the biblical books. No apparent discrepancy in the Bible truly qualified as an error—that is, something affirmed in the original autograph, interpreted according to its intended sense, and actually contradicting "some certainly known fact of history, or truth of science, or some other statement of Scripture certainly ascertained and interpreted."[35] After a lengthy summary, Patton could say concerning the Mosaic authorship of the Pentateuch, "There is no good reason for disbelieving it."[36] Green once again was more rhetorical: "May we not say of the latest critical attempt to roll the Pentateuch off its old foundation, that it has not achieved success? It has enveloped Mt. Blanc in a cloud of mist, and proclaimed that its giant cliffs had forever disappeared. But, lo, the mist blows away, and the everlasting hills are still in place."[37]

THE CONSERVATIVE EVANGELICAL STANCE

In the end, Hodge, Warfield, Green, Beecher, and Patton defined a position which became both normative and typical for many later evangelicals. It displayed several features which continue to mark the study of the Bible which followed in their train.

(1) The conservatives were scholars. While there has always been a popular, anti-intellectual contribution to evangelical discussion about the Bible, the conservatives writing in the *Presbyte-*

rian Review foreswore intellectual shortcuts, affirmed academic credibility, and practiced careful scholarship. Their camp would always sustain intimate relationships with more popular, less scholarly approaches, and the line would sometimes blur between popular activity and respectable academics. Yet a strong scholarly tradition was present at the beginning of the critical era and would never entirely pass away in what followed.

(2) The conservatives saw themselves as *critical* scholars. They did not abandon criticism, for they, like most academics in nineteenth-century America, regarded the careful, inductive, scientific sifting of evidence as the royal road to truth. It was not criticism as such but what they perceived as prejudiced criticism, criticism corrupted by bias, unbelieving criticism, that they attacked.

(3) The conservatives were sharply aware of the role of presuppositions in scholarship. Long before it became fashionable to talk about the sociology of knowledge, long before Michael Polanyi and Thomas Kuhn, these scholars assigned great weight to the standpoints from which scholars did their work. At least in this one limited area, they stood against the view of science as a disinterested, objective enterprise that was so powerful in the United States at the end of the last century.

(4) The conservatives were not afraid to acknowledge that they too came to their academic work with presuppositions, though they saw their predispositions arising from regeneration and the work of the Spirit rather than from the influence of academic conventions. Even as they claimed to look at the text objectively, they confessed that they held to a traditional view of the Bible's truthfulness, and that this truthfulness meant accuracy of fact as well as of religious sentiment. Furthermore, most of them held that such views deserved to have a place of influence in the exercise of the critical task. It was self-deception to think that the Bible could ever be studied "like any other book," as Benjamin Jowett had proposed in a famous paper for the British book *Essays and Review* in 1860.[38]

(5) At stake in the new critical discussions were matters of greatest consequence. If the Bible perpetrated errors of fact in history, science, or the accounts of its literary origins, it could not be relied upon to describe the relationship between God and humanity, the way of salvation, or the finality of divine law. As Hodge and War-

field put it, since "no organism can be stronger than its weakest part, that if error be found in any one element, or in any class of statements, certainty as to any portion could rise no higher than belongs to that exercise of human reason to which it will be left to discriminate the infallible from the fallible."[39] The choice, in other words, was between the infallible words of God or the volatile opinions of men and women.

(6) Still, the conservatives were not entirely inflexible in the conclusions to which they came concerning the Bible. Even those engaged in this early exposition of this evangelical position were able to accept nontraditional conclusions about certain matters in Scripture, provided only that such conclusions could be framed as reinterpretations of the infallible Bible rather than as examples of biblical error. Thus Green would adjust the genealogies of Genesis to accommodate an ancient age for the earth; Warfield would read early Genesis as supporting, or at least not denying, a kind of theistic evolution; and Beecher could be somewhat flexible when he examined critical questions concerning the historical and prophetic books.[40]

(7) Finally, the conservatives were more concerned about new views of the Old Testament than of the New. Part of the reason for this relative lack of interest in New Testament criticism can be ascribed to their confidence in the work of conservative British scholars, which we will examine in due course. Another part was their awareness that in the 1880s critical conclusions about the Old Testament were more radical than for the New. In any event, early emphasis on the missteps of Old Testament criticism established a pattern which has left evangelical Old Testament scholars further removed from the main arena of academic activity than their associates who work with the New.

Firm as the conservative position was on many matters, however, ambiguities did remain. These too have continued to be of interest in the tradition which they helped to establish.

BIBLICAL INSPIRATION

Differences of opinion existed as to the precise place of the doctrine of biblical inspiration in the critical task. Hodge and Warfield gave it great influence—the *onus probandi* lies with those who question biblical factuality. Since "the presumption" lies with the

Bible's accuracy as stated, "positive and conclusive evidence" is necessary to substantiate "each alleged instance of error."[41] Beecher, on the other hand, spoke as if a naive neutrality could in fact be reached: "That the critical inquiry into the nature of the Scriptures may be independent, it must reject all evidence which is based on the assumption that the Books are inspired, just as it rejects that which is based on the assumption that they are not inspired. While it is in progress it has nothing to do with inspiration."[42]

At stake in this difference of opinion was a clash between two traditional loyalties, to scientific scholarship as a neutral, objective inquiry, and to the Bible as the factually accurate Word of God. Both commitments have been hereditary possessions of American evangelicals, both remain important for the heirs of Hodge, Warfield, Beecher, and Patton. Both also require further analysis when we examine more closely the way in which evangelicals have studied the Bible.

NEW INTERPRETATIONS

A slightly different question concerns not the possibility of error in the Bible but the possibility of new interpretations. Conservative evangelicals have usually supported both high views of biblical infallibility and firm commitments to traditional views on the composition of the biblical writings. That is, Moses wrote virtually all of the Pentateuch, the prophet Isaiah wrote the entire book which bears his name, the book of Daniel dates from the fifth or sixth century B.C., Jonah is history not parable, the gospels report actual events and words from the life of Jesus in roughly the order they occurred, Paul wrote Ephesians and the Pastorals, and so on. These conclusions rest on a straightforward, commonsensical reading of the relevant passages.

The practice and stated principles of these early Presbyterian evangelicals suggests, however, that different views were held concerning the fixity of these literary opinions. Francis Patton, at one extreme, rang down the curtain on newer views about the origin of the Pentateuch by adducing the words of Jesus.

In support of the Mosaic authorship of the Pentateuch we urge the testimony of Christ and the writers of the New Testament. . . . We put the words of Jesus above the induction of the critics, and are sure that the responsibility of Moses for the books that are called by his name must be understood according to the plain implication of the passage which speaks of them as "his writings."[43]

Hodge and Warfield, on the other hand, profess more willingness to let "induction" take its course and (perhaps) to doubt what merely appears to be "the plain implication" of biblical passages. For them, the recovery of the texts "in all their real affirmations" is the key. They stress that the books of the Bible "were not designed to teach philosophy, science, or human history as such," and that the writers depended on "sources and methods in themselves fallible." All of this does not mean the Bible errs when its writers speak on history or literary origins. It simply means that "the affirmations of Scripture of all kinds" are true when "ascertained and interpreted in their natural and intended sense."[44] In this reading, Patton to the contrary notwithstanding, it would seem that even the words of Jesus need to be studied inductively concerning "their natural and intended sense" about the composition of the Old Testament.

These considerations do not concern evangelical affirmations about the errorlessness of Scripture. They do, however, raise the possibility that certain critical conclusions were acceptable, if it could be successfully argued that biblical statements, which earlier generations took as affirmations about the literary character of earlier books, were not actually intended to be judgments about critical matters. This is in fact what happened with a limited range of traditional interpretations for some of these early conservatives.[45] It left open a limited flexibility toward criticism which reappears from time to time in the later development of these evangelical positions.

PRESUPPOSITIONS

Drawing attention to issues of interpretation immediately raises the question of whether these conservatives were as conscious of their own presuppositions as of those held by the critics. Certainly, they acknowledged their indebtedness to the doctrine of biblical infallibility. At the same time they were not particularly alert to the historically rooted origin of other convictions concerning Scripture. Thus Beecher's view of critical neutrality was as much a function of eighteenth-century scientific fashions as W. Robertson Smith's developmentalism was of those in the nineteenth. Patton's conception of the "plain implication" of Jesus' words may have had something to do with how historical narratives were read in the nineteenth century as well as with how they were written in the first. Questions about the self-awareness of their own presuppositions are as valid for contemporary evangelicals as for their predecessors in the nineteenth century. This matter will remain a focus of our attention as we now pick up the story after this signal episode in the early 1880s.

CONTINUING VIGOR: 1880–1900

For the next two decades, the conservatives largely succeeded in maintaining the positions articulated in this exchange, and in maintaining them with academic rigor. It even appeared for a time as if the conservative evangelical response to the new criticism might be as successful at the end of the nineteenth century as it had been at the beginning.

During the 1880s and 1890s most of the major denominations took steps to protect theological education from the newer opinions. Critical views found readiest acceptance among the Congregationalists, where a rapid turnover in the faculty of Andover Seminary in the 1880s led to greater acceptance of liberal views generally. Yet the first responses of Congregational conservatives to these trends seemed successful. They were able, as an example, to oust Professor E. C. Smyth, one of the new "Andover liberals," from the seminary in 1885 for his use of the new Bible scholarship. The tide soon turned, however; Smyth was reinstated in 1892, and other efforts to discipline the Andover faculty came to naught.[46]

Baptists in the South were largely exempt from exposure to the newer opinions. The one exception was Crawford H. Toy, who taught Old Testament at Southern Baptist Seminary in Louisville from 1869 to 1879. When he came to accept Kuenen's account of the evolution of the Pentateuch, he resigned his post and eventually accepted a position in Hebrew and oriental languages at Harvard University.[47]

Baptists in the North tolerated a broader range of views, but there was no rush to accept modern criticism. Newton Theological Institution in Massachusetts dismissed Professor Ezra P. Gould in 1882 for advocating some of the critical conclusions in his classrooms. Although Baptists who began to accept the newer views remained popular in the denomination, none was given a position in the seminaries until the 1890s. Even then, the cautious embrace of critical conclusions at Colgate Seminary and the divinity school of the University of Chicago was offset by the continuing conservative stance at Newton, under its long-time president Alvah Hovey; at Rochester Seminary, where Howard Osgood, who supported the work of Princeton's William Henry Green, exerted great influence during the last quarter of the century; and at Crozer Seminary, where George D. B. Pepper articulated a balanced defense of biblical inerrancy.[48]

Biblical criticism also received attention from the Methodists, who continued to follow the conservative paths of the nineteenth century. When Hinckley G. Mitchell of the Boston University School of Theology questioned the Mosaic authorship of the Pentateuch, bishops brought charges against him. The proceedings went on for ten years, from 1895 to 1905, but eventually Mitchell was removed from his position.[49]

In these same years, three prominent Presbyterians—Charles Briggs, Henry Preserved Smith, and A. C. McGiffert—either lost judicial battles brought on by their advocacy of the new criticism or chose to resign from the denomination under threat of similar action.[50] Among Presbyterians the proceedings involving Briggs were most noteworthy. Briggs and A. A. Hodge had enjoyed a reasonably satisfactory relationship as coeditors of the *Presbyterian Review* in the early 1880s, but harmony deteriorated when first Francis L. Patton and then B. B. Warfield succeeded Hodge as the coeditor of the review.[51] Finally in 1889, the clash of personalities, as well as differences of opinion between Briggs and Warfield over the proposed Presbyterian revision of the Westminster Confession, led to the demise of the journal. When Briggs presented his inaugural address as professor of the newly created Chair of Biblical Theology at Union on January 20, 1891, the conservatives felt compelled to take action. This address, later published as "The Authority of Holy Scripture," appeared dangerously radical to the conservatives. Alongside the Bible, Briggs listed the church and reason as essential authorities for Christians. Even more worrisome to conservatives was Briggs's attack on six "barriers" which stood between Scripture and its usefulness in the church. These barriers included convictions like verbal inspiration, inerrancy, and the traditional opinions on literary matters that were firmly fixed among the conservatives. In order to leave no doubt about his convictions, Briggs affirmed "as the certain result of the science of the Higher Criticism . . . that Moses did not write the Pentateuch . . . Isaiah did not write half of the book that bears his name."[52]

Reaction came swiftly. The July 1891 number of the *Presbyterian and Reformed Review,* a successor to the *Presbyterian Review* under more thoroughly conservative control, contained a vigorous attack by Talbot W. Chambers, minister of the Collegiate Reformed (Dutch) Church of New York, president of the Presbyterian Alliance in 1892, and the only pastor to serve on the Old Testament committee of the American Revised Version. Chambers conceded Briggs's "sincerity and good faith," but concluded that he had "simply fallen a prey to the *Zeitgeist.* He has been borne along by the tide which has been steadily rising for half a century. . . . Standing inside the Church and holding a prominent position in a seminary of high character, he has borrowed the thoughts and the language of known errorists, and made a great stir by reproducing them after a fashion of his own."[53]

Briggs's New York Presbytery upheld him when charges were brought, but the denomination's general assembly in 1893 agreed with Chambers and suspended Briggs from the ministry. Briggs eventually found ordination as an Episcopalian, and Union Seminary, in order to extricate itself from the control of the general assembly, became independent. Ecclesiastical control seemed fully on the side of the conservatives.[54]

Nor were any weaknesses apparent in the intellectual marketplace. Conservatives were active on many fronts, and the quality of their work continued to command respect. Theologians acquainted with recent scholarship advanced sophisticated arguments in defense of infallibility and of conservative literary conclusions. In this effort B. B. Warfield led the way. His work was both negative, to strip concepts of "inerrancy" of mechanical or dualistic connotations, and positive, to affirm the right of critical, scientific study of the Bible within reasonable confessional guidelines.[55]

Other traditionalists added refinements to the concerns which Warfield learnedly expounded.

Scholars holding the conservative positions were also active in the new professional organizations. Early presidents of the Society of Biblical Literature and Exegesis (SBL), founded in 1880, included Talbot W. Chambers (1891–1894) and Willis J. Beecher (1904), whom we have already met as defenders of conservative positions, and several others with roughly similar sympathies. Papers presented at the SBL's annual meeting regularly advocated conservative views like the Mosaic authorship of Deuteronomy (Edwin C. Bissell, 1883) or the Pauline authorship of the Pastorals (M. J. Cramer, 1887). As Thomas Olbricht has pointed out, the "founding fathers" of the SBL were a largely moderate body; many were students or otherwise under the influence of Andover's conservative Moses Stuart.[56] Conservatives also served the Society in other ways. The SBL for its part early extended an honorary membership to Charles John Ellicott, Anglican Bishop of Gloucester, who had led opposition to the reinterpretation of Christ's self-consciousness contained in the famous revisionist book, *Lux Mundi*, edited by Charles Gore.[57]

Scholarly efforts to roll back the assured results of modern criticism also continued. Preeminent in this effort were Presbyterians, and preeminent among the Presbyterians was William Henry Green, who celebrated his fiftieth year of teaching at Princeton Seminary in 1896.[58] Green engaged William Rainey Harper in a lengthy, courteous, but resolute defense of a Mosaic Pentateuch in Harper's journal, *Hebraica*, a performance that he repeated in the somewhat friendlier pages of the *Presbyterian and Reformed Review* in 1893 and 1894.[59] In these and other efforts, Green weighed the new conclusions in the balance and found them wanting, both as science and as theology. He began his exchange with Harper, for example, by stating his case forthrightly:

If the critics were content with attempting a partition of Genesis (or even of the so-called Hexateuch) on purely literary grounds and with drawing what might fairly be reckoned legitimate inferences from such a partition, this would be a matter of curious interest but nothing more. The serious aspect of the affair is that there are presuppositions involved in the arguments employed and there are deductions made which are prejudicial to or subversive of the credibility and inspired authority of the sacred record. . . . I am accordingly only concerned to show, first, that the partition proposed by the critics in itself and apart from unfriendly prepossessions warrants no such destructive conclusions; secondly, that many of the arguments urged in support of the current critical partition are clearly invalid.[60]

Green was joined in these conclusions by others who, if they did not quite share Green's philological and casuistical skills, nonetheless partook of his determination to combine academic rigor with traditional reverence in approaching the text.[61]

While much of this conservative evangelical work took place in the North and among Presbyterians, other denominations and regions also witnessed a vital conservative scholarship at the end of the century. New Testament scholarship of unusual quality appeared, for example, from conservatives teaching at the Southern Baptist Seminary in Louisville. John Broadus (1827–1895), Southern's first professor of New Testament, published a *Commentary on Matthew* in 1886, which received positive notices from throughout the English-speaking world. His belief, "that the inspiration of Scripture is complete, that the inspired writers have everywhere told us just what God would have us know," did not prevent him from embarking on a full historical and linguistic study of the first gospel.[62] Nor did it impair his reputation in such academic centers as the new Johns Hopkins University, where he was invited to lecture.

Broadus's younger colleague, A. T. Robertson (1863–1934), devoted himself to linguistic concerns with even greater success. His *Grammar of the Greek New Testament in the Light of Historical Research,* first published in 1914, was the product of a lifetime's diligent attention to the best contemporary scholarship, mostly from the Continent. Long after the contributions of other conservatives from this era were forgotten, Robertson's grammar continued to be singled out for commendation in the wider world of biblical scholarship.[63]

In sum, although no discernible weakening appeared in strongholds of the new criticism before the turn of the century, conservative evangelical scholarship did not appear to be in serious danger. Nor had it lost its place in the general academic community. Its theological grounding seemed secure, its scholarship sound. Within a generation, however, all would be different.

3. Decline: 1900–1935

Is the position of modern criticism really compatible with a belief in the Old Testament as a divine revelation? The problem before us is not merely literary, nor only historical; it is essentially religious, and the whole matter resolves itself into one question: Is the Old Testament the record of a Divine revelation? This is the ultimate problem. It is admitted by both sides to be almost impossible to minimize the differences between the traditional and the modern views of the Old Testament.

W. H. GRIFFITH THOMAS, *The Fundamentals*

Robert W. Funk, a former president of the Society of Biblical Literature, has correctly observed that the period "roughly 1890–1920" was a "watershed" in American biblical study. During these years, "the lines in biblical scholarship were drawn very differently than in the preceding period." According to Funk, "our whole subsequent history has been shaped and, to a large extent, tyrannized by the fresh demarcation."[1] For conservative evangelical scholars, a redrawing of the lines meant a rapid decline from their position of relative strength in 1900. A number of reasons account for the eclipse which occurred after the turn of the century. Some were internal, reflecting the structure of evangelical beliefs and the quality of evangelical work. But others were external and involved matters over which evangelicals had no control. Of these, the most important was the rise of the modern university in the United States.

CHANGING TIMES: ACADEMIC PROFESSIONALIZATION

Great changes overtook American higher education between the Civil War and World War I. The number of students in college, and the number entering the country's many new high schools, increased dramatically. Funds for education were made available in unprecedented amounts from government, through land grants, but especially from private business. The prestige of science was at its height. Faculties grew and aspired to worldwide respectability. This process, which was underway everywhere in the North Atlantic community, involved the professionalization of academic life.[2] How this professionalization developed in America had a great impact on the study of the Scriptures.

As late as 1875, virtually every American who could be called an expert in the study of Scripture sustained some kind of a denominational connection and devoted the results of biblical scholarship primarily to the ongoing spirituality of the church. Change was dramatic. By 1900, as G. Ernest Wright once summarized it, "The productive Old Testament scholar had become for the most part an orientalist and a technical philologian; his interest in Israelite faith was largely governed by the current methodologies of comparative religion and by the almost exclusive interest in historical growth and development."[3] It was only slightly different for those who studied the New Testament.

Behind this rapid professionalization lay new emphases in scholarship which created a new academic environment.[4] To simplify a complex picture, this professionalization involved at least the following commitments: (1) rigorous inquiry; (2) specialized study; (3) orientation to academic peers instead of the general community; (4) a German model of scholarship stressing scrupulous objectivity; (5) a commitment to science in organic, evolutionary terms instead of mechanical, static ones; and (6) an iconoclastic, progressive spirit.

Evangelical Bible scholars did not adapt well to the new academic life marked out by these commitments. To be sure, they had no difficulty with rigorous inquiry, for the evangelical seminary of the nineteenth century had been the only American institution regularly encouraging such activity on a graduate level. Nor were they opposed in principle to specialized study, even though the most admired theologians of the era were versatile scholars like Philip Schaff, Charles Hodge, or Edwards Amasa Park who moved easily from exegesis to popular exposition, church history, and systematic theology. In addition, nineteenth-century theological journals often featured specialized essays on biblical topics, even while they also gave much space to more general theological discussions and to considerations of science, literature, and current events.

Real difficulties began only with the reorientation away from students and constituency to academic peers. The Bible for evangelicals was the church's book. It was much more important as a guide for the community of faith than as an object of study to a guild of scholars. Thus the Presbyterians, from 1881 through 1883, did not find it strange to spend so much time and effort discussing whether the newer critical theories could be accommodated to the denomination's doctrinal standard, the Westminster Confession. To divorce study from the ecclesiastical community was to take something away from its essential character.

A similar problem attended the German seminar. Evangelicals, whose stake in objective scientific inquiry extended back at least to the early years of the republic, nonetheless did science more after the British than the German model. That is, scientific learning was subordinate to larger social purposes. Important as science was in its own terms, it was even more important for its contribution to the process of character formation and for the enlightenment of the public at large. German academic freedom, which regularly appeared more liberating to visiting American scholars than it was in actuality for the Prussians, worried evangelicals. They had come to take it for granted that the results of scholarship could not be separated from the wider values of a community.

Most distressing to the evangelicals was the spirit in which denizens of the new university pursued the new science. American evangelicals had gone a long way toward making their peace with biological evolution by the end of the century.[5] What they could not accept was the European assumption—fueled more by Hegel than by Darwin—that later was always better, earlier always more primitive. This assumption, when joined with the anti-traditionalistic effects of the new scholarship, repelled evangelicals. They had no trouble using their minds; they welcomed appeals to science. What they could not tolerate was a science that seemed to accomplish so much by definition, that seemed to exclude what they felt were legitimate deliverances of responsible inquiry.

The result was a divide between two groups who shared little more than a general commitment to hard academic work. On what it meant to study, on the context in which study should occur, and on the acceptability of possible academic conclusions the two were far apart. Two such different orientations to academic work had the expected results—groups holding the radically different views began to accuse each other of not doing scholarship at all.

Although the process of academic professionalization was well under way by the 1890s, it did not greatly affect study of the Bible until the next decade. But then the implications became obvious with a vengeance.

One simple calculation illustrates the disengagement. A succession of Presbyterian journals—*Presbyterian Review* (1880–1889), *Presbyterian and Reformed Review* (1890–1902), and *Princeton Theological Review* (1903–1929)—published a great deal of the conservative Presbyterian scholarship of the period. Professors at Princeton Seminary were important for all three journals (coeditor of the first, managing editor on behalf of a number of Reformed scholars for the second, and sole editors of the third), but the journals were never entirely parochial. A fair number of Baptists, Congregationalists, and Europeans contributed to the *Presbyterian Review*. Even John Dewey made a brief appearance in the *Presbyterian and Reformed Review*, where he was joined by Lutherans, Congregationalists of both liberal and conservative persuasion, and many Europeans. And the *Princeton Theological Review*, though narrower in its editorial policy, still had room for many varieties of Presbyterian and Reformed thought from Europe, Canada, and America, and for the writing of Anglicans, Baptists, and Lutherans as well. Editorial content became more narrowly theological over the period, but these journals still continued the nineteenth-century tradition of comprehensive scholarship: Authors treated literature, politics, and science as well as theology and the Bible in nearly every issue.

The great change was not in the journals themselves, but in the participation of their authors in the professional world of Bible scholarship. Serious academic work on the Bible was a constant. It was every bit as important for the editors of the *Princeton Theological Review* in 1929 as it had been for the editors of the *Presbyterian Review* in 1880. After the turn of the century, however, writers who published in the Presbyterian reviews no longer published, as a general rule, in the professional journals. Twelve (8 percent) of the 150 individuals who published articles or notes in the *Presbyterian Review* (1880–1889) also contributed to the *Journal of Biblical Literature* from 1882 to 1901. Nineteen (7.5 percent) of the 252 authors in the *Presbyterian and Reformed Review*'s first decade (1890–1899) likewise placed essays in the *Journal of Biblical Literature* over the same period. But only two (0.7 percent) of the 275 authors who wrote for the *Princeton Review* from 1903 to 1929 contributed to the *Journal of Biblical Literature* during the period 1902 to 1941, and the last such contribution appeared in 1909.[6] B. B. Warfield published several essays in the *Journal of Biblical Literature* in its earlier years. His successor as the mainstay of Princeton orthodoxy, J. Gresham Machen, who had specialized more narrowly in New Testament work than his predecessor, nonetheless did not publish in the *Journal of Biblical Literature* or other professional periodicals.

By 1920, then, the professional study of Scripture, which had begun in the 1880s, was beginning to divide the academic community in two. Appearances before the turn of the century had been deceptive. Two tendencies were at work to create this division. Professional Bible scholars had less and less patience with those who did not accommodate themselves to critical conclusions. Conservative evangelicals had less and less patience with those who did.

REALIGNMENT

The denominational politics of the 1890s and the academic professionalization of the period 1880 to 1920 brought about a grand restructuring in the world of biblical scholarship. The turmoil that led to the ousting of moderate critics from the denominations hardened conservatives in their resistance to modern critical conclusions. As the ideal of science as iconoclastic naturalism secured its hold on American university life, academic professionals became less tolerant of theological objections to their critical conclusions. Two results followed, both pointing in the direction of new alignments for conservative students of Scripture. The first was a rapid decline in what could be called the middle party, evangelicals who sought accommodation with, rather than rebuttal of, criticism. In its early years the Society of Biblical Literature came close to being dominated by this group.[7] So long as these opinions were strong in the SBL, that organization and professional scholarship generally remained open to voices from both "right" (evangelicals who valued scholarship but attacked critical conclusions) and "left" (nonevangelicals who accepted critical methods and conclusions both). When the denominations ousted "liberal evangelicals" like Briggs and Henry Perserved Smith from their ranks in the 1890s, the result was a wider gulf in the academic community between conservative and moderate evangelicals. At the same time, these ecclesiastical proceedings were evidence to nonevangelical scholars that conservative theological convictions were incompatible with professional, academic study of Scripture.

By 1915, members of the middle group were beginning to lose their influence in the field of biblical scholarship. Conservative evangelicals continued to look upon them as dangerous radicals, but the academy was beginning to consider them hopeless reactionaries. The assessment of Charles A. Briggs made in 1914 by a rising star in the religious academy, Gerald Birney Smith, illustrates what Lefferts A. Loetscher once called "the rapid movement toward theological reconstruction in early twentieth-century America." Briggs, according to G. B. Smith, was so conservative on doctrinal matters that the only well-known American with whom he could be compared was B. B. Warfield.[8] The effort which Briggs had made to function as both an evangelical and a critic of moderate views had failed. The day of mediation was nearly over. The bridge individuals like Briggs had constructed between conservative evangelicals and academic nonevangelicals was in decay. No longer could it sustain the traffic it once had borne.

The isolation which resulted for conservative Bible scholars led to a second important development. Conservative evangelicals, either locked out of or alienated from the academy, turned for support to non-scholars who shared similar theological convictions. In this way, the conservative Bible scholars of the 1880s and 1890s, and their successors, became fundamentalists.

The passing of time has obscured how remarkable the alliance between conservative scholars and popular revivalism, the main ingredient in the making of fundamentalism, really was.[9] In nineteenth-century evangelical America such a close alliance had been unthinkable. To take but one instance, the best-known conservative biblical scholar and theologian at the turn of the century, B. B. Warfield, stood opposed to many of the prominent characteristics of the revival tradition. Warfield was a careful student—of the Scriptures, of European learning, of the classics and church history —where the revivalists had given formal learning short shrift. He was a sharp critic of perfectionism, or extravagant claims for the work of the Holy Spirit, at the very time when such beliefs were

becoming ever more powerful within American conservative Protestantism. For their part, the revivalists who emerged as fundamentalists were becoming nervous about evolution; they were increasingly likely to advocate a dispensational theology that
featured eschatological speculation prominently, and they tended
toward an ahistorical mode of proof-texting in their use of Scripture. Warfield, to the contrary, could countenance a conservative
version of theistic evolution. His Reformed theology left him
unimpressed with either dispensationalism as a system or apocalyptic speculation as an emphasis.[10] And he insisted on making the
effort to ascertain what Bible passages meant according to their
historical intention. Warfield's positions resembled most of the
other scholars who used learned argument to defend conservative
positions on the Bible in the decades around 1900. In other words,
it was the pressure of events, the expanding terrain of modernism
in the churches and of naturalistic scholarship in the academy, that
drove conservative scholars and revivalistic populists together into
a fundamentalist movement.

THE FUNDAMENTALS AND FUNDAMENTALISM

When the twelve-volume series of booklets known as *The Fundamentals* was published between 1910 and 1915, there was no fundamentalist movement. Only after World War I would disquiet with
liberal trends coalesce into organized efforts among northern
Presbyterians and Baptists to rescue their denominations from the
perils of modernism.[11] Before that time the various characteristics
of the later fundamentalism had emerged—militant defense of the
faith, concern for the reduced supernatural emphasis in the
denominations, skepticism about modern intellectual fashions,
and a leaning toward dispensational theology—but these existed
amorphously. The divisions were still blurred. Not everyone who
eventually accepted the fundamentalist label exhibited them all.
Some were found among individuals who never identified with the
later movement.

Given the relative fluidity in the first two decades of the century,
it is not surprising that the essays on the Bible and criticism in *The
Fundamentals* mingled both the academic conservatism and populist revivalism, which were coming closer together in opposition to

modernism. For our purposes, two things are important about the biblical articles of *The Fundamentals*. First what they affirmed, and second the effect those affirmations had on the world of biblical scholarship. On the first score, *The Fundamentals* represented more a competent restatement of received positions than a new defense. On the second, we have something quite different from what had gone before.

Almost a third of the nearly one hundred articles in *The Fundamentals* were devoted to Scripture.[12] Nearly all of these sought to confirm the trustworthy character of the Bible as a sure foundation for the church's life. And almost all set their face against the methods, assumptions, and conclusions of what by that time was becoming the critical orthodoxy. Essays in *The Fundamentals* spoke for a new generation of conservatives, taking the place of those who had first articulated the positions of the 1880s. But though there were new faces, the arguments were almost the same.

Scholarly investigation of the Scripture was still important. "The desire to receive all the light that the most fearless search for truth by the highest scholarship can yield," affirmed Canon Dyson Hague of Ontario, "is the desire of every true believer in the Bible. No really healthy Christian mind can advocate obscurantism."[13] Some of the protestations on behalf of criticism appear merely perfunctory. But other writers evidenced a sincerity to which arguments conformed.[14]

In addition, however, the authors in *The Fundamentals* emphasized with all the vigor of their predecessors, and more, that the real issue in the modern discussion was point of view. The testimony of a professor at Southwestern Baptist Seminary in Fort Worth, J. J. Reeve, concerning his own turn from the higher criticism, illustrated this prevalent note: "upon closer thinking I saw that the whole movement with its conclusions was the result of the adoption of the hypothesis of evolution."[15] At nearly every point, the exposure of a critic's presuppositions carried great explanatory significance. So, "the fundamental postulates" which grounded a belief in the plural authorship of Isaiah are "unsound"; "Modern objections to the Book of Daniel were started by German scholars who were prejudiced against the supernatural"; "the assumptions" of "the agnostic scientist, and the rationalistic Hebraist" must "be watched with the utmost vigilance and jealousy."[16] Although several of the papers do sift carefully through evidence, the heightened sense of clashing world views is the most prominent feature of the conservative argument.

Like their predecessors, authors in *The Fundamentals* still show much more interest in critical theories concerning the Pentateuch than in any other matter. To be sure, by the time of *The Fundamentals*, a fresh round of critical conclusions were being brought to bear for the New Testament (see, for example, 1901, William Wrede, *Das Messiasgeheimnis in den Evangelien;* 1906, Albert Schweitzer, *Von Reimarus zu Wrede,* later translated as *The Quest of the Historical Jesus;* and in English the article on the gospels by Paul W. Schmiedel in the 1901 edition of *Encyclopedia Biblica*). But concern in *The Fundamentals* was almost exclusively for the Old Testament. Of the twenty-seven biblical articles, twelve deal largely or exclusively with the Pentateuch, twelve are more general considerations of the question of inspiration, one each treats critical problems of Isaiah and Daniel, and only one (a brief meditation on the Gospel of John with no references to academic work) concerns the New Testament.

In general, these articles are a competent restatement of evangelical views.[17] The authors with professional credentials, like James Orr of the United Free Church College of Scotland, George Frederick Wright of Oberlin, or George L. Robinson of McCormick Seminary in Chicago, reasoned with care and gave evidence of prolonged study of the relevant literature. Yet for all the skill with which the booklets recapitulated evangelical positions, subtle changes had taken place since the first full-scale response to criticism a generation before.

For one thing, many of the articles are unabashedly derivative. The first two of several essays on inspiration, by James M. Gray of Moody Bible Institute and the evangelist L. W. Munhall, are little more than abridged summaries of the Warfield-Hodge paper of 1881. In several of the essays, reference to scholars holding conservative positions replaces articulation of the positions. Thus, Dyson Hague in his "History of the Higher Criticism" marshalls several counterarguments, but also makes much of reputed triumphs over the new views—for example, "Professor Winckler, who has of late overturned the assured and settled results of the Higher Criticism from the foundations"; "Green and Bissell are as able, if not abler, scholars than Robertson Smith and Professor Briggs."[18] For many, in other words, arguments about arguments are taking the place of the arguments themselves.

The Fundamentals also makes a somewhat more self-conscious appeal to the populace at large for an adjudication of the critical questions. Hague defends the right of "the average Christian," who "may not be an expert in philosophy or theology" but who possesses "common sense," to a judgment on the authorship of the Pentateuch and the dating of Daniel. Franklin Johnson, identified only as "D.D., LL.D.," was even franker in defending the rights of the pew against the academy: "As the sheep know the voice of the shepherd, so the mature Christian knows that the Bible speaks with a divine voice. On this ground every Christian can test the value of the higher criticism for himself." The same kind of appeal to the common person also shows through in occasional rhetorical flourishes, as when Sir Robert Anderson of London warned Christian scholars that they jeopardized their place among fellow Christians if they did not "disassociate themselves from the dishonest claptrap of this crusade ('the assured results of modern criticism' . . . and so on—bluster and falsehood by which the weak and ignorant are browbeaten or deceived) and acknowledge that their 'assured results' are mere hypotheses, repudiated by Hebraists and theologians as competent and eminent as themselves."[19] A democratic appeal was not absent from the earlier work of Hodge, Warfield, Beecher, and Patton, but it assumed a larger role in *The Fundamentals.*

A final difference from the earlier evangelical stance is the nearly complete abandonment of the idea that criticism can be a neutral task. For at least a few of the authors, absolutely everything hung on the assumptions brought to the Scriptures. Dyson Hague argued that unless the Bible is treated as "unique in literature," as a book full of "the spiritual and the infinite," it could not be understood properly—"the ordinary rules of critical interpretation must fail to interpret it aright." Hague's fellow Canadian, William Caven, suggested that "the principal external and internal evidences for the divine origin of the Scriptures" are so clear that they deserve to dominate the exercise of criticism.[20]

All of this is to say that the biblical essays in *The Fundamentals* occupied a transitional stage. Some of them were genuinely learned; all of the authors seemed to feel that it was important to continue a public dialogue with advocates of Higher Criticism; many of them expressed a high value for criticism within proper limits. Yet other tendencies were also present, like the great stress on the difference for scholarship between faith and rationalism, the propensity to play to the galleries, or a defensive listing of authorities, which pointed in the direction of a more complete divide between evangelical Bible scholarship and the study of Scripture in the academy.

Before leaving *The Fundamentals* it is important to note that its volumes encompassed a variety of evangelical positions. By far the largest group of biblical essays took critical arguments seriously, but only as a foil for counterarguments reestablishing traditional positions. Authors adopting this stance made much of internal disagreements among the critics to argue for the weaknesses of criticism itself.[21] The testimony of Jesus concerning the Mosaic authorship of the Pentateuch, the historicity of Jonah, and the early date of Daniel is a theme that appears frequently.[22] Those who practice this critical anti-criticism also stress the testimony of archaeology, ancient history, and modern philological discoveries in support of the traditional views.

It is hard to avoid labeling this position a defensive one. To be sure, the authors often argue it with skill, as when George Robinson carefully summarized the historical, literary, linguistic, and prophetic arguments against a unified Isaiah, only to find them inconclusive. But it also a position that could verge toward the bombastic, as when Dyson Hague paused in an exposition of early Genesis to comment on evolution:

Man was created, not evolved. . . . When you read what some writers, professedly religious, say about man and his bestial origin your shoulders unconsciously droop; your head hangs down; your heart feels sick. Your self-respect has received a blow. When you read Genesis, your shoulders straighten, your chest emerges. You feel proud to be that thing that is called man. Up goes your heart, and up goes your head.[23]

Although the earlier conservative thought of the 1880s and 1890s went somewhat beyond this position, the critical anti-criticism of the 1910s is a genuine if somewhat restricted heir of that earlier work. In turn it constituted a very important stance among conservative scholars in the generations that followed.

A somewhat less polemical position is also present in *The Fundamentals*. Especially in the three essays by James Orr we see similar arguments put to similar uses, but also some effort to benefit from newer approaches while rebutting their naturalistic aspects. Orr, for example, does not defend a twenty-four-hour day in his essay on early Genesis; he concedes that the long-lived patriarchs of Genesis 5 may have been tribes and not individuals; and he suggests that the flood was not necessarily universal.[24] In his essay on "Holy Scripture and Modern Negation," he is not so much concerned to engage "the question that has divided good men as to theories of inspiration—questions about inerrancy in detail, and other matters." He rather wishes to move "from these things at the circumference to the centre," to the Bible's faithful testimony to God and his acts, and to the salvation in Christ which that divine revelation brings.[25] In addition, Orr goes out of his way at several places to play down conflict between the Bible and science. He concedes that evolution, though not Darwin's "natural selection," is plausible, and that " 'Evolution' . . . is coming to be recognized as but a new name for 'creation.' "[26] Yet though he assumes this more accommodating posture, Orr's views are unabashedly conservative. He contends for the Mosaic provenance of Genesis 1–11 and against an evolutionary view of Hebrew monotheism. He argues that the accounts in early Genesis enshrined "the knowledge or memory of real transactions." And he regards the rejection of miracles as unprincipled dogmatic rationalism.[27] What is distinctive about Orr's position is not its conservative conclusions, but his willingness to absorb a good deal of modern thought on the way to those conclusions. It is also undoubtedly significant that Orr brought a British perspective to his American assignment.

There is yet a third stance toward criticism in *The Fundamentals*. This position comes close to denying the value of the modern scholarly enterprise as an aid for understanding Scripture. Franklin Johnson could find "no position of intellectual consistency" between the "natural view of the Scriptures" and "the lofty church doctrine of inspiration."[28] Canon G. Osborne Troop of Montreal concluded his meditation on "The Internal Evidence of the Fourth

Gospel" with the assertion that when we recite the book's contents, "we feel ourselves instinctively in the presence of truth."[29] While Johnson, Troop, and others who emphasized the spiritual apprehension of the Bible's message did not explicitly rule out the value of criticism as a lower-order means for understanding Scripture, they helped prepare the way for those to whom the spiritual and the critical were antithetical rather than merely different approaches.

Important as positions on the study of the Bible were in *The Fundamentals,* even more important for our purposes may be the reception which the wider world of Bible scholars accorded these positions. In sharp contrast to the situation during the 1880s and 1890s, the academic world as a whole paid very little attention to the evangelical arguments in *The Fundamentals.* A nearly complete disengagement seems to have taken place. It is difficult to make a case on the absence of evidence, but a fairly broad survey of contemporary academic periodicals—conservative, modernist, academic, denominational—reveals almost total disregard for *The Fundamentals.*[30] As William Hutchinson has shown, even such centers of conservative scholarship as Princeton Seminary paid almost no heed to the efforts in these booklets.[31]

This silence, like the dog whose bark Sherlock Holmes did not hear, is important. Arguments of *The Fundamentals* are not significantly different, nor are they argued in significantly inferior fashion, from the arguments that appeared in major theological journals, professional periodicals, and at meetings of the SBL a generation earlier. Now, however, conservatives are talking to the evangelical rank and file rather than to the academy. In these years before the emergence of the fundamentalist movement, the separation from the world fundamentalist leaders would advocate in the 1920s was already coming into existence. In retrospect, then, *The Fundamentals* mark an important stage in the development of evangelical scholarship not so much for the dignified work which they contain, for few responded to that work on that level. They are important, rather, as an indication of the estrangement of evangelical scholars from the academic marketplace and their turn toward the evangelical populace as the audience to which they will present their learned work on the Scriptures.

The reasons for the estrangement to which *The Fundamentals* testify are debatable. Those today who are inclined to continue earlier theological conflicts may point to the bigotry of intellectual fashion or, from the other side, the obscurantism of the evangelicals. A less volatile perspective is found in terms which Thomas Kuhn made famous in his book on *The Structure of Scientific Revolutions*.[32] Kuhn's discussion of "normal science," "paradigm shift," and "revolutionary" situations has been applied promiscuously to far too many historical developments. But here, at least, it really seems to fit. A period in which normal science proceeded under a secure paradigm (the Bible is the Word of God to be interpeted by the conventions of common sense) gave way to a period when anomalies in the old theories seemed to proliferate (new knowledge about world religions, new conceptions of historical development, new advances in research, new standards of professional study—and all exacerbated by social and economic changes in the community experiencing the anomalies). After a brief period of dialogue between those working in the old paradigm and those struggling toward something different (roughly 1880 to 1900), a new paradigm emerges for the practice of normal science (the Bible, however sublime, is a human book to be investigated with the standard assumptions that one brings to the discussion of all products of human culture). The first generation that accepts the new paradigm, that is, the first generation after the "revolution," then looks upon advocates of the old paradigm as almost literally beneath contempt. For their part, those continuing to do the "normal science" of the pre-1880 years still consider their work to be utterly scientific. The result is that individuals working in the two distinct paradigms regard the supposedly academic labor of the other as sheer quackery.

The one serious difficulty in the use of Kuhn's categories is that defenders of the old paradigm and workers within the new both considered their clash to be about the *truth* of the matter. Neither were satisfied with a sociology of knowledge, except as a way of explaining their opponents' mistakes. Thus, however helpful a consideration of paradigm shifts may be in describing what went on, it is far less useful for evaluating the truth-claims of the participants.

In any event, the lack of academic attention to *The Fundamentals* was a harbinger. Though the scholarship in *The Fundamentals* was more like evangelical work of the 1880s than of the 1930s, its relationship to the academic world was more like the latter period than the former. The outbreak of heated fundamental-ist-modernist strife after World War I drove the wedge deeper. As the years moved on, the place of scholars among conservative evangelicals, which had never been an exalted one, was reduced still further in deference to evangelists, missionaries, and pastors. In the world of academic scholarship, less and less work was done by evangelicals, less and less account was taken of that work by others.

The situation that developed was well described by two "main-line" observers who at mid-century wrote brief evaluations of Old Testament scholarship over the previous fifty years. Both George Ernest Wright of McCormick Seminary and Raymond A. Bowman of the University of Chicago were chastened liberals who chroni-cled unwarranted excesses of an earlier day. Yet neither was able to describe much of a contribution from evangelicals in restraining the excesses of criticism. Wright, whose survey appeared in 1951, spoke briefly and without prejudice of *The Fundamentals*, but then commented more generally on what followed:

. . . one of the chief characteristics of American fundamentalism of the twentieth century has been the steady decline in its scholarly work, and very little of real significance in the field of Old Testament study has been published. The fundamentalist atmosphere of largely negative reaction has not been conducive to the production of brilliant, flexible, highly trained, sensitive and scholarly work.[33]

Four years earlier in a similar survey, Bowman could say that by the end of World War I the Graf-Wellhausen theory of Pentateu-chal sources "was accepted by all reputable scholars." He did take notice of demurrals from "conservatives," but the only names he considered significant in this conservative camp were Germans and an occasional Frenchman or Englishman whose research in Semitic languages, Egyptian hieroglyphics, or similar fields had led to questions about one or another aspect of the documentary hypothesis. Bowman did not consider the arguments in *The Funda-mentals* or by their successors worthy of mention. Even the recon-dite efforts by German scholars to rescue the Mosaic authorship of the Pentateuch, he said, "have won no following among reputable scholars."[34] Other retrospectives concerning Bible scholarship for the years 1915 to 1940 likewise pass over the work of American evangelicals in silence.[35]

The professionalization of the university, the rise to dominance of critical conclusions in the new university, the growing irrelevance of evangelical scholarship to the world of the university, the fascination of university scholars with world religions, and the marriage of convenience between conservative scholars and the revivalist tradition led to a radical disengagement of conservative evangelicals from the broader world of Bible scholarship. *The Fundamentals* were not fundamentalistic, at least as that term came to be used in the 1920s, but they did anticipate the isolation that would characterize evangelical scholarship in the two decades after their publication.[36]

PRINCETON *CONTRA MUNDUM*

One group of conservative scholars constituted a significant exception to that generalization. Almost alone among the earlier centers of conservative scholarship, Princeton Theological Seminary continued to engage the modern questions through vigorous academic inquiry. Yet even as an exception, the Princeton scholars were becoming increasingly isolated. Because their work was so forthrightly conservative, it no longer had much of a place in the larger academic world. Because these men were so frankly academic, they sustained an ambiguous relationship to the popular world of theological conservatism. Yet the evangelical scholarship which continued at Princeton into the 1930s, as also the scholarship from Westminster Seminary, founded by Princeton conservatives after the reorganization of the older seminary in 1929, was important. It sustained a tradition of conservative academic work and paved the way for the contributions of other evangelicals who began to seek professional training after the standoffs of the 1920s gave way to a less polemical environment.

The importance of Princeton Seminary as a center for conservative evangelical scholarship rested in part upon the skills of its own faculty. But it also had something to do with trends in the wider circle of conservatives. Some groups, which conservative Presbyterians had numbered as allies on Scripture at the end of the previous century, moved into more liberal orbits. Others, though they retained a general conservatism, adopted theological principles that minimized the importance of academic biblical scholarship.

Congregationalists, who as late as the 1880s had accepted the largely conservative approach to the Bible, moved rapidly away from that position. The wholesale turn of Andover Seminary in a liberal direction symbolized the denomination's theological orientation, In addition, an unwillingness to promote further ecclesiastical conflict after the trials which followed the change at Andover also led to a situation in which fewer and fewer Congregationalist voices were lifted in support of conservative scholarship on Scripture.

IDEALISM, SUBJECTIVITY, AND THE BAPTISTS

The story of the Baptists was more complicated than the simple liberalization of the Congregationalists. Baptists both North and South remained staunchly conservative in theology. Critical conclusions had made only slight headway in the North by 1930, and almost none in the South. Yet the nature of theological conservativism among the Baptists left them little inclined to the active purusuit of biblical scholarship.

Intellectual leaders among Baptists in this period made less of detailed apologetical argumentation and more of subjective approaches to faith generally. Early in the century many Northern Baptists disassociated themselves from liberals at the University of Chicago. The founding of Northern Baptist Seminary in Chicago in 1913 as a conservative alternative to that University testified to the denomination's general uneasiness with the results of the new criticism. Yet this turn from modernism did not rest on technical biblical work so much as it did upon an intuitive sense that the new critical conclusions compromised important aspects of the Christian tradition. Since the end of the previous century, at least some Baptists had been giving subjectivity a higher place in the construction of their faith than a strict defense of biblical inspiration. As the conservative E. H. Johnson of Crozer Seminary had phrased this spirit at the 1884 Baptist Congress,

If your only ground for believing the doctrines of Christianity is that they are in the book, every question of the higher or of the lower criticism shakes your faith, and you are alarmed at such questions. And why? Because you believe in the doctrines of Christianity, since they are grounded in your religious consciousness, and you simply imagine that they are grounded only in the authority of the book. But, brethren, take courage from your fear. It is because we have found the doctrines of the Bible true, inwardly true, because we have tested them through and through, that we have reason not to fear.[37]

Even before 1900, A. H. Strong (1836–1921), the president of Rochester Seminary and author of a widely used *Systematic Theology*, came to exemplify an approach which joined doctrinal traditionalism with theological subjectivity. Strong was by no means a reactionary. He made his peace with evolution and also countenanced the possibility that some of the new critical conclusions about the Bible were correct, like the documentary view of the Pentateuch, dual authorship of Isaiah, or the allegorical character of Daniel and Jonah. Yet Strong also became greatly perturbed at the apparent implications of the new biblical scholarship. For him it was axiomatic that "the Bible is a revelation of Christ" and that this fact undergirded "the unity, the sufficiency, and the authority of Scripture."[38] Critical conclusions that undermined these convictions were suspect.

Strong's response to misguided criticism was not, however, a detailed anti-criticism. He was a theological idealist who had absorbed much from the "personalism" of Borden P. Bowne (1847–1910) of Boston University. In this philosophical position, all reality was personal, and God was the ultimate person. Bowne opposed all forms of evolutionary naturalism or simple materialism as violating the essential nature of reality. But he also opposed dogmatism and literalism and was skeptical about the value of minute investigations into causes and effects in the material sphere. The development, expression, and realization of personhood was what really mattered. With this perspective, Strong came to place less reliance on the static-mechanistic apologetics of the eighteenth and early nineteenth centuries. Ideas of development, so long as they could be tied to the divine, were no threat. While he remained opposed to the axioms of the new critical orthodoxy, he did not rest his defense on refutations at the level of a counter-criticism. His confidence was that the Spirit of Christ undergirded and suffused the processes of history.[39]

Baptists in the South had less contact with the newer criticism than their coreligionistis in the North. Only 9 of the SBL's 198 members in 1901 lived in points south of Washington, D.C., only 24 of 264 in 1921. The professionalization of academic life also proceeded at a slower pace in the South. After the departure of Crawford Toy from Southern Seminary in 1879, little interest in critical conclusions remained.[40] Southern Baptist efforts to maintain traditional faith, however, paralleled those of Strong's in finding more support from inner spirituality than from academic Bible scholarship.

The dominant Southern Baptist theologian during the first third of the century was E. Y. Mullins (1860–1928), president of Southern Baptist Seminary in Louisville from 1899 to his death. Mullins's importance for Southern Baptist attitudes to Scripture is suggested by a recent symposium on biblical scholarship in that denomination. Three different authors examined liberal, moderate, and fundamentalist approaches to Scripture among the Southern Baptists; each cites Mullins as contributing something essential to the stream he describes.[41] Mullins's own views on critical issues were traditional, though he supported a broad liberality of approach. Of greatest significance for a history of Bible scholarship is the fact that Mullins, like Strong, played down the objectivist, scientific approach to apologetics. Mullins was the most significant American conservative advocate of a subjectivist philosophy in the early twentieth century. He expressed his point of view succinctly in a contribution to *The Fundamentals:*

Christian experience sheds light on all the unique claims of Christianity. . . . Thus Christ acts upon the soul in experience as God and manifests all the power of God. . . . In this way Christ becomes final for the man, final for his reason, final for his conscience, final for his will, final for his intellect and most of all, final for his faith, his hope and his love, his aspirations. Nothing higher can be conceived. . . . Christian experience transforms the whole problem of Christian evidences to the sphere of practical life.[42]

When he made these assertions, Mullins was not denying the importance of traditional views about the Bible. These he helped to affirm by enlisting an old description of the Bible ("it has God for its author, salvation for its end, and truth, without any mixture of error, for its matter") for the Southern Baptist Statement of Faith and Mission in 1925.[43] Rather, Mullins was asserting that technical arguments about the Scriptures, while important, were not as significant for faith as the experience of Christ. This point of view, when combined with the cultural isolation of the South from the centers of the new criticism, meant that a low premium would be placed upon critical biblical scholarship among Southern Baptists until well after World War II.

The general conservatism of Baptists both North and South, though it did not lead to increased efforts at academic biblical scholarship in this period, would later prove to be a fertile medium for the cultivation of serious scholars. Much the same could also be said about Holiness, Wesleyan, and Pentecostal communities, and about the European confessionalists in immigrant communities during this same period. In the first decades of the century, however, the Presbyterians at Princeton flew the banner of conservative scholarship in the battlefields of the day pretty much by themselves.

SCHOLARSHIP AT PRINCETON SEMINARY

The scholarship of these Presbyterian conservatives continued the heritage of rigor, breadth, and learning which marked a wider range of conservative work in the nineteenth century. It was a scholarship tilted toward a theological more than an empirical approach to the Bible, but one which nonetheless did not slight exegetical, historical, and philological investigation.

In the work of Warfield, who continued active almost until his death in 1921, the conservatives enjoyed a learned theology of Scripture.[44] Warfield turned to other concerns in the first years of the twentieth century—most notably to historical studies on the Westminster Confession and Calvin, a lengthy series of attacks on perfectionism of both liberal and conservative varieties, and an immense range of reviews on the theological literature of Europe and America. But he still wrote learnedly on the subject of inspiration. His 1915 essay on "Inspiration" for James Orr's *International Standard Bible Encyclopedia*, as one notable example of such work, recapitulated his reading of crucial texts and allowed him to restate the conviction that the biblical testimony to the inspiration of Scripture "gives to the books written under its 'bearing' a quality which is truly superhuman; a trustworthiness, an authority, a searchingness, a profundity, a profitableness which is altogether Divine."[45] So long as Warfield lived, the conservatives possessed a champion whose views on the nature of biblical inspiration provided a sturdy canopy for other efforts.

This is not to imply that the consideration of critical proposals or the learned scrutiny of literary and historical particulars received any less attention. On the contrary, a substantial group of well-trained scholars continued the careful evaluation of individual arguments which William Henry Green had carried on in the previous generation. John D. Davis (1854–1926), who attended Princeton College and Seminary before pursuing advanced study at several universities in Germany, remains best known for his *Bible Dictionary*, first published in 1898. But his more technical work, especially on questions concerning the history of the Israelite monarchies, combined careful testing of critical conclusions and counterexposition of contested passages.

Davis summarized "Princeton Opinion" on the methodological questions at issue in a programmatic inaugural address for his induction as Professor of Oriental and Old Testament Literature in 1902. Princeton Seminary, he averred, had an explicitly "scientific" interest in these questions. Furthermore, "It has nothing that it regards as indispensable staked on the issue." Apart from the critical assumption that different accounts of similar events implies a real contradiction, Davis held that "the literary analysis is not in necessary conflict with any cherished convictions or vital doctrines." Anti-supernatural bias and the evolutionary presupposition that the sophisticated forms of Hebrew law had to be composed after the more simple were the real opponents of the Princeton position.[46]

Davis was joined in the study of the Old Testament by two scholars who eventually left Princeton to assist in the founding of Westminster. Robert Dick Wilson (1856–1930), after training at Princeton College, Western Seminary, and the University of Berlin, made a speciality of defending the historical character of the book of Daniel. His younger colleague, Oswald T. Allis (1880–

1973), who studied at Penn, Princeton Seminary, and Princeton University before taking a Ph.D. in archaeology and Assyriology from the University of Berlin in 1913, carried on the work of Green in contending for traditional views of the Pentateuch. Wilson's prefatory comments to his *Scientific Investigation of the Old Testament* (1926) suggest the nature of Princeton's Old Testament work in this period. He chose not to use prophecy or miracles in support of his conservative conclusions about the Old Testament, nor was he concerned about the controverted chronology of Old Testament events. Rather, he professed a reliance upon "the evidential method," that is, "the Laws of Evidence as applied to documents admitted in our courts of law," to settle the most important questions. It is "the evidence of manuscripts and versions and of the Egyptian, Babylonian, and other documents outside the Bible" which counts. Putting to use the facts "made known in the documents of the nations who surrounded and influenced the people of Israel through all its history from Abraham to Ezra," Wilson came to the following conclusions: (1) "that the Pentateuch as it stands is historical and from the time of Moses, and that Moses was its real author, although it may have been revised and edited by later redactors . . ."; (2) "that Joshua, Judges, Ruth, Samuel, and Kings were composed from original and trustworthy sources; though, in the case at least of Kings, they were not completed till about 575 B.C."; (3) that traditional dating for the prophets is correct; and (4) that the wisdom literature was all written by 400 B.C., and much of it considerably earlier.[47]

Davis, Wilson, Allis, and a few other Old Testament colleagues did not lack for learning, but their learning was not having much of an impact on American academic life of the time. Wilson published his *Scientific Investigation* and other scholarly works with the Sunday School Times Company in Philadelphia; similar in-house publishers brought out most of the books of these scholars. Academic essays appeared regularly in the *Princeton Theological Review*, but rarely in professional journals. And only infrequently did other professionals review their work.

The situation was different for the New Testament. Here Princeton succeeded in bringing together technical expertise and theological acumen in such a way as to participate, to at least some degree, in the wider academic world. For reasons discussed in the next chapter, New Testament scholarship was still much closer to traditional patterns than was the Old. The Princeton New Testament men were able to take advantage of this situation. Most prominent were William P. Armstrong (1874–1944), who studied at Princeton, Marburg, and Erlangen; and J. Gresham Machen (1881–1937), a graduate of Johns Hopkins and Princeton Seminary who also studied at Marburg and Göttingen. Both were conservatives who yet encouraged an unencumbered examination of current scholarly options. A student at Princeton Seminary in the mid-1920s has recently written, for example, to praise Armstrong and Machen for spending "more time [in class] teaching us the liberal rather than their own conservative point of view."[48]

Machen's New Testament work was the high point of conservative evangelical scholarship in the 1920s. He was soundly grounded in the classics. His *New Testament Greek for Beginners* (Macmillan, 1923) enjoyed a wide popularity and continues in print to the present. Machen also recognized the importance of modern critical questions and the importance for evangelicals to respond to the new scholarship on its own terms. In 1921 he published *The Origin of Paul's Religion*, (Macmillan) which set out to establish the continuity of Jesus' work and the mission of Paul. The best explanation for that mission, according to Machen, was that it rested on the supernatural character of Jesus' ministry. The book takes into consideration the mainstream of German criticism from Baur through Ritschl to Harnack, and the more recent technical studies of Wrede, Brueckner, and Bousset; it also benefited from, while yet criticizing, the work of Kirsopp Lake and J. Weiss. Although Machen by no means convinced all his readers, he made a substantial contribution to the discussion of first-century Christian history. In this and other works he largely succeeded in blending concern for theological principle with scholarly care in historical reconstruction.

Machen's *The Virgin Birth of Christ*, published by Harper & Brothers in 1930, was a similar effort to defend a traditional view through reasoned academic discourse, careful scrutiny of historical and linguistic research, and theological and philosophical criticism of counter positions. His argument was that only the unique circumstances of Jesus' life can account for the origin of the idea of his virgin birth; alternatives that trace it to contemporary circumstances are flawed by logical or historical defects. Machen drew his book to a close by acknowledging that the virgin birth represents "a stupendous miracle" opposed to the "enormous presumption" of ordinary human history. Yet, he argued, "that presumption can be overcome . . . when the tradition of the virgin birth is removed from its isolation and taken in connection with the whole glorious picture of the One who in this tradition is said to be virgin-born. What shall we think of Jesus Christ? That is the question of all questions, and it can be answered aright only when the evidence is taken as a whole."[49] Machen was continuing the earlier evangelical tradition. He valued the proposals of the new critics; he weighed carefully the historical and linguistic evidence; but he also insisted that point of view—"what shall we think of Jesus Christ?"—could never be set aside.

Machen's biblical scholarship, unlike Princeton work in the Old Testament, received serious attention in the broader world. Both his major works were reviewed widely in the academic and popular press; both were the occasion for serious responses from liberal scholars.[50]

The Princeton faculty in this period also enjoyed the services of Geerhardus Vos (1862–1949), a son of Dutch immigrants who had studied at the denominational seminary of the Christian Reformed Church in Grand Rapids, Michigan, at Princeton Seminary, and at the universities of Berlin and Strassburg, from which he received a doctorate in Arabic. From 1893 to 1932, Vos held the chair of biblical theology at Princeton. He was an accomplished exegete who did his share in turning back critical conclusions on Old Testament literature.[51] Vos, however, is most important for his contention that historical development was the central principle in the Scriptures. As a recent student has phrased it, Vos gave "pointed, systematic attention to the *doctrinal* or *positive* theological significance of the fact that redemptive revelation comes as an organically unfolding historical process."[52] To Vos, the revelation of Scripture did not constitute primarily a series of statements of fact (though the Bible is factual) so much as it offered a divinely inspired interpretation of God's redemptive work. The Bible was preeminently the record of a developing covenantal relationship between God, creator and redeemer, and the world. Vos rejected the common evangelical tendency to move past the historical particulars toward the timeless principle. Instead he focused on the way in which every part of the Bible is implicated by the historical relationship which it sustains to every other part. Vos, in other words, was attempting to roll back the assumption, prevailing since the late seventeenth century, that historical consciousness was the natural ally of rationalistic views of the Bible. From his earliest days as a Princeton professor, and increasingly in published work after the turn of the century, Vos used this conception of "biblical theology" to expound the biblical sense of covenant, Paul's view of salvation, Jesus's teaching on the Kingdom, the Gospel of John, the Epistle to the Hebrews, and other subjects.[53] To the more strictly doctrinal affirmations of Warfield and the learned defenses of Wilson, Machen, and the exegetes, Vos added an unusually fresh and creative note.

The study of Scripture at Princeton in the early twentieth century never succeeded in setting the tone for either the academic or the popular worlds. It was too conservative for the first, too learned (and Calvinistic) for the second. Nonetheless, it represented a significant strand of biblical scholarship which brought into the twentieth century the conservative convictions that had prevailed more widely during the previous period. It did so, moreover, by continuing the dialogue between conservative convictions and the current biblical scholarship of the day.

NADIR: 1930–1935

Events from the mid-1920s seemed to suggest, however, that even the sturdy work at Princeton would not be enough to sustain a viable conservative scholarship. The long conservative tradition at Princeton itself was placed in jeopardy when that seminary reorganized in 1929 to become a school reflecting the theological pluralism of the northern Presbyterian denomination.[54] Machen, Wilson, and Allis responded by founding a new seminary, Westminster, in Philadelphia, to carry on the "Old Princeton" tradition. But in spite of lofty goals and a capable faculty, Westminster found its influence restricted in the larger world of biblical scholarship. It was not clear, at first, whether Westminster could sustain even a shadow of the Old Princeton work. Machen, the ablest scholar, chose to pour his energy into church politics rather than academic work. From the time of Westminster's founding in 1929 to his death in 1937, he had little freedom to pursue studies in New Testament. Similarly, O. T. Allis devoted his attention to the theological controversies that eventually divided the separatistic Presbyterians among themselves. These struggles during the 1930s and 1940s led to major works from Allis exposing the errors of dispensational premillennialism as well as books engaging critical scholars on their methods and conclusions. The effective labors of the older Princeton conservatives—R. D. Wilson, Geerhardus Vos, and William P. Armstrong—also seemed finished. Wilson died in 1930 after only one year at Westminster. Armstrong, who was known for his brilliance in the classroom more than for his written scholarship, chose to remain at Princeton. Vos, never an active partisan in ecclesiastical controversy, did the same until he retired at age seventy in 1932. Vos's ideas, moreover, fell upon stony ground; some of his books were not even published for another two decades. But his scholarship was kept alive by professors at Westminster Seminary and now enjoys a growing, if still modest, reputation among conservative Presbyterians and in the Christian Reformed Church.

The last major institutional support for a conservative evangelical scholarship seemed, in other words, almost played out. Moreover, the larger world of fundamentalist and evangelical life beyond Princeton and Philadelphia seemed to have little concern for learned study of the Bible.

In that larger world conservative Protestantism was rapidly acquiring a reputation for atavism, anti-institutionalism, and even anti-intellectualism. The Scopes trial of 1925 represented a telling symbolic event. In the eyes of the learned culture, William Jennings Bryan had made a fool out of himself by defending the Genesis creation. But to a fair number of fundamentalists, Bryan had betrayed the faith by denying a creation of the world in six literal, twenty-four days.[55] Bryan's amateur attempts at interpreting early Genesis served only to drive the worlds of academic biblical scholarship and popular fundamentalist piety farther apart.

Even more important in this same regard was the rapid spread of dispensational theology. Dispensationalism grew out of the work of John Nelson Darby (1800–1882), a clergyman in the

Church of Ireland who became disenchanted with the compromises of that body and went on to help found the Plymouth Brethren. Darby stressed the division of history into a number of discrete epochs or dispensations, during which God offered salvation under differing methods. The basis for this view was a strict literalism in the interpretation of the Bible, especially its prophetic parts.[56] The Darbyite views first gained popularity in the United States during major conferences on prophecy which were held in the 1880s and 1890s. The affinities of Darby's views to assumptions about the static nature of truth, which were widespread in nineteenth-century America, made for its ready acceptance. In 1909 Oxford University Press published an edition of the Bible edited by C. I. Scofield (1843–1921) whose annotations set out a dispensational interpretation of the text. The Scofield Bible sold in breathtaking numbers and remains a mainstay of dispensational biblical interpretation.[57]

The rapid spread of dispensational convictions affected study of the Bible in three ways. It first provided an accessible scheme for making sense of the Scriptures—simple enough for ordinary people who would study hard, yet complex enough to afford the exhilaration of special knowledge. It brought the ancient book into the modern world simply, efficiently, and understandably. This feature of dispensationalism, unlike the next two, would eventually aid the academic study of Scripture by helping to create a reservoir of disciplined Bible readers from whose number professionally trained specialists would eventually emerge. The prominence of Plymouth Brethren scholars in later evangelical history bears out this long-term benefit. The Brethren, founded by Darby and his associates, encouraged a lay familiarity with Scripture. In turn, the various subgroups of this denomination, some of which are no longer dispensational, have contributed a disproportionately large number of scholars to evangelical biblical work in the twentieth century.[58]

Second, dispensationalism emphasized the supernatural character of the Bible to such an extent that the historical contexts of Scripture receded into the background. At a time when critical fashion was playing down the divine element in Scripture, such a reaction was not only to be expected but was also beneficial (from the standpoint of those who believed in the inspiration of Scripture). The difficulty came, however, when the effort to understand Scripture according to its divine character undermined efforts to grasp its historical contexts. Under this impetus, the Bible was all too readily taken out of history and read as an artificially unified text. In an extreme form, this tendency led spokesmen to urge parishioners simply to "select some word and with the aid of a good concordance, mark down . . . the references to the subject under discussion . . . thus presenting all the Holy Ghost has been pleased to reveal on the topic."[59] For those who accepted this approach, the historical, philological, and literary studies which made up the academic discipline were worse than irrelevant. They were dishonoring to the divine character of the Bible.

It is worth noting in passing that this dispensational emphasis on the divine character of Scripture provided the point of contact with conservative scholars from Princeton and elsewhere. At Princeton the Bible's divine character was never, at least in theory, divorced from its humanity. Thus Princeton scholars and other conservatives regularly showed considerable impatience with dispensational methods, exegesis of prophecy, and general orientation. Yet because both the dispensationalists and the Princeton conservatives shared a belief in the divine character of the Bible, they entered into an uneasy alliance against those whom they perceived as calling that divine quality into question.[60]

Third, dispensationalism flourished in communities that distrusted professional scholarship. Most of its major proponents were neither academically trained nor professionally certified students of Scripture. Darby was well educated and versed in the major European languages, yet devoted his energies to itinerant evangelism and popular writing. Scofield was a lawyer turned lay annotator. Lewis Sperry Chafer, who published a multivolume dispensational *summa* in 1947, attended Oberlin College for three years before beginning a pastoral career. To Chafer and other dispensationalists it was a positive advantage not to be contaminated by the accumulated learning of the centuries. He once was quoted as saying, "The very fact that I did not study a prescribed course in theology made it possible for me to approach the subject with an unprejudiced mind to be concerned only with what the Bible actually teaches."[61] The modern university was a place of danger. Not only its promotion of naturalism, but also its methods of scholarship were suspect.

The climate set by dispensationalism was a good one for treating the Bible seriously. But in the first forty years of this century it also contributed to a process that rendered academic study of the Bible —inquiry relying upon detailed, professionally trained investigation of the Scriptures and their times—nearly extinct among conservative evangelicals.[62]

Besides, for these Christians, the appeal of scholarship was a faint whisper in comparison to the imperative for action. The 1920s and 1930s witnessed a remarkable outpouring of conservative activity, whether organizing to defend the fundamentals in "mainline" denominations, or establishing separate agencies outside the denominations. The university world may have fallen to enemies, but vast arenas for service still remained in mission work, evangelism, popular publication, the new medium of radio, Christian colleges and Bible schools, and so on.[63] The effects of this activism could be seen everywhere, but one illustration from the Southern Baptists is sufficient to suggest its effects on biblical scholarship. At Southern Seminary in Louisville, the most accomplished Bible scholar after the passing of Robertson and Broadus was John R. Sampey, an Old Testament specialist who taught there from 1887 to 1942. Sampey had early studied with William Rainey Harper and remained Harper's lifelong friend. Although Sampey possessed solid academic credentials, he made very few contributions to scholarly literature. One reason may have been his growing conviction that some of the more modest critical conclusions, such as the division of Isaiah into two parts, were correct and yet still too radical for a Southern Baptist constituency. But the major reason was that he was so active in what he called "extramural work." For Sampey, this included great energy poured into work on the International Sunday School Committee, a long pastorate of forty years, and extensive traveling as a revivalist and as a visitor to the mission field.[64]

In sum, a combination of factors during the first third of the twentieth century—the loss of institutional bases within the older denominations, a shrinking corps of active Bible scholars, the spread of dispensationalism, the ascendency of activism, the distrust of the university, the disruption of the fundamental-ist-modernist controversies—led to an eclipse of evangelical biblical scholarship. Even mid-level journals like *The Biblical Review,* published by the Biblical Seminary of New York City, and *Christian Faith and Life,* which had published solid popularizations since the 1890s, ceased publication in the 1930s (1932 and 1939, respectively). A few denominational publications continued to report on more specialized evangelical work. Older books which had addressed critical questions continued to be reprinted. But when J. Gresham Machen died on January 1, 1937, an era seemed to be over. An evangelical scholarship which was supported by formidable institutions, which enlisted scholars of ability, which advocated thorough academic preparation, which was skeptical of exclusively popular interpretations, and which took an interest in the results of professional scholarship seemed to have come to an end.

In fact, appearances were as deceptive in the mid-1930s, when there seemed to be scant evangelical scholarship, as in 1900, when evangelicals seemed to be carrying the day. Already developments had begun which would bring evangelicals back to the marketplace of ideas and win back a partial hearing in the academy. These were taking place in immigrant communities, which had earlier shown little interest in broader American concerns; in the theological world more generally, and among fundamentalists themselves; and they were also taking place in Great Britain. Events across the Atlantic were of particular importance for the recovery of an evangelical Bible scholarship in America. But to see them in perspective, it is necessary to pause briefly to summarize the course of biblical criticism in Great Britain from the 1860s. Many of the questions Britons faced were the same as those confronting Americans. The pattern of answers, even among those who shared an evangelical theology, was not, however, exactly the same. The unfolding of these British developments deserves separate consideration before the story in America continues.

4. An Alternative: Great Britain, 1860–1937

> The inspired record must be, and is, sufficient to convey to us, in purity and faithfulness, the whole will of God for our salvation and guidance. But the course of the discussion, and survey of the Biblical facts, suggest also certain *limitations* with which the doctrine of inspiration, in its application to the several parts of Scripture, must necessarily be received. This is an aspect of the subject which, as arising out of the *data* presented in Scripture itself, likewise requires attention.
>
> JAMES ORR, *Revelation and Inspiration*, 1910

Britons began to pay serious attention to modern biblical criticism only a short time before their American colleagues. In England and Scotland the same range of responses was present as in the United States—some welcomed German views as a means of escaping from traditional conceptions of Christianity, others sought to appropriate the new views within an older orthodoxy, and still others rejected critical conclusions as an assault upon the faith. As in the United States, evangelicals could be found among both moderate appropriaters and conservative opponents of the new views. For all the similarities, however, major differences also separated British evangelicals from their American counterparts. To put these in perspective, the place to begin is with a definition of evangelicalism in Great Britain.

British evangelicals were those members of the established Episcopal Churches of England, Wales, and Ireland; the Presbyterian churches of Scotland and Ireland; or the nonconforming denominations, who traced their lineage to the evangelical revivals of the eighteenth century, and beyond that to the Protestant Reformation. Within the Anglican church a distinct evangelical party had emerged by the late eighteenth century. It was set over against a broad church group moving toward theological liberalism, and a high church party which, after the Oxford Movement of the 1830s and 1840s, stressed the Catholic character of Anglicanism. By the time of the Oxford Movement, Anglican evangelicals possessed a clear set of commitments: (1) to the Book of Common Prayer and the Thirty-Nine Articles of Religion interpreted as Protestant documents of the Reformation; (2) to the Bible as authoritative in faith and practice and to Bible-reading as an activity for home as well as church; (3) to the centrality of the cross in theological construction; (4) to justification by faith as the foundation of Christian good works; (5) to the importance of conversion for bringing people into relationship with Christ; and (6) to the necessity of evangelism and missions at home and abroad.[1] Toward the end of the century, the evangelical bishop of Liverpool, J. C. Ryle, began a definition of his party by noting that "the first leading feature in Evangelical Religion is the *absolute supremacy it assigns to Holy Scripture,* as the only rule of faith and practice, the only test of truth, the only judge of controversy." Scripture was the normative standard for all other religious authorities, whether the Fathers, tradition, the Prayer Book, or conscience. Upon this belief hung the second and third defining convictions of an evangelical, belief in personal human corruption and personal redemption in Christ, truths which Ryle set against formal, external, or merely sacramental kinds of the faith.[2]

In the nonconformist, dissenting, or free churches, the same range of emphases defined the same kind of faith. Wesleyan and other Methodists employed small cells to encourage confession, prayer, and Bible study. Baptists, some Congregationalists, a few English Presbyterians, a number of Welsh bodies, and a goodly contingent of Anglicans kept alive Calvinistic forms of evangelical theology, an allegiance that also survived in the established and nonestablished Presbyterian churches of Scotland. Some of the newer groups that arose in the nineteenth century, like the Plymouth Brethren, stressed a lay-oriented study of the Scriptures as the key to religious life. By definition, most dissenters felt that a proper Christianity could best be served beyond the boundaries of a state-church establishment. In many other respects, however, evangelicalism among dissenters closely resembled that among the Anglicans.

The major difference from America was the prominence of Anglicans among evangelicals. As members of the establishment as well as often of the lesser aristocracy, these Anglicans enjoyed access to Oxford and Cambridge, and they occasionally received preferment in the state church. In sum, their participation in the establishment encouraged both a traditional conservativism and a pragmatic tolerance for others. For most of the century, the evangelicals most visible in the formal study of Scripture were members of the Church of England.

A further difference was the presence in England of another traditionalist non-Roman Catholic body which shared a good number of orthodox convictions with the evangelicals. High church Anglicans, while preferring the Fathers to the reformers, sacraments to conversion, and learning to activism, still shared a thorough supernaturalism with evangelicals. Although they approached the interpretation of Scripture with a different hermeneutic, they agreed with evangelicals on the inspiration and infallibility of the Bible. Particularly after the excitement over the Oxford Movement began to subside, evangelical and high church Anglicans sometimes found themselves taking common positions on the study of Scripture. The result was a relationship without direct parallel in the United States. While antagonisms between evangelicals and Anglo-Catholics were too strong for the creation of an actual alliance, high church attitudes toward the Bible amounted to a respected conservative voice on questions of biblical criticism to complement opinion on the subject from the evangelicals themselves.[3]

THE EARLY REJECTION OF CRITICISM

Attempts at mid-century to introduce critical conclusions about Scripture met a nearly universal rebuff.[4] In 1860 seven Church of England ministers published a volume entitled *Essays and Reviews,* which was meant, among other things, to encourage open, unhindered discussion of the Bible. The essayists shared the conviction that the best modern learning on Scripture was being ignored in England because of a hidebound traditionalism. Although they differed widely in quality, the essays were united in tone. All assumed that the modern mind had rendered certain traditional formulations suspect. The Bible especially required reexamination. Much more attention needed to be paid to the poetic, religious, parabolic, or even mythic and legendary aspects of Scripture than to its character as a reporter of historic actualities. In fact, the essayists argued, all that the Thirty-Nine Articles of the Church of England required of a clergyman was to believe simply in the inspiration of Scripture; nowhere did the Articles specify how this inspiration was to be interpreted. Benjamin Jowett, Regius Professor of Greek at Oxford, who wrote on the intepretation of the Bible, raised the most far-reaching questions. Jowett asserted that "in what may be termed the externals of interpretation, that is to say, the meaning of words, the connexion of sentences, the settlement of the text, the evidence of facts, the same rules apply to the Old and New Testaments as to other books." It was necessary for the interpreter "to read Scripture like any other book . . . to open his eyes and see or imagine things as they truly are."[5] The same reversals of settled judgments concerning text, authorship, and interpretation which regularly appeared in classical studies should be expected in work on the Bible. At the same time, Jowett also spoke as if it were possible to transcend the details of the Bible to find its uniquely spiritual message.

Nonconformists joined evangelical and high church Anglicans in denouncing *Essays and Reviews.* The Anglican bishops agreed unanimously that its opinions transgressed the ordination vows of their communion. Many books and countless articles attacked one or another of the assertions in the volume. Some of these displayed a scholarship far exceeding that in *Essays and Reviews,* which was not a profound book; some of the attacks played unashamedly to the crowd.[6] The general reaction to *Essays and Reviews* lends credence to the somewhat exaggerated assessment that Stephen Neill once made concerning the Bible at mid-century:

Almost all good Christians in England were what would now be called "fundamentalists". Whether it was Mr. Newman [high church Anglican who had converted to Roman Catholicism] or Dr. Pusey [Anglo-Catholic], Lord Shaftesbury or Dean Close [Anglican evangelicals], Mr. Gladstone [high church statesman] or Dr. Dale [Congregationalist], there was very little between them; all accorded the Bible an unqualified reverence, and all believed that, if its inerrancy were successfully impugned, the whole Christian faith would collapse.[7]

Ironically, this unified reaction to *Essays and Reviews* paved the way for a much more open attitude to criticism. Some moderate or conservative scholars were distressed by the heavy-handed way in which traditionalists attacked the critics' views.[8] To them it did not seem fitting to adjudicate intellectual proposals through appeals to the courts of church and nation.

In addition, the judicial processes that arose in the wake of the book's publication heralded a greater openness for new critical views. The Church of England's official review resulted in a one-year suspension for two of the authors, Rowland Williams and H. B. Wilson, but also in a statement that the Anglican confession did not specify what were permissible views on most of the modern critical questions. These suspensions, moreover, were overturned in 1864 by a judicial committee of the privy council, whose majority declared that nothing in the book violated the constitutions of the Church of England.

The result was predictable. The church-state establishment was not able to quash the new conclusions through legal manuevers. Yet such political maneuvering had disenchanted some scholars who felt that the arguments of *Essays and Reviews,* however insubstantial, deserved to be addressed on their own merits. Critical views did not flourish in the wake of these events. Yet no longer did institutional barriers stand against their advance.

The next serious incident was similar to the controversy over *Essays and Reviews.* In 1862 the Bishop of Natal in South Africa, John William Colenso, published a quirky book, *The Pentateuch and the Book of Joshua Critically Examined.* It purported to be a study of the numbers in the earliest portions of the Bible. To Colenso many of them, like the size of the army Moses led toward Canaan, were absurd. Colenso concluded that the narratives of the Old Testament were not necessarily meant to report historical fact, but rather were vehicles for religious truth of a different sort. Colenso's opponents did not have much difficulty pointing out flaws in his arguments, but the significance of the case was not diminished for all that. Here was an Anglican bishop stating that portions of the Bible Christians had regularly regarded as factual history were nothing of the kind. Some of the leaders of new thought in England, like the scientists Charles Lyell and Charles Darwin, contributed to Colenso's defense fund as a means of showing their support for unencumbered academic inquiry. Finally, the bishop was suspended by his metropolitan, Robert Gray of Cape Town, a suspension which led to great complications because of the tangled legal and ecclesiastical bonds tying South Africa to Britain. A small number of Natal Anglicans followed Colenso in the establishment of a separate church, almost the last occasion in larger British history where disagreements over Scripture led to ecclesiastical schism.

The Colenso affair gave further publicity to the Continental opinions which were calling into question traditional stances to the Bible. It gave further offense to those who felt that the proper response to innovation was reason rather than the courts. And it helped keep alive questions of higher criticism until more responsible voices brought them again to the public attention.

EVANGELICAL CRITICISM

The William Robertson Smith case in the Free Church of Scotland, which was of so much interest to Americans, marked the beginning of a new relationship between British evangelicals and biblical criticism. Smith freely applied the criticism of the Continent to the Old Testament, but he did so while maintaining a belief in miracles, personal divine revelation, and the supernatural. At the end of a complicated series of hearings, Smith lost his professorship in 1881, but retained his status as an ordained minister. Of this action it was said that the Free Church secured its liberty in biblical criticism by the sacrifice of one individual.[9] Smith's convictions resembled those of Charles Briggs in the United States, except that Briggs was probably more cautious in using the new criticism. With Briggs, Smith shared the belief that it was possible to employ critical methods within an orthodox Christian framework. Unlike the fate of Briggs's ideas in the United States, however, Smith's general convictions became prominent in the United Kingdom.

A series of circumstances in England at the time of the Smith affair led to the development of an evangelical mode of criticism. The most important actors in this development were a trio of great Christian scholars, who had trained together at Cambridge and who had agreed to devote their lives to a coordinated study of the New Testament. These included an exacting textual critic, Fenton A. J. Hort (1828–1892); a commentator of unusual insight and scholarly depth, B. F. Westcott (1825–1901); and a meticulous historian of the early church, J. B. Lightfoot (1828–1889).[10] This

"Cambridge triumvirate" played a leading part in many of the significant discussions of their day. While not themselves members of the evangelical party in the Church of England, they were orthodox and pious. Their labors marked out a path for evangelicals to follow.

They were important, first, for their leadership in the preparation of a critical edition of the New Testament. Scholars had known for decades that the text used as the basis for the King James Translation was defective. As a result of the new scholarship on the Continent and a large number of successful forays into the Middle East, older and better manuscripts of the New Testament were now available. But what was to be done with the thousands of minute discrepancies in these manuscripts? Did they imperil Christian faith by making the Bible uncertain? As early as 1853 Westcott and Hort turned themselves to this task. Although the final results were not published until 1881, their work had much earlier attracted the attention of other scholars who shared their academic and Christian commitments. Westcott, Hort, and their colleagues succeeded in establishing a refined critical consensus which overturned many readings in the "received text" undergirding the Authorized Version. Their critical edition, for example, omitted several important passages that appeared in the Authorized Version because the scholars considered them later interpolations into the original text. These included the last twelve verses of Mark, the story in John 8 of the woman taken in adultery, and the trinitarian formula of 1 John 5:8. In addition, they concluded that in many other places it was simply not possible to decide with finality which of variant readings was closest to the original documents. Yet for all this reconstruction of older textual foundations, the work of Westcott and Hort was fundamentally conservative. They showed conclusively that although questions remained on many details, the essential message of the New Testament as a whole, and for each of its books, rested on secure textual foundations. The New Testament was more thoroughly and more clearly attested than any other volume from the ancient world.

This work on the text of the New Testament text had two important consequences. First, it encouraged conservatives to think that critical scholarship could end by defending, at least in large outline, traditional views. As pioneered by Westcott and Hort, criticism (the willingness to research new problems from scratch) had yielded conservative results. This aspect of their work left an enduring legacy on both sides of the Atlantic where textual criticism became a widely pursued academic task for evangelical scholars.

At the same time, however, study of the New Testament text promoted criticism more generally. If it were possible to research the text of the New Testament through unencumbered academic inquiry, should it not be possible to pursue other critical questions —literary, historical, and the like—through the same means? Hort, whose views on authorship, dating, and editorial reconstruction were less conservative than Westcott's or Lightfoot's, was more aware of the implications in this regard than were the others.[11] Yet their work as a whole pushed further into the background the older view of the Bible as simply a divine gift from heaven.

The second accomplishment of these scholars was to explode the radical New Testament criticism of the Tübingen school. Earlier in the century, German scholars led by F. C. Baur had proposed an extensive reordering of the New Testament on the basis of Hegelian presuppositions. Baur assumed that all history moved dialectically from thesis through antithesis to synthesis. As he studied the New Testament he came to the conclusion that the synoptic gospels and Acts represented a synthesis of Peter's teaching (embodying Old Testament and Hebraic emphases) and the teaching of Paul (shaped by Hellenistic influences). The synthesis of these views in the New Testament's historical books could only be explained by postulating a very late date for their composition. These books could have been written only in the second half of the second century, since it would have taken that long to move through Petrine thesis and Pauline antithesis to this synthesis. Such assumptions led to thoroughly radical views. Most of the New Testament books came from the second century. Few were written by the authors whose names introduced the books and whom the church had accepted throughout its history. This was a Bible scholarship even more alarming than the contemporary criticism of the Old Testament because it struck at the portrait and early interpretation of Jesus.

J. B. Lightfoot assumed most of the burden for assessing these views. His first important examination occurred in response to a book, *Supernatural Religion,* published anonymously in 1874. The author of this volume, J. A. Cassels, presented a superficial distillation of Tübingen views to advance the idea that supernaturalism hurt religion by overwhelming its proper ethical content. In the course of his study, Cassels criticized the integrity of B. F. Westcott's work. Lightfoot jumped to the defense of his friend in a series of essays published in the *Contemporary Review*. Lightfoot could show that the gospels possessed a much firmer historical character than the radical Germans allowed; he demonstrated the paltry character of Cassel's scholarship; he vindicated the judiciousness of Westcott; and he provided a persuasive attack on the theory-laden character of the radical views. Cassel's volume created a sensation when it first appered, and the book sold in great numbers. As a consequence of Lightfoot's response, however, publishers were forced to dump vast quantities of the volume onto the remainder market.[12]

Lightfoot also provided a more extensive response to this radical criticism in his masterful editions of the Apostolic Fathers, which began to appear in 1869. One of the linchpins of the Tübingen position was its contention that the works of Ignatius and Clement, traditionally dated around A.D. 100, had in fact been written much later. These writings were important because they quoted or cited most of the books of the New Testament and, furthermore, gave no evidence of the Pauline-Petrine tension so important to Baur's arguments. When Lightfoot published his edition of these and other early Christian writers, Tübingen's house of cards collapsed. Through detailed, painstaking historical reconstruction, Lightfoot showed that traditional dating for Clement's epistles from Rome to Corinth in the 90s and for at least several of Ignatius's epistles *circa* A.D. 110 was correct. With these works placed securely around the turn of the first century, it moved consideration of virtually all New Testament books back before this time. Whatever else one might argue about the composition of the New Testament, Lightfoot had effectively demolished the most radical criticism of his day.

Once again the Cambridge scholars had undermined skepticism through the use of scholarship. Again, it seemed as if the faith were not threatened by the application of careful historical work. Scholarship could work in harmony with orthodoxy. It was the critical scholars who displayed anti-intellectual tendencies by shaping their work to fit preconceived philosophical notions. Lightfoot's historical work, when added to the disciplined textual study of Hort and Westcott, convinced even many evangelicals that criticism had its place. More now were ready to attempt their own critical studies because it had become apparent that radical results were not the foregone conclusions of critical inquiry.

The Cambridge scholars were also important for the general place they held in the scholarship of the late nineteenth century as well as for their specific achievements. They were students of the New Testament who had applied criticism for the establishment of reasonably conservative conclusions. In Britain the success of this conservative New Testament criticism seemed to have something to do with the acceptance of a more liberal criticism of the Old Testament. The Cambridge trio and a number of scholars who followed in their train had secured the words and deeds of Jesus, they had established a preponderance of evidence in favor of traditional views concerning the apostolic writings, and they had justified a treatment of New Testament narratives as historically plausible. Did not these successes in the New Testament make for more latitude in the acceptance of newer views on the Old? Especially when the most prominent Old Testament critics were men like William Robertson Smith and Oxford's Samuel Rolles Driver, individuals who affirmed the supernatural character of Hebrew experience, the tendency was to allow conservative views on the New Testament to serve as a balance for more liberal views on the Old. No one could question the Christian seriousness of Hort or the orthodoxy of Lightfoot and Westcott, both of whom became bishops. If such ones could pursue criticism as an exercise of their faith, then perhaps criticism was a legitimate vocation for all. In addition, if these had used criticism to yield greater confidence in the New Testament, could historical and literary criticism of the Old Testament really do much harm?

In Britain during these years a certain ambiguity clung to terms like "criticism." It applied both to scholarly inquiry in itself and to the results of scholarship predicated on the new historical consciousness. In addition, a certain naiveté still attended the supposed ability to work on such issues with strict academic detachment. Yet for all these ambiguities, the work of the Cambridge scholars provided the most powerful model for critical study of the

Bible by evangelicals, even as it offered a nonthreatening way for criticism as a whole to become more firmly established in Great Britain.

This, at least, is one explanation for the rapid acceptance by evangelicals of Old Testament criticism during the period between 1880 and 1900, the continued prosecution of a conservative New Testament criticism over the same period, and the relatively subdued nature of evangelical protest against the newer views.

THE TRIUMPH OF CRITICISM

Moderate forms of critical scholarship came to dominate the British world of biblical scholarship with relative speed and with relatively little strife. The thesis argued by Willis Glover and others seems persuasive: In Britain, unlike the United States and the Continent, traditional views gave way without serious trauma because champions of the new criticism also succeeded in presenting themselves as defenders of the old faith.[13]

Several significant publications in this twenty-year period suggest the nature of that triumph. When S. R. Driver (1846–1914), the Regius Professor of Hebrew at Oxford, published his *Introduction to the Literature of the Old Testament* in 1891, he provided readers of English with an informed summary of the more recent Old Testament criticism. The book affirmed the multiple authorship of the Pentateuch and Isaiah, it dated Daniel in the second or third century B.C., and it conveyed many of the other critical conclusions about the Old Testament that had become conventional on the Continent. The significance of Driver for the acceptance of criticism in Britain, however, was his insistence that these critical conclusions did not imply a reduced view of biblical revelation. The critical conclusions were a necessary adjustment to unimpeachable scholarship: "It is impossible to doubt," he wrote, "that the main conclusions of critics with reference to the authorship of the books of the Old Testament rest upon reasonings the cogency of which cannot be denied without denying the ordinary principles by which history is judged and evidence estimated." Theologians who opposed such conclusions did so needlessly; they betrayed the same shortsightedness as those who once opposed newer views in astronomy, geology, and biology.

It is not the case that critical conclusions, such as those expressed in the present volume, are in conflict either with the Christian creeds or with the articles of the Christian faith. Those conclusions affect not the *fact* of revelation, but only its *form*. . . . They do not touch either the authority or the inspiration of the Scriptures of the Old Testament. They imply no change in respect to the Divine attributes revealed in the Old Testament; no change in the lessons of human duty to be derived from it; no change as to the general position (apart from the interpretation of particular passages) that the Old Testament points forward prophetically to Christ. [Even on this view the whole of the Old Testament] is subordinated to the controlling agency of the Spirit of God, causing the Scriptures of the Old Testament to be profitable "for teaching, for reproof, for correction, for instruction, which is in righteousness."[14]

Driver represented a large group of scholars who felt they could show the compatibility, rather than the reverse, between criticism and faith.

A second important development was the acceptance by many High Church Anglicans of at least moderate critical positions. Most notable in this regard was the publication in 1889 of *Lux Mundi: A Series of Studies on the Religion of the Incarnation* under the editorship of Charles Gore (1853–1932). The papers in this book represented statements by the rising generation of High Churchmen on Christ as the Light of the World. While the volume as a whole was moderate, reverent, and reasonably orthodox, it also no longer contested critical conclusions on the Bible. The most important essay for these purposes was a paper by Gore on "The Holy Spirit and Inspiration."

Gore used this opportunity to defend a traditional view of the Holy Spirit, and a relatively conservative view of biblical criticism. Thus the Pastoral Epistles must be given as much canonical authority as any of the New Testament documents. The Gospel of John did not distort "the record, the personality, the claims of Jesus Christ." And "there is nothing to prevent our believing . . . that the [historical] record from Abraham downward is in substance in the strict sense historical." At the same time, however, Gore made a place for modern criticism, especially on the Old Testament. So long as the supernatural and miraculous were not ruled out of consideration, nothing restrained the Christian from letting criticism take its own course in deciding whether

Jonah and Daniel were history or drama. Furthermore, "within the limits of what is substantially historical, there is still room for an admixture of what, though marked by spiritual purpose, is yet not strictly historical—for instance, for a feature which characterizes all early history, the attribution to first founders of what is really the remoter results of institutions."[15]

In this accommodation to criticism, Gore addressed directly the encumbrance which more than anything else kept conservatives from appropriating the new views of the Old Testament. Did not Jesus himself testify to the Mosaic authorship of the Pentateuch, the historicity of Jonah, and other traditional beliefs? On such matters, how could a Christian prefer the most recent *eureka* from Germany in favor of Jesus himself? Gore responded by proposing that the Incarnation involved Christ in a self-emptying or *kenosis* (following Philippians 2:5–11). This meant that Jesus' references to authors, dating, and interpretation of the Old Testament were not meant to settle questions of modern criticism. "Thus the utterances of Christ about the Old Testament do not seem to be nearly definite or clear enough to allow of our supposing that in this case He is departing from the general method of the Incarnation, by bringing to bear the unveiled omniscience of the Godhead, to anticipate or foreclose a development of natural knowledge." While Christ "revealed" God perfectly, in his Incarnation he *"used* human nature, its relation to God, its conditions of experience, its growth in knowledge, its limitation of knowledge."[16] Gore did not set aside his conservative convictions about Scripture through these means. He rather affirmed a way to maintain them in concert with the moderate conclusions of the new criticism.

Not everyone by any means was satisfied with Gore's proposal. Yet it was still of great significance for the progress of criticism in Britain. Now the argument seemed less compelling that to accept the lordship of Christ prevented one from appropriating some variety of critical work on the Bible.

By 1900, in other words, British Christians had made an important transition. While maintaining certain features of older views on the inspiration of Scripture, churchmen and dissenters of at least relatively conservative theology still had made their peace with the new criticism. Those who moved in this direction were supported by the conservative achievements on the New Testament from the Cambridge triumvirate. They possessed examples of Old Testament scholars who had combined piety and criticism. And they seemed satisfied to practice what modern commentators have called an "evangelical," "devout," or "believing" criticism of the Scriptures.[17]

CONSERVATIVE REACTION

This is not to say that all evangelicals within the Church of England or outside of it accepted the newer views. In fact, a substantial number continued to look upon accommodation to criticism as conformity to the world. Yet these nay-sayers, as opposed to their fellows in the United States, succeeded in establishing only weak counterorganizations, and they did not erect a conservative scholarship worthy of the name.

Charles Haddon Spurgeon (1834–1892), the great Baptist preacher, was the best-known opponent of modern criticism. One of his concerns in the famous Down-Grade Controversy of 1887–1888, when he attacked other members of the Baptist Union for departing from traditional faith, was the increasing acceptance of critical views of Scripture. To Spurgeon, such opinions contributed to the Baptists' slide from traditional Christianity. When Spurgeon resigned from the Union in 1888, one of the reasons was its lack of resolution to oppose criticism. Spurgeon, however, was a preacher who opposed the new views especially for the spiritual devastation he feared they would wreak in the church. Yet he did not take upon himself the task of providing scholarly answers to the newer views.

Others, however, made this attempt. The Congregationalist Alfred Cave (1847–1900) published *The Inspiration of the Old Testament Inductively Considered* in 1888 as an effort to overthrow the criticism of the continent which was now coming into Britain. This work represented a competent restatement of traditional views; but it was marked by careful rather than deep learning. Cave rarely employed Hebrew or Aramaic in his arguments, and his grasp of historical and literary questions was not profound. The book also displayed a certain ingenuousness about method. It proposed to study "all the facts concerning inspiration presented by the Old Testament . . . as far as possible without bias or prepossession, with a view to ultimately ascertaining the conclusions these facts warrant. The familiar conclusions of Protestant theology are not to be assumed at the outset."[18] Cave did adduce many important facts in the course of his book, but it was clear from the outset where his argument was headed. While the volume was not as disreputable as modern commentators have suggested, it was not a pathbreaking effort, in either scholarship or theology.[19]

Toward the end of the nineteenth century other attempts were made to shore up conservative views. A group of mostly Anglican authors, for example, published in 1894 *Lex Mosaica: Or the Law of Moses and the Higher Criticism,* a book containing some serious work. Among its contributors, pride of place was given to the archaeologist A. H. Sayce, Professor of Assyriology at Oxford, who was in the process of becoming an active opponent of critical views. Sayce's prominence in the volume suggests something of the character of the conservative scholarship of the day, for Sayce was always more a critic of the critics than a champion of traditional opinions.[20] The book as a whole featured theological, commonsensical, and logical argumentation more than detailed historical or linguistic study. It was a good, but not particularly academic, inquiry. Not as much can be said for the effort by John Kennedy, honorary professor in New College, London, who published *The Book of Daniel from the Christian Standpoint* in 1898. This defense of the traditional view was predicated almost entirely upon two factors extrinsic to the book's historical circumstances. For Kennedy, Jesus' references to Daniel in the New Testament and the consistency of Daniel's messianic theology with New Testament themes determined the issue.

British conservative response to criticism contained many of the same elements as the American. It too was concerned about the practical implications of accepting the new criticism; it too proceeded on several fronts in response to conclusions from the Continent. On the whole, however, the British conservatives did not display the academic ability or the theological acumen characteristic of the American conservatives active before 1930. The Methodist *London Quarterly Review,* which had provided steady resistance to the new views for some time, came to this conclusion in 1890 after a fairly sympathetic review of the most significant conservative British books on the subject from the previous decade. "It is to America we must go," the essay ran, "if we would find an adequate reply to modern critics. Professor W. H. Green of Princeton . . . Professor Bissell . . . Dr. Ives Curtiss, and Mr. Vos . . . have all written better books than England has to show on this side of the argument." William Robertson Nicoll, the moderately conservative editor of the *Expositor,* gave the same opinion when he wrote in 1894 that "the only *respectable* defenders of inspiration" were "the Princeton school of Green and Warfield."[21]

These are well-considered judgments. British efforts to rebut criticism were marked by a substitution of popular appeal for careful scholarship, which did not take place in America to the same degree until World War I and after. In addition, British conservative leaders did not provide focused attention to the biblical questions. Spurgeon, for example, was the most prominent public opponent of the new criticism. But he found it worth his while to diffuse polemical efforts by quarreling with other conservatives on matters unrelated to the Bible or on minute particulars of the biblical issues. At the time of the Down-Grade Controversy he thus carried on a lengthy public dispute with the London Congregationalist Joseph Parker over Parker's attendance at the theater, even though this "foe" defended views on Scripture that were as conservative as Spurgeon's. And Spurgeon would not recommened Cave's defense of traditional views because Cave tolerated the idea that there may have been minor editing of the Mosaic documents.[22]

Nor was British conservative scholarship as searching as American. One has only to compare the theological essays by Warfield to Cave's "inductive" study to note the greater weight of the former. Where Warfield understood the importance of theological assumptions, Cave wrote as if they were of little importance. Where Warfield employed an immense range of learning for his conservative tasks, Cave's scholarship tended toward the derivative. The same conclusions pertain for other comparisons. A world of difference separated John Kennedy's popular defense of a sixth-century Daniel from the learned disquisition on the Aramaic of that book which Robert Dick Wilson produced in 1912.[23] British conservatives enjoyed many capable writers, but not profound scholars. Their relative weakness in the face of both critical consensus and the example of believing critics helps to explain the absence of a well-grounded conservative tradition of biblical scholarship in Great Britain.

The situation which resulted is illustrated by the case of George Jackson, a Methodist minister appointed to his denomination's Didsbury College in 1913.[24] Of all the dissenting denominations in the decades before World War I, the Methodists had been the most consistently conservative on Scripture. Acceptance of the new criticism came more slowly than among the Baptists, Congregationalists, or Presbyterian. But by the turn of the century, some Methodist leaders had begun to adopt moderate positions. One of these was George Jackson, who held successful pastorates in Edinburgh and in Toronto. While in Canada, however, Jackson became involved in several small controversies over the use of criticism, and this had been enough to mark him as a person with "advanced views." After he was appointed to the Didsbury position, considerable opposition arose within the denomination. It was significant, however, that this opposition did not lead to excessive polarization of the denomination, it did not bring about the formation of strong conservative organizations, and had no long-range effect in retarding the acceptance of criticism. By 1913, in other words, even the more conservative dissenting bodies had made an accommodation to the new scholarship.

STEADY STATE: 1900–1937

From the turn of the century to nearly the start of World War II, evangelical Bible scholarship in Britain proceeded in a steady state. Fundamentalist-modernist controversy on the American scale was not present to focus attention on controversies over Scripture and other theological matters. Britons were concerned about more pressing things: the destruction caused by World War I, long controversy over revision of the Anglican Book of Common Prayer, and general uneasiness over a loss of religious influence in the country. Although among both Anglicans and dissenters some maintained conservative evangelical views on the Bible, and although several sophisticated theologians published generally conservative works on the subject of biblical inspiration, it is difficult to find the kind of self-conscious conservatisim on biblical scholarship which by this time had come into being in America.

To be sure, a small number of groups and individuals with relatively limited influence on British church life continued to resist criticism of every sort. Yet the important leaders who combined a conservative view of Scripture and a repudiation of modern criticism had passed from the scene before the turn of the century—for example, the Baptist Spurgeon and the Anglican preacher in Oxford and London, H. P. Liddon (d. 1890)—or shortly thereafter—for example, the Congregationalist Parker (d. 1902), Bishop Ryle (d. 1900), and the Bishop of Durham, H. C. Moule (d. 1920). Effective preachers like Congregationalists J. H. Jowett (d. 1923) and G. Campbell Morgan (d. 1945), and the Baptist F. B. Meyer (d. 1929), who were active in the first third of the century, would not tolerate the notion of errors in the Bible.[25] But such convictions did not lead to a biblical scholarship.

Another group of evangelicals, who functioned within the more central church bodies, published distinctively conservative theories of the Bible. Even here, however, the tendency ran away from an utter skepticism concerning modern criticism to an affirmation of both the Bible's general trustworthiness and the appropriate use of criticism. It is significant that recent surveys find no leading evangelical spokesmen who insisted upon a strict view of biblical inerrancy from the period after 1900 until World War II.[26] The Scottish theologians James Denney (1856–1917) and James Orr (1844–1913) were representatives of the stance that then prevailed.

Denney is best known as a defender of the substitutionary atonement against Albrecht Ritschl's view of atonement through subjective influence.[27] He also offered cogent criticism of kenotic theories concerning Christ's person. The skill with which Denney plied these defenses set him apart as one of the weightier evangelical voices at the turn of the century. On Scripture, however, Denney was able to make significant adjustments in light of criticism. His experience with the opponents of criticism during a trip to the United States left him unsettled, for he found them manifesting an unhealthy interest in "the millennium, premillennial notions, and in general the fads of the uneducated and half-educated men."[28]

For Denney, Scripture was *"the* means through which God communicates with man. . . . No Christian questions . . . that God actually speaks to man through the Scriptures, and that man hears the voice and knows it to be God's." But once this truth-telling character of the Bible is established, and so long as no *a priori* anti-supernaturalism intrudes, "criticism is free to do its appropriate work." Denney conceded that "the evangelists may make mistakes in dates, in the order of events, in reporting the occasion of a word of Jesus, possibly in the application of a parable . . . ; we may differ—Christian men do differ—about numberless questions of this kind; but . . . even though in any number of cases of this kind the *gospels* should be proved in error, the *gospel* is untouched."[29] Moreover, it was not appropriate to decide whether to apply the new scholarship moderately or excessively. "The answer to the critic's questions are not moderate or extreme, but true or false; and of all men a Christian ought to be willing to go any length with truth."[30]

James Orr, one of the rare Britons of the period to bring both evangelical convictions and technical expertise to bear on the Old Testament, did not concede as much as Denney to the new views. Orr's major works on the subject expanded the positions he would later take in *The Fundamentals.* In *The Problem of the Old Testament* (1906) Orr argued, with careful attention to recent literature and sophisticated use of exegetical tools, that criticism based on an unsupported evolutionism or the arbitrary rejection of the miraculous was not persuasive. Traditional views or modifications of them were far sounder than academic fashion indicated. Yet in this nay-saying there was also a positive appreciation for modern work. For example, Orr found concepts of development (that is, progressive revelation) useful as means to explain the history of Hebrew religion.

Orr appreciated the theories of A. A. Hodge, Warfield, and other American evangelicals. Yet substantial theological agreement with them did not lead him to adopt their response to criticism. A major statement on *Revelation and Inspiration* in 1910 allowed him to address these questions directly. He did deny that the Incarnation involved a radical kenoticism, and he asserted that Jesus' expressed opinions on the Old Testament must lead even the modern Christian to affirm that "the truths of God's revelation were not in the air. They became the possession of mankind through *real* events and *real* acts of God. Revelation, in a word, was *historical.*" Yet he could go on to say "that when Jesus used popular language about 'Moses' or 'Isaiah,' He did nothing more than designate certain books, and need not be understood as giving *ex cathedra* judgments on the intricate critical questions which the contents of these books raise." Similarly, Orr held that the American inerrantists were correct "in affirming that *the sweeping assertions* of error and discrepancy in the Bible often made cannot be substantiated." He agreed that a theory of inerrancy yielded a positive view of Scripture as "supernaturally inspired to be an infallible guide in the great matters for which it was given." At the same time, however, he accepted a criticism which called details of the historical record into question. The presumption that "unless we can demonstrate what is called the 'inerrancy' of the Biblical record, down even to its minutest details, the whole edifice of belief in revealed religion falls to the ground," was "a most suicidal position."[31]

Denney and Orr, in short, were British evangelicals who did not find modern critical conclusions persuasive, but who also did not feel threatened by critical study or the adoption of occasional critical conclusions.

Still another group of scholars occupied a position that counted as conservative within the academic context, but which represented a more complete accommodation to modern criticism than either British or American evangelicals accepted. Numbered in this group were scholars in the tradition of Westcott, Lightfoot, and Hort (for example, H. B. Swete, Armitage Robinson, A. E. Brook, and later E. G. Selwyn and C. F. D. Moule),[32] High Church Anglicans like Charles Gore, the Congregationalist P. T. Forsyth (perhaps the most important theologian in the prewar period), and rising scholars among the dissenters like C. H. Dodd. What these scholars held in common was a twin commitment to the divine character of Scripture and to the value of an unfettered research. For them, the results of a moderate criticism were given; but this did not entail a commitment to unbelieving rationalism, Hegelian evolution, Spencerian naturalism, or any of the other major heterodox assumptions which had played such a large role among the nineteenth-century German critics.

Yet another factor in the evangelical use of the Bible during this period were the conservatives active in the churches. The evangelical party in the Church of England as well as a conservative evangelical coalition among the dissenters survived with some vigor, although both were also weakened by the religious lassitude of the times. In 1925, members of the Fellowship of Evangelical Churchmen (that is, Anglican) published a volume entitled simply *Evangelicalism.* The aim of this book was to counteract both the "aggressive sacerdotalism" of the High Church and the "growing movement [toward] modernism" of the Broad Church.[33] Several of these essays were competent popular statements, but they did not constitute an academic defense of evangelical convictions. The paper on "The Inspiration and Authority of the Bible" by G. T. Manley presented firm, but modest views on Scripture. It was informed by fairly wide reading, but it did not itself engage the most pressing academic questions. Manley aligned Anglican evangelicalism with the historic positions of the church. He insisted that "the claim to inspiration which the Bible makes necessarily involves the claim to truth, and this must be granted no less to the historical than to the doctrinal parts," even though he conceded that "this argument cannot be pressed so as to prove verbal inerrancy in detail." When Manley applied these theological convictions to the question of modern criticism, he was somewhat indecisive. He described what seemed to him "the present almost chaotic condition of Old Testament and New Testament criticism," a situation that arose due to the fact that "the majority of theological teachers in our universities have accepted most of the literary and historical conclusions of the German school, whilst either rejecting or giving a hesitating acceptance to their rationalistic theory." Manley did not want to deny that "a wealth of scholarship and labour" over the last century had increased understanding of the Scriptures. But he stood resolutely against the "professed rationalists" whose "conclusions are based on arguments penetrated in every direction by their prejudice against the supernatural."[34] Manley's essay was representative of evangelical work at this time.

INTER-VARSITY FELLOWSHIP

One other concentration of evangelicals deserves attention, for it would come to play a major role in the rejuvenation of conservative biblical scholarship: the evangelical student organizations in British universities.[35] As a legacy of efforts by Charles Simeon and other Anglicans, a strong evangelical presence had been sustained at Cambridge University throughout the nineteenth century. *Ad hoc* evangelistic efforts (such as the Jesus Lane Sunday School and the Cambridge University Church Missionary Union) as well as a vigorous devotional life (the Daily Prayer Meeting, for example) eventually led to the formation of the Cambridge Inter-Collegiate Christian Union (CICCU) in 1876. After the turn of the century CICCU was associated briefly with the Student Volunteer Movement and its sister organization, the Student Christian Movement (SCM), in the promotion of missions, evangelism, and spiritual renewal. Soon, however, tension between the more theologically inclusive SCM and the more conservative CICCU led to a new evangelical organization following the heritage of the CICCU. This was the Inter-Varsity Fellowship of Evangelical Christian Unions, officially established in 1928, but the product of annual meetings involving evangelicals from several colleges, universities, and medical training institutions that had taken place since 1919. The Inter-Varsity Fellowship (IVF) soon became a catalyst for intellectual as well as spiritual renewal among evangelicals involved in British higher education.

As early as 1933, IVF students training for the ministry joined to form the Theological Colleges Prayer Fellowship. This was a harbinger of more intensive cooperation among students and scholars of Scripture. In 1937 the first theological colleges conference took place in Digswell Park at the direct instigation of a young Cambridge graduate, John W. Wenham. Although it was a small beginning, this was a most significant event. Organized effort by conservative evangelicals pointing toward serious academic work was now a reality for the first time in Great Britain. A number of other important developments followed closely on the heels of this conference. In 1938 the IVF formally organized a Theological Students Fellowship (TSF, known until 1946 as the Theological Students' Prayer Union), which defined one of its purposes as the promotion of evangelical scholarship. In 1939 a "Biblical Research Committee" was organized under the leadership of Anglican ministers, including the same G. T. Manley who had written on Scripture in the 1920s, young scholars (among them F. F. Bruce, then a lecturer in Greek at Leeds, and Norval Geldenhuys, a South

African doing postgraduate work at Cambridge), and IVF staff. The aims of this group were not modest. They have been summarized by the IVF's historian:

Its first task would be to survey the position and then to plan appropriate action to meet the more urgent needs. This would be by the production of conservative commentaries on the books of the Bible and a scholarly re-examination of the linguistic and historical problems connected with the text of the Old and New Testaments. A major interest would also be the hope of encouraging post-graduate students with the necessary linguistic training to undertake research at the growing points from the point of view of conservative scholarship.[36]

In 1941 a conference on "The Revival of Biblical Theology" drew together the same individuals plus Dr. Martyn Lloyd-Jones, minister of London's Westminster Chapel, and Dr. W. J. Martin, Rankin Lecturer in Semitic Languages at Liverpool University. This body proposed to urge university work upon budding scholars, to fund graduate studies once the war was over in order to prepare evangelicals for university careers, and to prepare commentaries on the Greek and Hebrew Scriptures. In 1942 the TSF organized the Tyndale Lectures in New and Old Testament. In 1943, IVF secured a house with ample grounds in Cambridge, soon called Tyndale House, as a library and study center. By that year as well plans were in place for a one-volume commentary on the whole Bible, for a series of professional but not technical commentaries on the individual books of Scripture, for a Bible dictionary, and for postwar fellowships to encourage advanced study.[37]

The year 1937, including the developments which led up to the meeting at Digswell Park, was a turning point. It reflected the ongoing nurture of traditional positions in the established church, a revitalization of evangelical student work, and a dedication to conservative labor on Scripture among dissenters, of whom the Plymouth Brethren exerted an influence all out of proportion to their size. A more self-confident evangelical scholarship which valued university level work was the result. It was not long until the effects were felt in America.

During roughly the first third of the century evangelicals in Britain retained considerable institutional vitality in the churches and among extra-ecclesiastical bodies. Yet this vitality did not include a powerful academic presence. As the evangelical historian H. D. McDonald has summarized the period, "Evangelicals were in the backwood as far as convincing Biblical scholarship was concerned."[38] On the other hand, barriers between evangelicals and the practitioners of modern biblical scholarship were not as formidable as those which separated conservative evangelicals in America from the practice of scholarship in their country. The most significant conservative Bible scholarship in Great Britain was being done by Christians working in the university world; their convictions, while not strictly evangelical, were reasonably traditional. From this setting a more distinctly evangelical scholarship emerged more easily than was the case in the United States. But it would also be an evangelical scholarship in which theological boundaries continued to exhibit the blurring characteristic of the British acceptance of criticism during the last years of the nineteenth century.

A BRITISH-AMERICAN COMPARISON

In light of the importance of British scholarship to American evangelicals, it is useful to compare more exactly the differences between evangelical study of the Bible in the two places, especially for the period when modern criticism began to exert its sway. In making such a comparison two kinds of differences are important, those which arose most obviously in the development of criticism itself, and those which pertained to the differing contexts of evangelical study.

Before examining these two sets of differences, however, it is well to remember that more things have united conservative evangelicals in America and Great Britain than have separated them. These commonalities include a confidence in the truth-telling character of Scripture, an exaltation of the Bible as the supreme religious authority, and a decided preference for traditional explanations of the Bible's authorship, dating, and interpretation. American and British evangelicals are both heirs of the Reformation and of the eighteenth-century revivals. Although their histories diverge more clearly after about 1800, evangelical expressions on both sides of the Atlantic still share a great deal in common.

But the differences are also significant. These differences are apparent for the decades immediately before and after 1900. In Britain, first, practitioners of modern scholarship were never as rationalistic or anti-supernaturalistic as the best-known critics in Germany and the United States. Scholars like William Robertson Smith and S. R. Driver, who upheld both recent critical conclusions and the supernatural character of God's dealing with Israel, became increasingly marginal in the United States after 1900. Such ones always occupied a prominent place in British scholarship.

Second, the most important conservative scholars in Britain deserve the label "believing critics" or "evangelical critics." Conservatives like Orr, Denney, the English Presbyterian Hugh McIntosh, and the Anglicans Henry Wace and E. A. Knox occupied a territory somewhere between the positions advocated by B. B. Warfield and by Charles Briggs.[39] With Warfield they opposed evolutionary assumptions and the sacrifice of the church's traditional interpretation of Scripture. But with Briggs they felt it was possible to make a place for modern critical conclusions, and to a limited extent for the idealism, historicism, and developmentalism which undergirded the new criticism. This group, moreover did not die out, but continued with varying degrees of strength to exert an influence among the churches and in the universities.

Third, more thoroughly conservative evangelicals never mounted a serious biblical scholarship in Great Britain. There simply were no conservatives holding the views of Warfield, Green, and Vos who displayed the academic abilities or the polemical skills of these Americans. In the absence of such a vital conservative tradition, it was easier for British conservatives to move closer to the conventions of critical scholarship, and harder for the evangelical opponents of modern criticism to gain a hearing for their convictions.

These differences between evangelical Bible scholarship in Britain and America are manifest. They are discussed in much of the serious literature on the subject. Not as apparent are the reasons for these different developments. At this point it is pertinent to sketch, however briefly, some of the conditions in Britain that affected evangelical scholarship there.

A principal difference was the church-state establishments in England and Scotland. The state-church in England (Episcopalian) and Scotland (Presbyterian) enjoyed inherited rights both in law and in the older universities. This meant, among other things, that parties within the church usually had some voice in Parliament and at the colleges of the ancient universities which, until the twentieth century, virtually monopolized formal theological education. Evangelicals in the Church of England and the Scottish Kirk therefore had access to education at the major universities and never totally lost their places in the legislative and academic establishments. In turn, the allegiance of these evangelicals to the establishment made them somewhat more tolerant of other parties within the churches than was the case in America where conservatives often created entirely separate ecclesiastical and educational structures. One result of this British situation was constant contact—as pupils, students, and denominational colleagues—among groups with different convictions about Scripture. Lines were never drawn as firmly between evangelical and other convictions; blacks and whites more easily gave way to varying shades of gray.

A factor related to the church-state establishment was the nature of change in the universities. As in America the British universities underwent a process of professionalization in the last half of the nineteenth century. But the secularization that accompanied this process, while unquestioned, was never as thorough as that in the United States. The tie between the ancient universities and the churches was weakened seriously, but did not give way entirely. In the period between 1881 and 1900, for example, 31 percent of Oxford dons were in orders; and as late as 1900, 53 (or 10 percent) of Oxford's resident M.A.s, who did most of the teaching, were Anglican clergymen.[40] In addition, as Oxford and Cambridge came to serve the needs of the nation more generally, dissenting denominations were able to establish colleges in these universities where at least some evangelical sentiments continued to be heard. C. H. Dodd, for example, taught from 1915 to 1930 at the Congregational Mansfield College, which had recently moved to Oxford from Birmingham. From this position Dodd's relatively conservative views exerted a considerable influence in the university at large.[41] In the new regional, or "red brick" universities, conservative voices also found a place. The first John Rylands Professor of Biblical Criticism and Exegesis at the University of Manchester, for instance, was the Primitive Methodist A. S. Peake, who continued to teach at his denomination's college in Manchester while filling the university chair from 1904 to 1929. Peake was a mediator between conservative evangelicals and more active proponents of modern criticism. Though not himself a conservative evangelical, he was probably closer to that viewpoint than any major university professor of Bible in the United States at the same time.[42]

At least one other aspect of British education differentiated British from American evangelicals, namely the continuing vitality of classical studies in the secondary schools and universities.[43] After the revolution in American education in the 1870s, the classics, which had been the mainstay of the American curriculum, rapidly lost their importance. Harvard, a bastion of conservatism on this question, after 1886 made it possible for students to enter without the traditional preparation in Latin and Greek, a provision which expanded rapidly in the following decades.[44] Soon more modern and more pragmatic subjects had replaced the classics almost entirely in the secondary school curriculum. In Britain, by contrast, study of Greek and Latin remained foundational for at least the elite educational tracks. This had two important consequences. So long as evangelicals did the regular secondary preparation, it kept them conversant with not just the ancient languages, but also classical history and literature. This offered a ready-made group of potential Bible scholars for whom it was second nature to study the ways in which ancient cultures differed as well as resembled the modern. It also offered a career path for evangelicals whose conservative views on Scripture might have kept them from gaining initial appointments in more strictly biblical study. More than one prominent evangelical Bible scholar in Britain during the twentieth century began a professional career as an instructor of classics, only to move over into professional study of Scripture as time went on.[45] The continuing vigor of the classics in Great Britain, in sum, offered a range of possibilities for the study of the Bible, which had become increasingly rare in the United States by the end of the nineteenth century.

It was not only the structure and curricula of the universities but also their intellectual atmosphere which shaped the context for biblical scholarship. At Oxford the idealist philosopher T. H. Green (1836–1882) exerted a considerable influence himself and through his disciples for many decades during this period. Green's idealism was much more amenable to theism than the naturalistic evolutionism of Herbert Spencer or the progressive scientism of Thomas Huxley, both of which enjoyed more academic influence in America than in England. Where American conservative evangelicals, especially those prominent as conservative students of Scripture, regularly looked upon all forms of idealism as so many signposts of heresy, the situation was different in England. Idealism, as well as non-naturalistic forms of evolution, became the ally of a range of theological positions, from modernist to quite conservative.[46] To the extent that evangelicals were comfortable with such intellectual positions, and to the extent that these same positions provided at least some grounding for the modern critical study of the Bible, British evangelicals found themselves in a position to mediate between conservative theological convictions and the practice of modern scholarship.

A final matter has more to do with internal religious life than external academic conditions. Evangelical teaching on the role of the Holy Spirit occupied a slightly different position in America than in Britain. A lively, vibrant tradition exalting the work of the Spirit had grown up in America through the expansion of the Methodists and the revivalism associated with Charles Finney, Dwight L. Moody, and the Keswick movement. But other American evangelicals, primarily among the Baptists and Presbyterians, looked with some suspicion on this emphasis. Significantly, the latter were most responsible for the careful, systematic evangelical Bible scholarship in response to modern criticism. The former—Methodists, most Congregationalists, some Presbyterians, and eventually Nazarenes, other Holiness bodies, and Pentecostals—while no less conservative concerning Scripture, linked its interpretation more closely to the work of the Spirit. The result was a fissure—evangelicals for whom the Spirit played a more prominent role tended not to engage in detailed Bible scholarship; evangelicals who championed a rational defense and interpretation of the Bible were most nervous about excessive interest in the Spirit. To the first group modern criticism was almost an irrelevancy, to the second it was a matter of life or death.

Among the British, by contrast, learned study of the Bible and an intense interest in the Spirit had never been sundered.[47] During the eighteenth century John Wesley had promoted a religion marked by both intense Bible study and a revolutionary new emphasis on the Spirit. At the turn of the nineteenth century the Cambridge rector Charles Simeon left a similar legacy to hundreds of Anglicans who became important in church and university. Like Wesley, Simeon combined serious learning with a Spirit-led interpretation of both life and the written page. The division among British evangelicals between those who leaned to the Spirit and those who leaned to reasoned apologetics was never as great as in America. As a result evangelicals in Britain tended to respond to the rise of criticism with somewhat less concern for rational precision than one group of Americans, and somewhat more interest in learned study than the other.

We will return to these more general contextual religious considerations later in the book, for they are crucial in understanding the nature of evangelical Bible scholarship. Now, however, we are in position to resume the story of American conservative scholarship in the mid-1930s. Assistance from Great Britain was one of the reasons why that scholarship began to arise so rapidly from the ashes.

5. Return: 1935–1974

Meanwhile, something has been happening within fundamentalism. Away from the centers of ecclesiastical power and theological education in the major denominations, there has been a remarkable renascence of intellectual activity among fundamentalist scholars, several of whom have studied in centers like Basel and Zurich and hold doctorates from such places as Harvard and Boston. The periodical *Christianity Today* has made its appearance, counting President Eisenhower's pastor among its contributing editors. The latest volume on apologetics from the pen of the president of Fuller Theological Seminary has been put before the public by a front-rank publisher. And Billy Graham storms city after city under the auspices of the "respectable" churches.

ARNOLD W. HEARN, *Christian Century*, 1958

The renewal of evangelical Bible scholarship depended upon several related developments. Some concerned intellectual stirrings among fundamentalists, others the growing involvement of immigrant confessional churches in American activities, and still others the fruitful use of evangelical scholarship from Great Britain. Shifts in the wider world of theology also made a contribution. Together, changes among evangelicals and changes in the intellectual climate nurtured a resurgence of evangelical thinking which continues to this day. This renewal has not led to the triumph of evangelical convictions among academics at large, nor has it meant the unity of evangelicals on the implications of traditional faith for scholarship. But it has witnessed a remarkable revival in the quantity and quality of academic work. This chapter treats some of the important parts of that story from the mid-1930s to the mid-1970s; Chapter 6 provides a more programmatic description of the return over the last decade.

A NEW CLIMATE

The rise of neo-orthodoxy in Europe and a related theological "realism" in America changed the context in which study of the Bible took place. Barth, Brunner, and the Niebuhrs, who largely accepted the conclusions of the new Bible scholarship, did not mean to encourage American fundamentalists. For their part, American conservatives in the 1930s and 1940s were prone to regard neo-orthodoxy as merely a variation of theological liberalism.[1] Nonetheless, the emphasis in the new theology on divine transcendence and the moral debilities of human nature encouraged a theological soberness which had a decided impact on the study of Scripture. What Amos N. Wilder of the Harvard Divinity School has called "the special impact of orthodoxy at one period on certain aspects of our [New Testament] studies," formed a backdrop to such cautionary messages as Henry Cadbury's *The Peril of Modernizing Jesus* (1937).[2] So rapidly did liberal certainties decay that, by the late 1940s, an occasional word was heard commending fundamentalists for their intransigence. Thus Nels F. S. Ferré in 1948 suggested that "fundamentalism, as the defender of supernaturalism, has . . . a genuine heritage and a profound truth to preserve. . . . We shall some day thank our fundamentalist friends for having held the main fortress while countless leaders went over to the foe of a limited scientism and a shallow naturalism."[3]

Alongside the altered theological climate, fresh insights into the historical dimensions of Scripture also lent plausibility to conservative critical conclusions. W. F. Albright's archaeological research undercut assumptions about the supposed ahistorical character of Old Testament writing before the prophets.[4] Other discoveries in the Middle East—both the Dead Sea Scrolls and the Gnostic texts at Nag Hammadi—were a serious embarrassment to those who had regarded great swaths of the New Testament as a thinly veiled Hellenism. In 1968 R. M. Grant concluded that the Dead Sea Scrolls forced "parallelomaniacs" who had sought the meaning of Christianity in "hellenistic mysteries or philosophy or in the remoter areas of Iranian thought" to reconsider the singularities of Palestinian events. Furthermore, Nag Hammadi required those who had read "a general idea of Gnosticism" back into the first century "in order to explain the more esoteric ideas of Paul and John and their opponents . . . to pass from the warm tub of speculation into the icy shower of historical evidence."[5]

The advent of neo-orthodoxy and the new Middle Eastern discoveries did not vindicate the earlier scholarship of conservative evangelicals. Nor did theologians like Ferré, archaeologists like

Albright, or biblical scholars like Grant abandon critical methodologies or conclusions originating in the nineteenth century. But neither did conservative positions in biblical scholarship seem as trifling or as ungrounded as had once been the case. It was far clearer at mid-century that theological point of view entered into scholarship at the deepest levels. "It is time to be done with the deceptive myth of neutrality," said one New Testament student, and other established scholars agreed.[6] A door to the academic marketplace which had been closed to conservative evangelicals opened a crack. It revealed a new generation of evangelicals knocking to get in.

FUNDAMENTALISTS AWAKE

It is an exaggeration to say that conservative evangelical Bible scholarship during the 1930s was confined to the faculty common room of Westminster Theological Seminary in Philadelphia. But not by much. A few other academically certified and intellectually responsible evangelicals, especially in the confessional European denominations, were still at work. And a good bit of competent popularization appeared in various evangelical forums. But beyond the remnant from Old Princeton now at Westminster—Machen, Wilson, and Allis—and one or two younger scholars who had joined that faculty—like Ned B. Stonehouse—very few evangelicals were engaged in the serious wrestling with ancient texts, the comparison of historical interpretations, and the weighing of contemporary research that constitutes scholarship on Scripture. Westminster was a link to an older tradition, it played an important role in the evangelical revival, and it continues as an important center of evangelical scholarship to this day. After the passage of only a few years, however, it no longer stood alone.

Fundamentalists reawakened to the value of scholarship for several reasons. The decade of the 1930s witnessed a new spirit, a fresh generation of effective leaders, a series of critical books, considerable institutional vigor, and an unprecedented commitment to graduate higher education.

Harold John Ockenga (1905–1985)—minister, educator, author, and organizer—is usually given credit for coining the term "new (or neo-) evangelical" to describe these postfundamentalist developments. To Ockenga, a "new evangelical" was someone who, while believing in traditional Protestant orthodoxy, also valued scholarship and took an active concern for society. The term was presumptuous, but was nonetheless useful for describing a general phenomenon.[7] A certain number of northern fundamentalists, trained at the movement's schools and nurtured in its separatist denominations, seem to have come to the realization nearly simultaneously that the intellectual boundaries of fundamentalism were too narrow. Without giving way on "the fundamentals of the faith," this group nonetheless found the sectarianism, the anti-intellectualism, the combativeness, and the world-denying character of their inherited religion too confining.

Ockenga himself exemplified the concerns of these leaders.[8] He graduated from Taylor University in Indiana, a conservative school of evangelical Methodist origins, before becoming one of the first students at Westminster. While serving as a Presbyterian minister in Pittsburgh he pursued advanced education, earning an M.A. and Ph.D. at the University of Pittsburgh. In 1936 he entered on a wider sphere when he became pastor of Park Street Congregational Church in Boston where he served until his retirement in 1969. At Park Street, Ockenga established both an extensive missions program and a concentrated outreach to the university students of the region. He was also a founder of Fuller Theological Seminary in Pasadena, California, which he served intermittently as president (by transcontinental commute) for two decades. Upon his retirement from Park Street he became president of Gordon-Conwell Theological Seminary north of Boston. He enjoyed a close association with Billy Graham, he recruited many of evangelicalism's emerging scholars, and he hoped to infuse evangelicals with the fortitude of the orthodox heritage of the Protestant Reformation.

Although Ockenga wrote much and spoke widely, his lasting influence was mostly institutional and inspirational. Among his associates, however, were several individuals who made scholarship a career. Edward J. Carnell (1919–1967), who spelled Ockenga for five years as president of Fuller Seminary, led in this respect. A graduate of Wheaton College and Westminster Seminary, Cornell earned doctorates at both Boston University (philosophy) and Harvard (theology). In his own work he interacted critically with Kierkegaard and Reinhold Niebuhr, and sought aggressively to secure a hearing for conservative positions in the academic world at large. His most significant book, *The Case for Orthodox Theology* (1959), tried to differentiate between the "cultic" aspects of modern fundamentalism and a more theologically balanced and intellectually responsible evangelicalism.

Bernard Ramm (b. 1916), who studied at Eastern Baptist Seminary, the University of Southern California, and under Karl Barth in Basel, attempted with Carnell to mark out a middle ground for evangelicals. He criticized fundamentalists who distrusted modern thought without reservation, even as he proclaimed an evangelical message throughout a prolific writing career. His *Christian View of Science and Scripture* (1954) was a milestone for its hearty endorsement of the scientific enterprise. Ramm called evangelicals to engage the world of thought with the assurance that they could discriminate between true advances in knowledge and unfounded extrapolations of non-Christian presuppositions.

Carl F. H. Henry (b. 1913) was a two-fold convert to evangelical theology, from a non-Christian background to faith, and from a career in journalism to one in teaching. His *Uneasy Conscience of Modern Fundamentalism* (1947), a series of lectures presented first at Gordon College and Seminary, attacked the fundamentalist withdrawal from society and its captivity to conventional American culture. It too marked a significant break from the past and a new appeal for an evangelicalism engaged with the world. Henry graduated from Wheaton and Northern Baptist Seminary before earning a Ph.D. in philosophy at Boston University. In the 1970s, he would emerge as the most visible evangelical theologian, especially through his multivolume *God, Revelation and Authority*. Well before then, however, he became a major force in the mobilization of evangelical energies, first as founding editor of *Christianity Today* (1956) and then as impresario of numerous books, symposia, and encyclopedias. Henry's editorial efforts always included encouragement for evangelical colleagues who had dedicated themselves to the study of Scripture.

One other individual deserves special mention for signal contributions to the recovery of an evangelical mind. The evangelist Billy Graham, by his own admission, is no scholar. Yet he has played a surprisingly large role in many of the ventures that advanced evangelical learning. Graham was the major force behind the founding of *Christianity Today*, which he envisaged as a magazine "that would give theological respectability to evangelicals," one that would, among other things, "also show that there was concern for scholarship among evangelicals."[9] He has served as a board member for many evangelical institutions of higher education, and he has gone out of his way to present an evangelistic message at many major universities in the United States and abroad. By his friendship with Ockenga, Henry, and like-minded leaders, he provided the evangelical equivalent of an *imprimatur* for serious engagement with the academic world. Perhaps more than any other figure, Graham has protected evangelical scholars from the anti-intellectual tendencies of the broader evangelical community.

This new leadership, whose efforts were critical for increasing evangelical attention to learning, also took in hand the revitalization of institutions. Already in the 1930s a few colleges with evangelical convictions were beginning to emerge from the trauma of fundamentalist separation. Under the guidance of conservative Presbyterian J. Oliver Buswell, Wheaton College in Illinois was for three years the fastest growing liberal arts college in the nation.[10] At the same time, Buswell also began seriously to search for an academically qualified faculty. Wheaton had never had a Ph.D. teaching Bible until Buswell appointed one in 1935. The trend, once begun, continued, so that by 1952 seven of the college's Bible professors held university level doctorates (three from Harvard, one each from Dropsie, Johns Hopkins, Chicago, and Princeton Seminary).[11]

Even more significant was progress in advanced study. During the 1940s, Fuller Seminary joined Westminster as a professional school dedicated not only to the preparation of ministers but also to the prosecution of research. Before another two decades had passed, other seminaries—Asbury in Wilmore, Kentucky; Gordon (which became Gordon-Conwell in 1969) north of Boston; Trinity in Chicago; and several of the Southern Baptist and Church of Christ schools—were also stressing academic thoroughness in a new way. The scholarly reinvigoration which resulted was especially visible in the study of the Bible. And the evangelicals involved in studying the Bible testified increasingly to outstanding academic preparation.

A RETURN TO GRADUATE EDUCATION

Among the most visible aspects of the new evangelicalism was its concern for academic pedigree. On the hustings, evangelists still got a rise by affirming that God looked not for abbreviations after a person's name but for humility in the heart. Many evangelicals, nonetheless, testified by their actions that academic certification meant a great deal. The commitment to graduate school was a momentous change, for it moved evangelicals closer to a scholarly exposition of their general convictions as well as their specific views on Scripture.

Especially striking was the number of young evangelicals who sought academic training at Harvard University beginning in the late 1930s. Aspiring scholars like E. J. Carnell, George Ladd, and Kenneth Kantzer went to Harvard partly to escape the strictures of fundamentalism, partly to test the mettle of their faith. Recent remarks by Kantzer, nearing retirement after service as chairman of the Bible Department at Wheaton, dean at Trinity Evangelical Divinity School, and editor of *Christianity Today*, illustrates the situation which his generation faced:

I began my own advanced study for the ministry when I graduated from college in the 1930's. I sought an accredited school committed to a consistent biblical theology, with a scholarly faculty, a large library, and a disciplined intellectual atmosphere. I couldn't find any. The nonevangelical schools had great libraries, strong scholarly faculties, and impressive reputations as accredited centers of learning. The evangelical schools had no libraries to speak of, unknown faculty (J. Gresham Machen, the last evangelical scholar, had just died), and no tradition of high scholarship. So I chose two schools: the first [Faith Theological Seminary], a rather typical fundamentalist school so new the ink was barely dry on its articles of incorporation; and the second [Harvard], a liberal school with a solid reputation for academic excellence.[12]

In a fine essay Rudolph Nelson has identified fifteen "fundamentalists at Harvard" from the mid-1930s to 1960.[13] Significantly, these individuals went on to careers at the institutions which led in the development of an evangelical biblical scholarship. Four taught at Fuller (Carnell, George Ladd, Paul Jewett, Glenn Barker), three at Wheaton (Kantzer, Merrill Tenney, Samuel Schultz), three at Asbury (Harold Kuhn, George Turner, Harold

Greenlee), and two at Gordon-Conwell (Burton Goddard, Roger Nicole). One of the Wheaton professors (Kantzer) later transformed Trinity Evangelical Divinity School from a small denominational Bible institute into a major seminary.[14]

The importance of the evangelical entrance into the academic mainstream cannot be overemphasized. On a relatively superficial level, the success of evangelicals at Harvard and other prestigious graduate schools carried a mythic significance in some circles. A reviewer of one of Carnell's books caught that note by lampooning "the new generation of brainy fundamentalists who have studied at Harvard in order to learn the arguments they will spend the rest of their lives attacking."[15] At a deeper level such educational adventuresomeness made possible the reawakening of evangelical intellect by exposing it to a harvest of learning from academia at large. It also made for potential conflict by introducing critical positions into an evangelical community that had little desire to give them room.

In its early stages, however, evangelical application to mainstream scholarship seems to have had little impact on evangelical methods or convictions. Certification rather than confrontation was the goal. Evangelical leaders wanted their institutions to be respectable. To be respectable in American education meant having a faculty with advanced degrees from established universities. In pursuing those degrees evangelical scholars seemed content to show that they could competently manipulate data and concepts. Fewer seemed eager to engage the general intellectual values of the modern university or the specific conventions of critical Bible scholarship. Their theses were mostly on historical subjects. When they did specialize in Scripture, they wrote dissertations on textual or extrabiblical subjects: for example, "The Eschatology of the *Didache*," "An Introduction to the Testaments of the Twelve Patriarchs," "The Quotations from Luke in Tertullian as Related to the Texts of the Second and Third Century," or "A Comparison of Masoretic and Septuagint Texts of Deuteronomy." In addition, only a few in this generation of evangelical scholars published for the academic world at large. Much more common was a pattern in which after beginning a teaching career, the scholar would set aside the dissertation and its technical concerns in order to pursue popular publications for evangelicals. When they were finished with their graduate education, moreover, the evangelicals returned to the separated networks from which they had come. Harvard would certify but not hire. Evangelicals would sample but not stay. All of the fifteen "Harvard fundamentalists" became professors in seminaries; and only one taught in a school which was not identified completely with a conservative constituency.

The higher education evangelicals began to pursue in the 1930s was, therefore, only a partial reintroduction to the larger world of learning. But it was nonetheless of great importance. It gave evangelicals a body of scholars who had done significant research, who had benefited from the study of nonevangelical sources, and who now were instructing a rising evangelical generation. Not the least of the important legacies in the return to graduate education was a more diligent prosecution of scholarship on the Bible.

AN ALLIANCE FOR SCHOLARSHIP

Still more, however, was needed to rejuvenate evangelical study of the Scriptures. The transformation of fundamentalists into "new evangelicals" was a necessary but not sufficient condition for meaningful biblical research. For that purpose the support of others was required, and it came primarily from conservatives within established American denominations, from broadening contacts between evangelicals and immigrant denominations of European background, and from increased involvement with the British.

Barriers between conservative Presbyterians and Baptists, on the one hand, and nonaffiliated fundamentalists, on the other, had never been high. They became less prominent in the 1930s and 1940s as some young fundamentalists became "new evangelicals." When Wheaton College was finding its intellectual bearings in the 1930s, it sent about equal numbers of prospective ministers to Westminster and Princeton. At Princeton Seminary, moreover, several confessionalists welcomed these and other evangelicals. In fact, a young Princeton instructor who began teaching in the 1930s, Bruce Metzger, would in time become one of the most respected evangelical scholars. Presbyterians and Northern Baptists helped fill the ranks of Fuller Seminary when it was founded in 1947 and provided other schools with teachers, and many classrooms with books, over the same period.

Assistance from the European confessionalists was even more strategic in support of an evangelical Bible scholarship. Partly as a result of contact in graduate school, but even more through the self-conscious efforts of leaders like Carl Henry, evangelicals made increasingly strong alliances with both Lutherans and the Dutch Reformed. Relations with Lutherans remained somewhat tenuous, for it was always easier for evangelicals to recruit Lutherans as contributors to books and periodicals than to establish long-lasting, mutually beneficial relationships. yet Lutheran traditions of orthodox scholarship, from Europe and among conservatives in America, became something more than a distant inspiration after World War II. When Carl Henry produced six symposia promoting evangelical convictions from 1957 to 1969, the eighty-five authors for these books included ten Lutherans.[16]

More important was the Christian Reformed Church (CRC), the less assimilated of the two major Dutch-American denominations. During the 1930s and 1940s this body continued to undergo a process of Americanization that had begun with some trauma during World War I. American evangelicals were always nervous about Dutch clannishness, pipes, and lager. And the Dutch-Americans reciprocated by self-consciously distancing themselves from "Methodism," a catch-all term applied generally to American superficiality.[17] Yet by 1930 a bridgehead was established when Westminster Seminary drew almost half of its new faculty from the Christian Reformed Church or from scholars who had done graduate work at the Free University of Amsterdam. Soon there were more involvements: The Christian Reformed Church joined the new National Association of Evangelicals in 1943; and when *Christianity Today* came into existence in 1956, its staff included several men from that denomination.

Evangelicals offered the Dutch Reformed an important reference point as they moved closer to American ways. Evangelicals were obviously pious and obviously orthodox on the main Christian convictions. If they were also flighty, separatistic, and millennarian, such traits were only to be expected from Christians so thoroughly imbued with American activism. In turn the Dutch Reformed gave evangelicals a heritage of serious academic work, experienced philosophical reasoning, and measured intellectual endeavor. If they were also Teutonic in expression, cold in personal relations, and blind to the evils of drink, that was only to be expected from immigrants so unfamiliar with the realities of the new world.

The most obvious contribution of the Dutch Reformed to evangelical biblical scholarship came through the press. Grand Rapids, Michigan, home of the CRC's Calvin College and Seminary, was also the center of an important publishing network. By 1930 several firms were busy producing books for the denomination and related groups. Especially important was the William B. Eerdmans Company which had been publishing serious confessional theology, sometimes in Dutch, since the 1920s. Shortly after World War II Eerdmans made a significant expansion in its lists to include neo-evangelical authors alongside Dutch and Dutch-American writers. Eerdmans brought out Carl Henry's *Remaking the Modern Mind* in 1946 and his *Uneasy Conscience of Modern Fundamentalism* in 1947. The next year it published two books from the "Harvard Fundamentalists," Carnell's *Introduction to Christian Apologetics* and Merrill Tenney's *John: The Apostle of Belief,* along with reprints of John Calvin's Commentaries in English and the first edition of Geerhardus Vos's *Biblical Theology.*[18]

Important as Eerdmans was in promoting American evangelical theologians, its greater significance for biblical research came through its partnership with British Inter-Varsity. William Eerdmans himself established the contacts which made his firm the link between British evangelicals and their American counterparts. The books produced in England and published here by Eerdmans lighted the way for American evangelicals. Inspired in part by such efforts, Americans sought increased contacts with their British counterparts, several of whom had obtained university positions. These university scholars eventually served as doctoral mentors for some evangelicals, and eased the way for others into British graduate work. As this process worked over time Eerdmans also began to publish significant works of biblical scholarship by Americans in addition to books from British and European authors. It was Eerdmans, for example, which brought out George Ladd's path-breaking study of the Kingdom in 1952 and many other important volumes in the period.

A Dutch-American publisher was the mediator, but the substance it transmitted was British. After World War II the efforts

British evangelicals had directed toward research began to pay significant dividends. The New Testament Study Group of the Tyndale Fellowship for Biblical Research, with F. F. Bruce as Chairman, led the way.[19] From the first, the annual lecturers in New and Old Testament at Tyndale House in Cambridge wrestled seriously with problems at the intersection of modern scholarship and evangelical conviction. British evangelicals also made remarkable progress in certifying scholars for university-level work. For a number of reasons relating both to conditions in the universities and capabilities of the evangelicals, these scholars were more successful than their American counterparts in securing posts at research universities as well as at evangelical training colleges. When in the mid-1940s the British Inter-Varsity Press made plans for its first major reference volume, its editors feared there would not be enough scholars to meet the need. The book which resulted, *The New Bible Commentary*, enlisted forty-three British contributors, only five of whom held university appointments, and two of these five were retired. By the mid-1950s, when work began on *The New Bible Dictionary*, the situation was dramatically different. One hundred and forty contributors were required, most needing technical expertise in linguistics, ancient history, archaeology, or biblical criticism. This time the problem was a surfeit of scholars. Of the group recruited to meet this need, over fifty held university positions or their equivalents.[20] Professionalization of evangelical Bible scholarship in Britain had proceeded more rapidly than the most optimistic could anticipate.

In the late 1940s, British IVCF established a separate imprint, Tyndale Press, to publish its more academic books. The purpose was to make such volumes available to those for whom the Inter-Varsity label denoted a mindless fundamentalism. Its first publications were the Tyndale Lectures, like F. F. Bruce's inaugural address from 1942 on "The Speeches in the Acts of the Apostles." Its first major work was Bruce's *Acts of the Apostles: The Greek Text with Introduction and Commentary* (1951). This book marked a major breakthrough. Bruce was then head of the Biblical Department at Sheffield University, and before this time he had divided his writing between essays for scholarly journals and more popular books for the Inter-Varsity Press. In 1951 the two parts of his work came together as an evangelical press issued this major and well-received reassessment of the text of Acts and its interpretation.[21] According to I. Howard Marshall, one of the British evangelicals who has followed in Bruce's footsteps, the appearance of this book marked "the decisive date in the revival of evangelical scholarship and in its recognition by other scholars."[22]

The American publisher of Bruce's book was the InterVarsity Press of Chicago, but most other volumes from British evangelicals appeared from Eerdmans. Also in 1951 the Grand Rapids firm issued the first volume in a *New International Commentary of the New Testament* (published in the United Kingdom by Marshall, Morgan, and Scott as the *New London Commentary*). This soon became the most widely used set of serious commentaries among American evangelicals. The editor was Ned Stonehouse from Westminster Seminary. But the authors, including F. F. Bruce with an exegetical commentary on Acts, were mostly from Britain or the circles of British IVCF. Six of its first thirteen authors were from the United Kingdom, two from Holland, two from South Africa, and one from Australia. Of the two authors living in America, one was a Scotsman trained in his native land. The content of the *New International Commentary* will concern us below. At this stage it is important to see how British research and Grand Rapids publishing combined to advance evangelical biblical work in America.

Eerdmans also played a key role in producing several other important British volumes in this period including in 1953 *The New Bible Commentary*. This volume represented a major effort by British Inter-Varsity to produce an intellectually responsible commentary on the whole of Scripture from an evangelical standpoint. The magnitude of that effort is suggested by the fact that British Inter-Varsity Press spent more than twice as much to print this one book than it had laid out for all of its publications the year before.[23] The then Publishing Director of IVP, Ronald Inchley, has written about the details of its production: "The first printing was 30,000 copies, an unbelievably large quantity for the Press in those days. Of these, 22,000 had been ordered and partly paid for in advance by Eerdmans and the IVCF in the USA."[24] The roster of authors for this joint effort indicates again how dependent Americans were on British conservatives for sound biblical work and how the Old Princeton tradition provided a link to British efforts. The four Americans who contributed taught at Princeton, Westminster, and

Faith Theological Seminary (the last a school serving the body which had separated from the Westminster Seminary Presbyterians). The other forty-six authors included twelve low-church Anglicans (ten from the United Kingdom, two from Australia), fifteen authors from Presbyterian bodies in Scotland, five Irish Presbyterians, ten members of English free churches, and four writers from evangelical denominations in Holland, Jamaica, Greece, and Canada.

Beginning in 1956, Eerdmans was also the American publisher for the Tyndale New Testament Commentaries, a more popular series produced entirely by Britons. In 1958, it brought out in America a book by the evangelical Anglican, J. I. Packer, entitled *"Fundamentalism" and the Word of God,* which was the most intelligent reassertion of biblical inerrancy since Warfield and Hodge. Eerdmans also contributed venture capital for the *New Bible Dictionary* (published 1962), which was edited by Bruce, Packer, the Scottish Presbyterian J. D. Douglas, the Anglican textual critic R. V. G. Tasker, and D. J. Wiseman, an archaeologist at the British Museum.

Eerdmans did not remain for long the only outlet for academic contributions by evangelicals. Soon it was followed by evangelical concerns like Zondervan and Baker (also in Grand Rapids), the American InterVarsity Press, and Word Books. Before too long the path Eerdmans pioneered was also being pursued by general presses like Harper & Row and denominational ones like John Knox, who began to make room for evangelical titles on their lists. Harper in 1960 brought out the introductory text *The Old Testament Speaks,* by Samuel Schultz, a Harvard Ph.D. teaching at Wheaton. This book was that firm's first work of conservative evangelical Bible scholarship since World War I. Its success with Elizabeth Eliot's account of missionary martyrs in Ecuador, *Through Gates of Splendor,* had encouraged it to follow Eerdmans and other evangelical publishers with such a venture.

The role of Eerdmans must not be overemphasized to the exclusion of other factors. It did not inspire the neo-evangelical movement in its earliest stages. It was only the expected place for Dutch-American scholars to publish as they ventured further into American academic life. It was dependent upon the increasing sophistication of British evangelicals for some of its major books. Yet as the mediator among these renewed centers of evangelical vigor, as the pioneer in publishing academic evangelical books, and as the firm which has most consistently issued serious conservative work since World War II, Eerdmans deserves substantial credit for the renewal of evangelical Bible scholarship in the United States.

NEW PROFESSIONAL ORGANIZATIONS

After World War II evangelicals also formed several professional organizations to cultivate academic study of the Scriptures. The Evangelical Theological Society, which met for the first time in 1949, and the Wesleyan Theological Society, organized in 1965, treat a range of theological issues in their journals and at annual meetings. But in each group questions of biblical scholarship and the doctrine of Scripture have always been in the forefront.

Two more recent organizations, formed in direct imitation of the British, are the Institute for Biblical Research and the North American Theological Students Fellowship (TSF). Professor E. Earle Ellis, who taught for many years at New Brunswick Theological Seminary, established the Institute in 1970 on the model of Britain's Tyndale Fellowship. It exists "to foster the study of the Scriptures within an evangelical context."[25] Membership, which is limited to professionally trained scholars, stood at approximately 150 in 1985. The Institute sponsors academic gatherings, often in conjunction with meetings of the Society of Biblical Literature, occasionally subsidizes publications, and promotes communication among its members.

In the August 10, 1973, number of *Christianity Today*, Ward Gasque of Regent College in Vancouver surveyed for American readers the state of evangelical academic life in Great Britain. Gasque, who had completed a Ph.D. under F. F. Bruce at the University of Manchester, pointed to the British TSF and the Tyndale Fellowship for Biblical Research as the principal reasons behind the robust health of evangelical scholarship on the Scriptures in Great Britain. In the essay he proposed "setting up . . . a group similar to the British Theological Students' Fellowship" as one means of reestablishing "the authority of evangelical scholarship in the world of biblical and theological research."[26] The next year, Clark Pinnock, then at Regent College and now at McMaster Divinity College in Ontario, led in the founding of the North American TSF. Pinnock, also a Bruce student, and like-minded scholars began a journal (*TSF Bulletin*), distributed literature from the British TSF, and helped to establish local chapters of evangelical students on seminary campuses and at universities with programs in religion. Under the leadership of TSF General Secretary Mark Lau Branson, the North American group has produced significant aids to biblical research. It has also been the distributor for the journal *Themelios* from the British TSF. That journal, its predecessor the British *TSF Bulletin*, and the annual *Tyndale Bulletin* have been for many years the finest regular sources of serious evangelical writing on the modern study of the Bible in the English-speaking world.[27] By making such work available in North America, as well as through its own productions, directors of the TSF have done for a broader group what the Institute for Biblical Research accomplishes for a more select number. The result in both cases is more exposure to excellent scholarship and more intense concentration on what it means to pursue that scholarship as an evangelical.

SCHOLARS

To show how evangelical scholarship developed from the mid-1930s, it will be helpful to sketch in somewhat greater detail the individual careers of significant pioneers in the academic study of Scripture. I have selected five individuals for this purpose, both because their work is exemplary and because each represents an important strand that contributed to the resurgence. Two are the heirs of the Old Princeton tradition (one at Westminster, one at Princeton); one illustrates the links joining diverse evangelical traditions; still another represents the self-conscious movement beyond fundamentalism; and the last stands for the generation that came to maturity in the 1950s. These five are not necessarily the best evangelical scholars, though each has done outstanding work. Nor do their views necessarily speak for evangelicals as a whole, though the conclusions of their research are widely accepted among their conservative peers.

NED B. STONEHOUSE

Ned B. Stonehouse (1902–1962), the successor of J. Gresham Machen in the chair of New Testament at Westminster Theological Seminary, maintained the Old Princeton commitment to academic thoroughness and evangelical conviction as a living tradition into the middle of the twentieth century. Born in Grand Rapids to Dutch-immigrant parents, he attended Calvin College before taking graduate degrees from Princeton Theological Seminary and the Free University of Amsterdam. His dissertation at the Free University was published in 1929 as *The Apocalypse in the Ancient Church*. Stonehouse assisted Machen in New Testament study from the founding of Westminster and succeeded his mentor when Machen died in 1937.

Stonehouse's importance lay in his willingness to interact with modern criticism of the gospels and to do so with a considerable degree of freedom.[28] In the preface to his first major work, *The Witness of Matthew and Mark to Christ* (1944), he affirmed that "any discussion of the contents of Mark which takes notice of modern opinion is obliged to deal more or less directly with the most influential critical views concerning it."[29] And in the sequel to this volume, *The Witness of Luke to Christ* (1951), Stonehouse rebuked both liberals and conservatives who fled from the witness of the texts to preconceived understandings:

Contemporaneous study of the New Testament abounds with modernizations of Jesus and the Gospels which betray a tragic lack of exegetical fidelity. Conservatives may and ought to do better, because they generally approach the exegetical problems with a sympathy rooted in their commitment to the Christian presuppositions of the authors of Scripture. But conservatives are prone to a traditionalism which is uncritical of the past and is not sufficiently alert to the distinction between what is written and what may have been erroneously inferred from the biblical text. In particular it has seemed to me that Christians who are assured as to the unity of the witness of the Gospels should take greater pains to do justice to the diversity of expression of that witness.[30]

In these and other works Stonehouse abandoned the widespread assumption that the evangelists wrote history according to the canons of the modern period. For him exact harmonization became considerably less important than it had been for other evangelicals. Mark, for example, did not set out to write a biography of the modern sort, but rather was proclaiming "the glad tidings of Jesus Christ, and this presupposes something different from the interest which a biographer has in his subject. . . . The gulf that separates Mark's historical method from the typical modern one is seen most clearly in the almost complete absence of the notion of development." Luke, for his part, "is least concerned with the chronological and topographical settings of the incidents and teachings which he reports."[31] In a later work, *Origins of The Synoptic Gospels: Some Basic Questions* (Eerdmans, 1963), given as lectures at Fuller Seminary, Stonehouse allowed that Matthew "exercised a measure of freedom in his literary composition of the narrative."[32] In these and other assertions, Stonehouse broke with a long evangelical tradition that had regarded the evangelists' sayings as simply reports of facts largely unrelated to the author's theological intentions. Stonehouse's final purpose in these protoredactional studies was anything but liberal or radical. It was precisely the truth of the message, the reality of the historic Christ, which Stonehouse expected to enhance by noting the literary purposes of the gospel-writers:

It is a thrilling experience to observe this unity, to be overwhelmed at the contemplation of the *one* Christ proclaimed by the four evangelists. But that experience is far richer and more satisfying if one has been absorbed and captured by each portrait in turn and has conscientiusly been concerned with the minutest differentiating details as well as with the total impact of the evangelical witness.[33]

Stonehouse's work was treated respectfully by American biblical scholars and greeted with manifest appreciation by British evangelicals, who invited him to lecture in Scotland and England, His selection to edit the *New International Commentary of the New Testament* also spoke of his standing in the Anglo-American world of evangelical scholarship. When British Inter-Varsity Press published the symposium which he edited on *The Infallible Word* in 1946, he became one of the few American evangelicals of his day to reduce the literary trade deficit with Great Britain. His work indicated that American evangelicals did not have to be reactionary in their conservatism.[34] Although Stonehouse's American contemporaries seemed largely oblivious to his creativity, he established standards of critical judgment, thoughtful conservatism, and scholarly exegesis which paved the way for more of the same to come.

BRUCE M. METZGER

Ned Stonehouse carried on the tradition of Old Princeton scholarship from Westminster. At Princeton Seminary itself, Bruce M. Metzger (b. 1914) exemplified an evangelical scholarship of similar integrity and even greater recognition.[35] Metzger, who graduated from Lebanon Valley College in Pennsylvania, Princeton Seminary, and Princeton University (Ph.D. in classics), began teaching at Princeton Seminary in 1938. More than any contemporary evangelical, Metzger has recapitulated the balanced virtues of the Cambridge Triumvirate. Like these scholars, he is cautious in reasoning and careful in research. His work most resembles Hort's in its concentration on textual criticism. Metzger's *Text of the New Testament: Its Transmission, Corruption, and Restoration,* first published by the Clarendon Press in 1964, has gone through several editions and has been translated into German, Japanese, and Chinese. It is a standard. Beyond this and many other works on the establishment of the New Testament text, however, Metzger has also served as an editor of the United Bible Societies' *Greek New Testament,* participant and eventually chairman of committees to revise the Revised Standard Version, and member of countless boards and councils for publishing projects on biblical and classical texts. In addition, as a painstaking and winsome historian of the early church, he partakes also of the legacy of Lightfoot and Westcott.

Metzger has written for a vast number of publications and worked with many different groups. Although he has displayed much more interest in textual problems than in theological controversy, his evangelical convictions have provided the foundations for his work. These convictions have led to close relations with many evangelical organizations. He has written for Eerdmans, Baker, and Zondervan, as well as for Oxford, Abingdon, and the University of Chicago; published in *Christianity Today* and *Eternity* as well as in academic journals; lectured at Asbury, Bethel, Dallas, Eastern Baptist, Houghton College, Southwestern Baptist, Westminster, and Wheaton, as well as in the great seminaries and universities of the world. For conservative students at Princeton Seminary and for younger evangelicals with a taste for textual criticism, Metzger has provided counsel and above all an indication of the contributions an evangelical can bring to the academic study of the Scripture.

Metzger typically states conclusions with learned caution. His presidential address to the Society of Biblical Literature in 1971 illustrated well the nature of his contribution. His subject, "Literary Forgeries and Canonical Pseudepigrapha," at first glance appears to be directed at conservatives. After carefully weighing a wide variety of evidence, Metzger offered these conclusions:

Instead of beginning with declarations of what is licit and what is illicit, one is likely to make more progress by considering the theological problem from a historical and literary point of view. It must be acknowledged that the inspiration of the Scriptures is consistent with any kind of form of literary composition that was in keeping with the character and habits of the speaker or writer. . . . If, indeed, an entire book should appear to have been composed in order to present vividly the thoughts and feelings of an important person, there would not seem to be in this circumstance any reason to say that it could not be divinely inspired. . . . In short, since the use of the literary form of pseudepigraphy need not be regarded as necessarily involving fraudulent intent, it cannot be argued that the character of inspiration excludes the possibility of pseudepigraphy among the canonical writings.[36]

The message to evangelicals was plain: A doctrine of inspiration does not necessarily require traditional ascriptions concerning the authorship of New Testament books. The message to the academic world was more subtle, but for that very reason more impressive: It is no detriment to research for a scholar, even the president of the Society of Biblical Literature, to presuppose the inspiration of Scripture before setting to work on the text.

EVERETT F. HARRISON

Everett F. Harrison (b. 1902) is a Presbyterian like Stonehouse and Metzger, but his career illustrates a different road to scholarship.[37] Harrison graduated from the University of Washington, the Bible Institute of Los Angeles, and Princeton Seminary, where he was a teaching assistant to Robert Dick Wilson. He received an M.A. from Princeton University in 1927, the same year in which he was ordained to the Presbyterian ministry. He then served briefly as a pastor in Nova Scotia and as a missionary in China before accepting a position at Dallas Theological Seminary (where he eventually completed a Th.D. thesis on "The Christian Doctrine of Resurrection"). Harrison thus moved in a more conservative orbit than Metzger and in a more dispensational circle than Stonehouse. In these early days he published several expository studies on Old and New Testament themes in Dallas's *Bibliotheca Sacra,* but seemed content to examine modern critical work from afar. From 1940 to 1944 Harrison was pastor of the Third Presbyterian Church in Chester, Pennsylvania. During this time he began studies in Hellenistic Greek at the University of Pennsylvania, which culminated in a dissertation on "The Use of DOXA in Greek Literature with Special Reference to the New Testament" (1950). In 1947 he became one of the founding faculty of Fuller Theological Seminary, where he taught for over thirty years.

Harrison typifies a very important segment of the new evangelical scholarship. He has chosen not to direct his energies to the academic marketplace, and he has remained content with traditional conclusions on debated matters in New Testament criticism. But for evangelicals he has produced a vast bulk of mid-level popularization which reflects consistent reading in the wider worlds of scholarship and responsible distillations of conservative positions. Harrison's books, like his *Short Life of Christ* (Eerdmans, 1968), his work for Moody Press (including several studies of New Testament books as well as editorial labors on the *Wycliffe Bible Commentary*), his essays in *Christianity Today* and the *Sunday School Times,* editorial contributions to the revised *International Standard Bible Encyclopedia,* and many reviews in evangelical publications on a broad range of New Testament books set out a middle road. Harrison was not convinced by the conventions or discoveries of modern critical scholarship, but he did consider them worthy of serious attention.

Harrison's 1958 essay on "The Phenomena of Scripture" in Carl Henry's symposium, *Revelation and the Bible,* suggests the character of this work. He began by asserting the inspiration and inerrancy of Scripture, but conceded that the testimony of Jesus could not be used woodenly to settle critical questions.

We can hardly say that Jesus' pronouncements on the Old Testament were framed in anticipation of the attacks which would be made on it many hundreds of years later. Consequently, his affirmations on Scripture cannot be invoked with the same force as though the modern issues were in his mind. On the other hand, . . . we rightfully expect that his comments on the Old Testament are fully reliable.

Furthermore, inspired Scripture "says nothing precise about its inerrancy," and if it did, it is not an easy matter to define exactly "what constitutes error" in biblical writing. Having made these adjustments in the direction of modern critical scholarship, Harrison discussed questions of chronology, numbers, harmonization in the Gospels, the historical nature of John, and other questions where the apparent meaning of texts upset traditional convictions. Harrison ended on the traditional side in addressing these matters, but he did so calmly and while noting the weight of objections to traditional views.[38] Harrison was not so much a pioneer in the reestablishment of evangelical scholarship as he was a facilitator for evangelicals who needed reassurance that it was possible to countenance discussion of traditional positions without giving up foundations of belief.

GEORGE E. LADD

Harrison's younger colleague at Fuller, George E. Ladd (1911–1982), built on that solid foundation.[39] Ladd was living in New Hampshire when he was converted in 1929 through the ministry of a woman graduate of Moody Bible Institute who was preaching at a small Methodist church. During the next twenty years Ladd graduated from Gordon College and Divinity School, served several churches as a Northern Baptist minister, studied ancient languages at Boston University, taught at Gordon College and Divinity School, and completed a Ph.D. in classics at Harvard. He moved to Fuller in 1950 because of the opportunity that institution offered for research, and stayed until his death. A recent poll has revealed that Ladd is the most widely influential figure on the current generation of evangelical Bible scholars. (See Appendix for details.)

Ladd's work shared the theological conservatism, intellectual integrity, and critical freedom that also marked the labors of Ned Stonehouse and Bruce Metzger. His first major publication, *Crucial*

Questions About the Kingdom of God (Eerdmans, 1952), gave an evangelical dress to themes made prominent by C. H. Dodd. Ladd addressed this issue because he had been troubled by dispensational interpretations of the question, even during the time when he too was a dispensationalist. He wrote in the preface that while he had found support for a dispensationalist view in the New Testament,

there remained a feeling of uncertainty as to the soundness of some of its positions. Accompanying this was a growing dissatisfaction with the quality of much of the literature which espoused this position. Most of the books I read seemed to assume the whole system rather than prove it. While many biblical passages were quoted, the exegetical problems involved appeared to me to be unsolved.

Ladd sought a solution to these issues through intensive study of the New Testament, but also by patient attention to modern research. He minced no words in chastening his fellow conservatives for opting out of the disciplines of scholarship:

Many conservative students have withdrawn from the movements of contemporary criticism and have not been concerned with the problems which have been raised by the many recent critical discussions. . . . There has not been written a comprehensive study of the kingdom of God in the New Testament from a conservative, premillennial position which takes into account the critical literature; in fact, there does not exist an up-to-date conservative critical treatment of the kingdom of God from any point of view.[40]

Against the dispensational interpretation, and making use of contemporary scholarship, Ladd argued that the Kingdom was a partially present reality. Intensive literary and historical research, rather than a presupposed theology, was required to understand the nature of this Kingdom teaching in the New Testament. Biblical eschatology was not a magic key to unlock the secrets of Scripture, but an element woven into the complex historical circumstances of the text.

Ladd continued to write on the Kingdom, eschatology, and the book of Revelation, but his interests also extended more broadly. His *Theology of the New Testament* (Eerdmans, 1974) culminated a lifetime of serious scholarship. The book was hailed by evangelicals and treated kindly in the wider academic world. Reginald

Fuller, in the *Anglican Theological Review,* noted that the book was "expressly designed to provide a conservative evangelical alternative to Bultmann," and that "while it is conservative (a very legitimate position) it is not fundamentalist (a hardly tenable position in a respectable scholarly enterprise)." After raising some strictures, Fuller concluded, "This work is to be highly recommended to the seminarian and the preacher, with a suitable warning about its critical limitations."[41]

Of Ladd's other major contributions, *The New Testament and Criticism* (Eerdmans, 1967) was important for what it revealed about the evangelical scholarship which emerged after the war. This book contended for the divine character of Scripture and for revelation as word as well as deed, but it did so in full recognition that the divine Word participated in the flux of human history. Criticism, as the effort to fathom these historical circumstances, must therefore be given its due. Ladd warned against the naturalistic presuppositions of literary, form, and historical criticism, but insisted upon their value nevertheless. He concluded that "an evangelical understanding of the Bible as the Word of God written is not *per se* hostile to a sober criticism; rather, an evangelical faith demands a critical methodology in the reconstruction of the historical side of the process of revelation."[42]

Stonehouse, Metzger, Harrison, and Ladd represented the first full generation of evangelical scholars after the trauma of fundamentalism. They had entered the academic marketplace as both scholars and evangelicals. Their work included contributions on technical questions, which the larger academic community acknowledged and put to use. It also included a forthright defense of conservative critical conclusions and a reiteration of questions about theological assumptions to which the academic world as a whole paid less attention. Perhaps most important, it also reestablished a tradition of conservative work on the Scriptures which nourished a numerous generation of rising scholars.

E. EARLE ELLIS

Several in this group have obtained standing in the world of biblical scholarship. The career of one representative repays attention in order to see more clearly how evangelicals took advantage of the door that opened to them in the 1930s. E. Earle Ellis (b. 1926), now at Southwestern Baptist Seminary in Fort Worth, graduated from the University of Virginia and the master's program at Wheaton College, before studying at Tübingen, Göttingen, and Marburg. He received his Ph.D. from Edinburgh in 1955 with a thesis on Paul's use of the Old Testament. Ellis has written extensively on nearly every aspect of the New Testament. He has lectured at major universities in this country and abroad, and has edited several *Festschriften* for British and Continental New Testament scholars. His own research stands in the tradition of European confessional conservatives who maintain evangelical convictions within the larger academic world. He is cautious on debated critical issues (for example, leaning to the Pauline authorship of the pastorals),[43] but willing after judicious assessment of evidence to modify traditional conclusions (for example, conceding that Luke's theological purposes sometimes overrode strict concerns for historical accuracy).[44] Ellis has avoided controversies over the exact nature of biblical inspiration, and he has restricted his writing to mostly academic forums. Nonetheless, he has never sought to hide his convictions about the divine character of Scripture.

Papers which Ellis has published in *New Testament Studies, Journal of Biblical Literature, Zeitschrift für die neutestamentliche Wissenschaft,* no less than his earlier teaching at Southern Baptist and Bethel Seminaries, his reviews for the *TSF Bulletin,* his involvement on behalf of the InterVarsity Christian Fellowship, his oversight of the Institute for Biblical Research, and his lectures at Wheaton, Trinity Evangelical Divinity School, Tyndale House in Cambridge, and North Park Seminary, testify to a coming of age. Not many evangelical scholars are of Ellis's caliber, and not all evangelicals share the conclusions of his research. Yet the nature of his career suggests something of the turnabout that has taken place since the 1930s, when few could have imagined the day when theological conservatives would again become participants in the academic world.

CONVICTIONS

Of course, it is one thing to regain a measure of professional respectability and another to make an impression through the force of research and the power of reasoning. The resurgent evangelical scholarship of the 1930s and 1940s was marked not so much by new positions, as by more learned, more reasonable defenses of the old. As the general theological world lost some of its confidence in previous certainties, evangelicals deployed a broader range of technical expertise and more penetrating arguments to defend positions which a liberal establishment thought it had permanently consigned to the dustbin of history. An evaluation of evangelical scholarship depends very much on whether one believes such a salvage operation is possible in principle, even more than on how well one feels about specific evangelical works.

This is not to say that evangelicals simply went on repeating the arguments of Warfield, Green, Spurgeon, or Cave, for the range of evangelical critical conclusions did expand. Stonehouse allowed for considerable individuality in the literary work of the evangelists. In this he was joined by Ladd who, while reluctant to question the historicity of gospel accounts, nonetheless asserted "the freedom with which the Evangelists arrange their narratives."[45] G. C. Aalders in the *New Bible Commentary* slightly modified traditional opinions on the earliest part of Scripture by suggesting that the Pentateuch "as we know it was compiled by an author at a somewhat later date (probably during the early days of the monarchy) who made use of extensive Mosaic literature together with some pre-Mosaic materials."[46] In the same volume A. J. Macleod, while affirming that the gospel of John was "a record of the revelation of the Word made flesh and must be studied in its historical context," concluded nevertheless that "the literary structure, the unity of teaching, the development of the claims of Christ, the clear transcript of the consciousness of Jesus in relation to great themes demand a *theological* explanation."[47]

It is important not to make too much of these and similar adjustments, however, for the main efforts of the "new evangelical" scholars were decidedly conservative. A more intimate knowledge of contemporary research and a more sophisticated presentation of evidence informed their work, but its conclusions were traditional. The Scriptures everywhere spoke the truth. Its authors also made reliable statements about the works which they wrote. Its narratives were essentially historical, its parts basically coherent.

These persistent affirmations continued to divide evangelical scholars from their academic counterparts, who sometimes reacted with exasperation to the reassertion of these views. When, in 1957, the High Church Anglican A. G. Herbert assessed the resurgent evangelical scholarship coming from British Inter-Varsity in *Fundamentalism and the Church of God,* he complained about the presuppositions of that work. The evangelical view of the Bible was "old fashioned"; "a rigid theory of factual inerrancy" was "too narrow."[48] James Barr, the Oriel Professor of the Interpretation of Holy Scripture at Oxford before becoming Regius Professor of Hebrew at the same university, restated this kind of criticism with a vengeance in the 1970s and early 1980s. He finds something "pathological" in much of the work of many conservative evangelicals.[49] Those who consider the views of conservative evangelicals appalling instead of merely quirky tend, like Herbert and Barr, to share faith in a transcendent deity with those whom they attack; but they have a very different view of revelation, history, and the nature of their interrelation.

Such critics notwithstanding, evangelical work has proceeded within the framework of affirmations that are conservative both theologically and critically. Given these boundaries, some general judgments are possible for the quality of the scholarship that appeared after World War II. Some of the best work has been done in textual, or lower, criticism. Bruce Metzger in the United States and R. V. G. Tasker in Great Britain stand out, but they have been joined by a host of others. Solid textual work is practiced in a full range of evangelical institutions, even ones of extraordinary theological conservatism. The persistent attention to Greek and Hebrew which characterizes American evangelical seminaries has paid dividends in the production of a learned audience for serious textual studies. While doubts about modern text-critical research continue to plague the generality of evangelical and fundamentalist churches, these scruples have long been set to rest among academically qualified conservatives.[50]

Evangelicals also succeeded early on in producing solid commentaries. These regularly reflected conservative conclusions on critical questions, but, following the lead of F. F. Bruce's 1951 literary and historical study of the Greek text of Acts, the conclusions have often been learned, detailed, and very much in dialogue with other opinions. Evangelicals continued to excel at the production of devotional and expository commentaries. But the number of commentaries sharing a definite concern for responsible interaction with modern criticism grew rapidly after 1950. While it is chancy to single out specific volumes, a number were outstanding, including in the *New International Commentary* volumes on John by Leon Morris, an Australian Anglican (1970), and by Bruce himself on Acts (1954) and Hebrews (1964); in the Tyndale Old Testament Commentary series on Proverbs (1964) and Genesis (1967) by Derek Kidner, sometime warden of Tyndale House, Cambridge, and on the Gospel of Luke by Earl Ellis (1966).

In 1974, William Lane's study of the book of Mark in the *New International Commentary* was published. This event may be said to mark the end of the beginning. It was the first volume by an American-born, American-trained scholar to appear in the series. Lane, a graduate of Wesleyan University, Gordon and Westminster seminaries, and Harvard Divinity School (Th.D., 1962), was then teaching at Gordon-Conwell, had studied with Stonehouse, the series editor, and enjoyed a close working relationship with F. F. Bruce, who assumed direction of the series after Stonehouse's death. Lane's commentary was probably the most thorough effort by an American evangelical since the publication of Broadus's *Matthew* nearly a century before. His notes took account of current scholarship; his text was a model of patient, judicious exegesis. His conclusions on critical issues were conservative, but the pathway to those judgments was marked by persuasive learning. Although work of Stonehouse, Metzger, Ladd, Ellis, and others had prepared the way for this volume, its appearance announced that American evangelical scholarship had attained a new level.[51]

Significant advance occurred also in other aspects of biblical work. With the publication of J. I. Packer's *"Fundamentalism" and the Word of God: Some Evangelical Principles* in 1958, evangelicals were in possession of a strong defense of Scripture's verbal inspiration. The "Fundamentalism" of Packer's title has been a source of some confusion in America, because he used it for the type of conservative evangelicalism represented in Britain by the TSF and the Tyndale Society for Biblical Research, bodies which have concentrated on academic pursuits far more extensively than have American fundamentalists. Packer defined the most important modern question as "the principle of authority." He argued, through an extensive use of Scripture itself, that the proper Christian attitude was to regard "the teaching of the written Scriptures [as] the Word which God spoke and speaks to His Church." It is "finally authoritative for faith and life." Packer made an effort to distinguish between this position and inexpert applications of it. For example, he decried the "pronounced anti-intellectual bias" of an earlier fundamentalism as well as "its adventures in the field of the natural sciences, especially with reference to evolution, [which] was most unfortunate." And he endeavored to show that a conservative view of the Bible did not have to be hermeneutically naive: "The idea that the doctrine of the inerrancy of the Word of God commits its adherents to a literalistic type of exegesis is groundless."[52] Evangelicals had not possessed as clear or as balanced a theology of Scripture since the passing of Warfield.

In other areas, however, the renewal of evangelical scholarship did not accomplish as much. Sophisticated work on the text of the Bible and persistent attention to the definition of biblical authority was not matched by more general theological construction. This weakness was connected with a studied lack of appreciation for the issues thrown up by the Enlightenment and nineteenth-century historicism. Evangelicals instinctively opposed most of these modern conceptions, even as their thought reflected them in subtle ways. Yet such ideas or their consequences did not receive sophisticated attention.

In 1965 Carl Henry used the pages of *Christianity Today* to assess evangelical scholarship as it had developed over the previous thirty years. He could point with satisfaction to the renewal of biblical work which has been the subject of this chapter; and he spared no feelings in contrasting the virtues of evangelical positions to the errors of liberals and the neo-orthodox. Yet Henry's review also contained a disquieting note, along with an unflattering comparison to European confessional orthodoxy:

If the strength of American evangelicalism rests in its high view of Scripture, its weakness lies in a tendency to neglect the frontiers of formative discussion in contemporary theology. . . . The element missing in much evangelical theological writing is an air of exciting relevance. The problem is not that biblical theology is outdated; it is rather that some of its expositors seem out of touch with the frontiers of doubt in our day. . . . Evangelicals need to overcome any impression that they are merely retooling the past and repeating cliches. . . . Unless we speak to our generation in a compelling idiom, meshing the great theological concerns with current modes of thought and critical problems of the day, we shall speak only to ourselves. . . . A comprehensive statement of evangelical theology from American sources, comparable to Berkouwer's *Studies in Dogmatics*, remains a necessary project.[53]

Henry's assessment was accurate. Evangelical achievements since the Depression had been significant, but were still far from complete. For purposes of biblical study, Henry could have added that the interpretation of an infallible Bible was still an issue to which few evangelicals paid serious attention. The hermeneutical question, however, could never be far from those who hoped to communicate an infallible Word in the fluctuating circumstances of human history. Willy-nilly evangelicals found themselves face to face with such matters as the resurgence in biblical work continued.

CONCLUSIONS

Three conclusions are inescapable. The first is that American conservatives benefited greatly from British research. The "new evangelicals," having left fundamentalism behind, still did not strike out on their own in the study of Scripture. It took the efforts of those associated with British Inter-Varsity to provide methods, strategies, goals, and conclusions for Americans to follow.

The second is that this process led to far greater success in New Testament scholarship than in Old. What Peter Craigie, a Canadian evangelical and an exemplary student of the Old Testament himself, wrote as recently as 1983 describes well the situation which has prevailed in Old Testament work for most of this century:

Conservative scholarship is continuing to contribute to the larger field of scholarship, but not in proportion to its numbers or potential for influence. The great debates of Old Testament scholarship during the last century were so loaded with theological overtones that conservatives have usually been on the defensive. For the most part, their writings have defended traditionalist views in a polemic tone. As a consequence, they have not been influential and they have not been widely read outside the conservative camp.[54]

A more fruitful Old Testament scholarship began to appear by the mid-1950s, but the standoff between evangelicals and the academy remained much more complete for the Old Testament than for the New.[55]

The third conclusion is that while American evangelicals trailed their British colleagues, and while Old Testament scholars had more difficulty reentering the world of research than New, evangelical scholarship in America has nonetheless continued a steady maturation since the 1930s. At the three-quarter mark in the century evangelicals had reached a takeoff point. They had achieved a critical mass. This, however, was not without its ambiguities. On the one hand, evangelical Bible scholarship burgeoned. On the other, evangelicals encountered painful tensions arising from their very success in reentering the marketplace of ideas.

Looking back from 1967, George Ladd well described the situation this chapter has chronicled.

The successors to the fundamentalists of the 1920s have divided in two directions. Some . . . have shown little interest, indeed, a strengthening negative attitude toward interacting with the main stream of culture, philosophy, and theology. . . . There is, however, a growing number of other scholars whose theological heritage is the older fundamentalism, who are convinced of the truthfulness of the fundamentals of the Christian faith but who do not reflect the basic defensive, apologetic stance of fundamentalism. They acknowledge their indebtedness to critical scholarship. They believe that if the traditional orthodox interpretation of the gospel is true, it should be capable of defense, not by the negative technique of attacking other positions, but by expounding its own view in critical but creative interaction with other theologies. These modern successors of fundamentalism, for whom we prefer the term evangelicals, wish, in brief, to take their stand within the contemporary stream of philosophical, theological, and critical thought.[56]

What Ladd could not see was how many achievements lay ahead for those who took the second direction. That is the theme of Chapter 6. Chapters 7, 8, and 9 seek to interpret this story by defining more carefully the range of evangelical convictions about scholarship on Scripture, the uncertainties that have accompanied the recovery of academic interest, and the contexts in which evangelical scholars go about their work.

6. The Recent Achievement

The emergence today of a new scholastic conservatism in biblical studies, distinguished from Fundamentalist views, presents a fresh opportunity in the minds of many members [of the Society of Biblical Literature] for a productive dialogue on the nature and authority of scripture as well as on the historical and philological issues.

ERNEST W. SAUNDERS, *Centennial History of the Society of Biblical Literature*, 1982

This chapter is a progress report. Considerations of quality and problems of interpretation are suspended in order to focus on the expansion of evangelical American scholarship since the mid-1970s. The remarkable turnabout in such work over the last fifty years deserves full documentation even at the risk of putting to sleep those who prefer their books with words and reasoning instead of numbers and tables. Charting the maturation of evangelical biblical research, however, makes a natural transition to more reflective interpretation. In this case, percentages and lists of books provide hints for a clearer understanding of what the evangelical resurgence has, and has not, accomplished; how different groups of evangelicals have accommodated themselves differently to the new emphasis on scholarship; and how American evangelicals as a whole can still be differentiated from their colleagues in Britain and Canada.

EDUCATIONAL PEDIGREE

In early 1983, Word Books, an evangelical publishing house in Waco, Texas, which had secured a place in the religious marketplace by selling a wide variety of popular books and phonograph records, announced the publication of an ambitious commentary on the entire Bible. Forty-six evangelical scholars from the United States, Canada, the United Kingdom, and Australia were listed as authors of the project's fifty-two volumes. The editors hoped that the series would "serve for a generation or more as the definitive work of scriptural exegesis for the Christian community." The

authors of the *Word Biblical Commentary* are a distinguished group
—seven hold doctorates from Harvard, nine received their final
academic degrees from Cambridge University, six from the University of London. Others were trained at Oxford, Manchester, the
universities of Scotland, and at some of the best American graduate schools. They teach in the United States' foremost evangelical
seminaries and in a wide range of institutions in Canada and the
United Kingdom. Their work represents, according to the prospectus, "A Harvest of Biblical Scholarship from the Evangelical
Renaissance."[1]

Although this series promises to take its place among the most
distinguished evangelical commentaries, the training of its authors
is now more a commonplace than an exception for such efforts.
Shortly before the inauguration of the Word Commentary, Zondervan in Grand Rapids issued the first volumes of another major
series, *The Expositor's Bible Commentary (EBC)*. Although this multivolume work was pitched at a slightly more popular audience
than the Word commentaries, and although Zondervan aims its
publications more consistently to the conservative end of the evangelical spectrum, the editors of this project assembled a team of
authors nearly equal in pedigree to the more self-consciously academic effort from Word. Six of the *EBC*'s twelve books had appeared by 1985—one introductory volume with approximately
thirty-five major articles on the contexts of biblical scholarship,
and the five volumes for the New Testament. The fifty-three authors employed in producing these six volumes included seven
who had obtained terminal degrees from Harvard, five each from
Cambridge and Edinburgh, four from Oxford, and three each
from Brandeis and the University of Pennsylvania.

Such resources in academically certified personnel have not always been available to editors of evangelical publications. For
instance, only twelve of the fifty contributors to the *New Bible
Commentary* in 1953 had obtained research doctorates (one
D.Theol, eleven Ph.D.s, eight D.D.s, thirty with B.A., M.A., B.D.,
or Th.M.). To be sure, this figure is deceptive. It seriously underestimates the academic quality of that production, several of whose
British authors had demonstrated their expertise not by the customary American procedure of obtaining doctoral certification,
but by making serious and sometimes—as in the case of F. F. Bruce

(M.A. Cambridge, M.A. Aberdeen)—prolific contributions to scholarship. Nonetheless, the fact that half of the fifty authors were serving as active clergymen rather than in academic posts suggested that evangelicals had made only a partial transition to the academic professionalization that had come to characterize formal study of the Bible in the twentieth century.

Within ten years the situation was beginning to change. When Carl Henry published a series of six symposia on *Contemporary Evangelical Theology* from 1957 to 1969, he was able to draw upon a body of authors with more impressive academic credentials. The eighty-five writers for these books included fifty-seven Americans, thirteen Britons, ten Europeans, two Australians, two South Africans, and one Canadian. Seventy-two had earned doctorates, and several who had not were productive research scholars. Nine had secured their terminal degrees from Harvard, six from Princeton Seminary, five each from Edinburgh and the Free University of Amsterdam, and three each from Dropsie, Pennsylvania, Boston University, London, and Cambridge.

The authors whom editor Walter Elwell, dean of the Wheaton College Graduate School, was able to recruit for an *Evangelical Dictionary of Theology* published in the mid-1980s by Baker illustrate the zeal with which evangelicals have continued to pursue academic certification. Its 288 contributors held 254 earned doctorates. Dallas Theological Seminary had made the largest contribution to this total, with nineteen Th.D.s, but close behind were Edinburgh (eighteen), Harvard (thirteen), Chicago (nine), Iowa (eight), Pennsylvania, Oxford, London, Aberdeen, and Manchester (seven each), Princeton Seminary (six), and Cambridge (five, with another six who had obtained an M.A. from that same university). Another recent team effort, the *Beacon Dictionary of Theology* (1983), edited by Richard S. Taylor and written for a Nazarene and Wesleyan constituency, revealed similar high standards of educational preparation. Ninety-seven of this volume's 153 authors (63 percent) had earned research doctorates.

Impressive as this general picture for evangelical scholars seems, it is, in fact, dimmed by the academic training of those who teach the Scriptures in evangelical seminaries. At four of the largest interdenominational evangelical seminaries during the early 1980s (Fuller, Trinity, Asbury, Gordon-Conwell), thirty-four of thirty-six professors of Bible held earned university doctorates. These Ph.D.s and Th.D.s were distributed in roughly four equal parts: one-fourth from Harvard, one-fourth from Dropsie and Brandeis, one-fourth from English and Scottish universities, and one-fourth from other universities in the United States. Just about the same qualifications are the norm for faculties at several Baptist seminaries (Eastern, Northern, Denver), the Reformed seminaries (Westminster, Calvin, Reformed), the Nazarene seminary in Kansas City, the Adventist seminary at Andrews University in Michigan, and the seminaries of the Lutheran Church–Missouri Synod, to mention only part of the full roster of evangelical institutions. Even at the seminaries of the Southern Baptist Convention and the more conservative evangelical groups, which as a rule provide doctoral training for their own faculties, a few professors have done advanced graduate work at widely respected research universities. (See Tables 1, 2, 3.)

The ability of evangelical seminaries to staff their faculties with well-trained scholars involves a greater achievement than appears on the surface. Evangelicals have not only been undergoing the rigors of academic professionalization; they have done so under the added responsibility of training increasing numbers of students. A population explosion in the evangelical seminaries has added to the demand for teachers. Of the country's ten largest accredited seminaries in 1956, only four Southern Baptist schools (Southern, Southwestern, Southeastern, New Orleans), and the Missouri Synod's Concordia, fell within the broadly conservative camp. By 1984 the situation was quite different. The ten largest seminaries in the country included five Southern Baptist schools (the same four plus Golden Gate), as well as Fuller, Trinity, and Gordon-Conwell. And the other two, Princeton and San Francisco, were both adding more faculty of generally evangelical convictions.[2] To fill more faculty slots while simultaneously upgrading the quality of those called to teach was no mean achievement.

The training of Bible professors at evangelical colleges is only slightly less impressive. Nearly two-thirds of those teaching Bible and religion at the thirteen member institutions of the Christian College Consortium in the early 1980s, for example, held university doctorates, and several more had earned Ph.D.s from seminaries. The university degrees, moreover, came from a wide variety

TABLE 1
Seminary and University Training for Bible Professors at Various Seminaries[a]

Type	Total Faculty	University Doctorates (%)	Foreign Doctorates	Attended This Seminary or Sister Institution[b] (%)
Evangelical (Asbury, Fuller, Gordon-Conwell, Trinity)	36	34 (94%)	10	14 (39%)
Conservative Evangelical (Dallas, Talbot, Grace)	35	7 (20)	4	30 (86)
Southern Baptist (Southwestern, Southern, New Orleans)	40	7 (18)	2	36 (90)
Northern Baptist (Eastern, Northern)	6	5 (83)	2	3 (50)
Conservative Baptist[c] (Denver, Western)	15	4 (27)	2	4 (27)
Reformed (Westminster, Calvin, Reformed)	15	11 (73)	6	13 (87)
Adventist (Berrien Springs)	6	5 (83)	0	6 (100)
Nazarene (Kansas City)	4	4 (100)	1	2 (50)
Missouri Synod (St. Louis, Fort Wayne)	16	9 (56)	2	12 (75)
Control (Harvard, Union)	10	10 (100)	3	0 (00)

(a) Information on the faculties came from the following catalogues: Asbury 1982–1983; Fuller ca. 1980–1981; Gordon-Conwell 1982–1983; Trinity 1981–1983; Dallas 1982–1983; Talbot 1980–1981; Grace 1982–1984; Southwestern 1980–1981; Southern 1982–1984; New Orleans 1982–1983; Eastern 1981–1983; Northern 1980–1981; Denver 1983–1985; Western 1980–1981; Westminster 1982–1984; Calvin 1981–1983; Reformed 1981–1982; Adventist 1982–1983; Nazarene 1982–1983; St. Louis 1980–1981; Fort Wayne 1980–1981; Harvard 1982–1983; Union 1982–1983.

(b) That is, a member of the same denomination, or a closely related school.

(c) Denver (three of five faculty with university doctorates); Western (one of nine).

TABLE 2
Distribution of University Doctorates from Four Large
Evangelical Seminaries[a]

University	New Testament	Old Testament	Other[b]	Total
Harvard	5	3	1	9
Dropsie		5		5
Brandeis		2	1	3
St. Andrews	2	1		3
Aberdeen	2			2
Cambridge	2			2
Drew		1	1	2
Basel	1			1
Columbia	1			1
Duke			1	1
Emory	1			1
Johns Hopkins			1	1
London	1			1
Manchester	1			1
University of Southern California	1			1
Total Doctorates	17	12	5	34
Total U.S.	8	11	5	24
Total U.K.	8	1	0	9
Total Europe	1	0	0	1
Total Faculty	17	13	6	36

(a) Asbury, Fuller, Gordon-Conwell, Trinitity Evangelical Divinity School
(b) Faculty listed in general biblical studies, without designation for New or Old Testament.

TABLE 3
Distribution of University Doctorates from All Evangelical Seminaries in Table 1

University	New Testament	Old Testament	Other	Total
Harvard	6	4	1	11
Dropsie		7		7
Aberdeen	3		2	5
Cambridge	4	1		5
Princeton Seminary	5			5
Brandeis		3	1	4
Johns Hopkins		2	2	4
Manchester	4			4
St. Andrews	2	2		4
Columbia	1	1	1	3
Duke	2		1	3
Free (Holland)	3			3
Claremont		1	1	2
Drew		1	1	2
Edinburgh	1		1	2
London	2			2
Washington–St. Louis			2	2
Basel	1			1
Boston		1		1
Case Western Reserve	1			1
Chicago	1			1
Emory	1			1
Fordham		1		1
Hamburg	1			1
Hebrew Union		1		1
Michigan		1		1
Oxford	1			1
Pacific School of Religion	1			1
Pennsylvania	1			1
Stellenbosch (RSA)	1			1
University of California Los Angeles		1		1
Union			1	1
University of Southern California	1			1
Vanderbilt		1		1
Wisconsin		1		1
Total	43	29	14	86
Total U.S.	20	26	11	57
Total U.K.	17	3	3	23
Total Europe/Africa	6	0	0	6
Total Faculty	82	65	26	173

of distinguished American and foreign institutions. (See Table 4.)

A recent survey of the Institute for Biblical Research, which elicited responses from over two-thirds its nearly 150 members, showed a degree of academic certification comparable to that of the evangelical seminaries where, of course, a number of the IBR members teach. Eighty-eight of 102 respondants hold doctorates from research universities, and another thirteen from seminaries. The distribution of these Ph.D.s and Th.D.s reflected the evangelicals' by now traditional schools of choice as well as a number of newer institutions: Princeton Seminary and Harvard (seven each), Brandeis and Manchester (six each), Cambridge and St. Andrews (five each), Dropsie, Aberdeen, and the Free University of Amsterdam (four each), and Chicago, the University of Southern California, Southern Baptist Theological Seminary, Claremont Graduate School of Theology, and Union Seminary (three each). (Fuller results from this survey, which included also members of the Evangelical and Wesleyan Theological Societies, are found in the Appendix.)

The data begin to numb, but their import is clear. Evangelical Bible scholars are no longer looking in from the outside at the distinguished centers of graduate education.

PROFESSIONAL PARTICIPATION

Not surprisingly, the growing number of evangelical scholars who have undertaken serious graduate education also are playing a larger role in the activities of professional organizations. Not since before the turn of the century have evangelicals participated in the larger scholarly community as they have done during the last two decades. The recent survey revealed that over three-fourths of the members of the Institute for Biblical Research (IBR) were also members of the Society of Biblical Literature (SBL), while nearly two-fifths also held membership in other professional societies. The same poll showed that almost a third of the members of the Evangelical Theological Society, whose ranks include many who are not Bible scholars as such, are also members of the SBL. (See Appendix for further details.) As might be expected, membership leads to participation. In 1982, at least 10 percent of those on the program at the annual meeting of the SBL came from the pro-

TABLE 4

Doctorates for Bible Faculty[a] in Selected Evangelical Colleges[b]

College	Total Faculty	University Doctorate	Seminary Doctorate	Total
Asbury	7	5	0	5
Bethel (MN)	8	4	1	5
George Fox	3	3	0	3
Gordon	5	4	1	5
Greenville	3	2	0	2
Houghton	6	1	1	2
Malone	4	2	1	3
Messiah	4	1	1	2
Seattle Pacific	9	7	2	9
Taylor	5	3	1	4
Trinity	4	4	0	4
Westmont	6	3	0	3
Wheaton	13	10	3	13
Total	77	49	11	60

University Doctorates (U.S.)		University Doctorates (Foreign)		Seminary Doctorates	
Boston	6	Manchester	3	Fuller	3
Brandeis	5	Edinburgh	2	Dallas	2
Iowa	4	Basel	1	Ashland	1
Chicago	3	Cambridge	1	Bethel	1
Hebrew Union	3	Glasgow	1	Concordia	1
Claremont	2	Oxford	1	Hartford	1
Duke	2	St. Andrews	1	Pittsburgh	1
Johns Hopkins	2			Southern	1
Michigan	2			Baptist	
NYU	2				
Vanderbilt	2				
Case Western Reserve	1				
Drew	1				
Dropsie	1				
Michigan State	1				
Northwestern	1				
Rice	1				
Total	39		10		11

(a) Assistant professors or above, listed as teaching Bible, religion, theology, or similar subjects.

(b) These are the colleges in the Christian College Consortium as of 1983. Catalogues: Asbury 1980–1982; Bethel 1982–1983; George Fox 1982–1984; Gordon 1982–1983; Greenville ca. 1980–1981; Houghton 1981–1983; Malone 1982–1983; Messiah 1982–1984; Seattle Pacific 1981–1982; Taylor 1981–1983; Trinity 1982–1983; Westmont 1981–1982; Wheaton 1982–1983.

fessedly evangelical colleges and seminaries, or from Baptist, conservative Lutheran, fundamentalist, or Adventist groups which also fit within the general evangelical category.[3] This figure has, if anything, increased since 1982.

These professionally active evangelicals have also begun to place their work with publishers and periodicals that had not traditionally served the evangelical community. One-fourth of the members of the IBR have produced books for university presses, commercial houses, or other nonevangelical publishers; and one-half have published articles in professional journals. Of the forty-six authors in the new Word Biblical Commentary series, more have published with Eerdmans than any other press (seven). And several have written books for Baker (three) and InterVarsity Press (three), as well as the Southern Baptist Broadman (five) and the Presbyterian Westminster (three). But five have also brought out books from Cambridge University Press, four from Harper & Row, and three each from Scholars' Press and E. J. Brill. In recent years something approaching 10 percent of the notes and articles appearing the *Journal of Biblical Literature*, and something over 10 percent of those in *New Testament Studies* have come from evangelicals.[4] While the numbers are not as impressive for the Old Testament journals, evangelicals also show up there.[5]

PUBLICATIONS

To note the quantities of evangelical work, however, is not as meaningful as to indicate the kind of works being produced. Any effort to do this will be impressionistic, skewed, and partial, but it is still worth the effort as a way of suggesting the boundaries of the recent achievement. No claims are made for the completeness of the following paragraphs; they are attempts, rather, to provide a flavor of the recent scholarship.

Most obvious is the profusion of outstanding commentaries. At least four academic series are currently being published, including from Eerdmans the last volumes of the *New International Commentary of the New Testament*, a matching series for the Old Testament, and the *New International Greek Testament Commentary*. The *Word Biblical Commentary* on the Old and New Testament had already published several volumes by 1985. At least six other semipopular series, which often contain careful consideration of critical matters, are in press as well: the *Tyndale Old Testament Commentary* and *The Bible Speaks Today* series from the American InterVarsity Press; the *Tyndale New Testament Commentary* and the *New Century Bible* from Eerdmans; the *Good News Commentary Series* from Harper & Row, and the *Expositor's Bible Commentary* from Zondervan. The *Wesleyan Bible Commentary* from Eerdmans, now reprinted by Baker, was completed in the late 1960s. Most of these series employ British authors as well as Americans, and some are exclusively British. But the American contribution is considerable. And each of the commentary series serves large numbers of American evangelicals. (See Table 5 for more information.)

In recent years the evangelical appetite for reference works on Scripture has stimulated the production of several competent volumes. Besides more general dictionaries of theology, Christian ethics, and church history, several books or series have addressed biblical matters directly: *Eerdmans Handbook to the Bible* published with Lion in Great Britain (1973); the *Zondervan Pictorial Encyclopedia of the Bible* (1975); Eerdmans' new revision of the *International Standard Bible Encyclopedia* (from 1979); Moody's *Theological Wordbook of the Old Testament* (1980); and a revision of the *New Bible Dictionary* (1982), published also with extensive graphics as the *Illustrated Bible Dictionary* (1980), from British Inter-Varsity Press and Tyndale House in America. In addition, Eerdmans is the American publisher for the English translation of the German *Theological Dictionary of the New Testament* and *Theological Dictionary of the Old Testament,* as Zondervan is for the *New International Dictionary of New Testament Theology.*

Evangelicals have also written several large introductions to the discussion of criticism as applied to both the Old and New Testaments. For the Old Testament, Gleason Archer's *A Survey of Old Testament Introduction* published by Moody (1964; revised 1974) is least accommodating to modern criticism; William Sanford LaSor, David Allan Hubbard, and Frederic W. Bush, *Old Testament Survey: The Message, Form, and Background of the Old Testament* published by Eerdmans (1982), is more willing to consider modern critical conclusions; and again for Eerdmans, R. K. Harrison's *Introduction to the Old Testament* (1969) is somewhere in between. For the New Testament, E. F. Harrison's *Introduction to the New Testament* for

TABLE 5
Evangelical Commentary Series in Press (1985)

New International Commentary on the New Testament
William B. Eerdmans Co., 1951 ff.
Ned B. Stonehouse, F. F. Bruce, eds.
15 volumes by 1985 (3 by Americans[a])

Tyndale New Testament Commentary
William B. Eerdmans Co., 1956 ff.
R. V. G. Tasker, ed.
20 volumes by 1985 (0 by Americans)

New Century Bible Commentary
William B. Eerdmans Co., reprint from Oliphants (Eng.), 1960 ff.
Ronald Clements and Matthew Black, eds.,
29 volumes by 1985 (4 by Americans)

Tyndale Old Testament Commentaries
InterVarsity Press, 1960 ff.
D. J. Wiseman, ed.
18 volumes by 1985 (0 by Americans)

New International Commentary on the Old Testament
William B. Eerdmans Co., 1970 ff.
R. K. Harrison, ed.
6 volumes by 1985 (1 by an American)

The Bible Speaks Today
InterVarsity Press, 1978 ff.
Alec Motyer and John R. W. Stott, eds.
14 volumes by 1985 (1 by an American)

New International Greek Testament Commentary
William B. Eerdmans Co., 1978 ff.
W. Ward Gasque and I. Howard Marshall, eds.
3 volumes by 1985 (1 by an American)

Expositors Bible Commentary
Zondervan Publishing Co., 1979 ff.
Frank E. Gaebelein and J. D. Douglas, eds.
53 different authors by 1985 (38 Americans)

Good News Commentary Series
Harper & Row, 1983 ff.
W. Ward Gasque, ed.
8 volumes by 1985 (6 by Americans)

Word Biblical Commentary
Word Publishing Co., 1982 ff.
David A. Hubbard and Glenn W. Barker, eds.
11 volumes by 1985 (5 by Americans)

[a] "American" means U.S.-born and those from abroad who have taught in the United States most of their academic lives. It excludes Canadians.

Eerdmans (1964), the major text by an American, is not as thorough as two widely used works by British evangelicals. Ralph Martin, who has taught for some years at Fuller Seminary, more often agrees with modern critical conclusions in his two-volume *New Testament Foundations* for Eerdmans (1975), than Donald Guthrie in his *New Testament Introduction*, published by Tyndale Press in Britain, InterVarsity Press in America (1970). Both books, and especially Guthrie's are marked by painstaking consideration of alternative views.

These introductions, as well as the reference works, differ considerably in scholarly expertise, in the aesthetics of bookmaking, and in the degree of willingness to learn from modern criticism. Some make stronger cases for their conclusions than others. Here the point is that evangelicals enjoy a range of learned books which address questions of criticism and which are marked by serious attention to the biblical scholarship of the last century.

Biblical translations also testify to the scholarly maturity of evangelicals. Frantic outbursts by evangelicals at the release of the Revised Standard Version, which never characterized more than a vocal minority, have almost entirely passed from the scene.[6] Evangelicals are now responsible for a number of popular paraphrases (like the *Living Bible*), but also for serious scholarship in the production of translations. The *New American Standard Bible* (1963) attempts to modernize the American Standard Version of 1901 while retaining that version's more literalistic approach to the translator's task. In 1978 the International Bible Society, in cooperation with Zondervan, brought out the *New International Version* (NIV), which sold nearly 11 million copies in its first six years. For this translation, moreover, critical reception has been largely favorable.[7] Over one hundred scholars, with a small army of support personnel, worked for more than a decade on this project. The result was a version solidly grounded in up-to-date textual study, cautious in its rendering of debated passages (especially for the Old Testament), yet also well adapted to modern English usage. Scholars have questioned details in this work, but it is nonetheless a superb effort.[8] One evangelical student of the Old Testament, after pointing out some questionable readings in parts of the NIV which fell within his expertise, delivered an opinion which deserves to stand for the entire effort: "When all is said and done the

OT NIV is a magnificent monument to Biblical scholarship. This is scholarship at its best, directed toward a practical end—namely, the clarification of the Biblical text through careful translation for present and future generations of English-speaking peoples."[9]

To keep impressive gains in perspective, it is necessary to acknowledge that American evangelicals have not produced a great quantity of first-rate scholarship on the interpretive contexts of Scripture. In spite of a flurry of recent attention to hermeneutics, for instance, two of the most perceptive evangelical interactions with recent academic discussions are a book and an essay by Britons.[10] Again, while questions of historicity for the gospels and the Pentateuch remain of great interest to Americans, British evangelicals have consistently produced the more intensive wrestling with these matters.[11] The Tyndale Fellowship for Biblical Research, which has commissioned several extensive projects to study such matters, has no counterpart in America. Americans suffer for lack of a similar agent of coordination.

American evangelicals also continue to draw attention to the presuppositions of modern critical scholars, but more general consideration of how convictions, whether modernistic or evangelical, affect understanding are in short supply. Among the few noteworthy American publications of this sort is Eerdmans' study of *Rudolf Bultmann's Theology* (1976), by the philosopher Robert C. Roberts, originally prepared as a dissertation at Yale University. But such work has to date received little attention from practitioners of biblical research. American evangelicals have produced a voluminous literature on the inerrancy of the Bible, but they have not been as concerned about other questions which may, in their own way, bear as significantly on the reading and understanding of Scripture as this issue.

Lacunas and lapses there are, beyond question, in the current research of American evangelicals. But the general picture, especially by comparison with the 1930s, is encouraging. In recent years a steadily growing number of well-qualified and widely published scholars have broadened and deepened the impact of evangelical scholarship. Again, it risks serious omissions and misrepresentations to single out individuals. Nonetheless, a roster of some who have made signal contributions is warranted as a way of providing a more general impression of evangelical expertise. In short, the work of Bruce Metzger, E. F. Harrison, Earl Ellis, and William Lane (who have continued to publish well into the 1980s) is only part of the harvest of evangelical scholarship.

Evangelical contributions have been especially noteworthy in New Testament study. Gordon Fee (Seattle Pacific, Southern California), who now teaches at Regent College after many years at Gordon-Conwell, has done outstanding work in textual criticism.[12] Robert Mounce (Washington, Fuller, Aberdeen), the president of Whitworth College, has written an especially fine commentary on the Book of Revelation.[13] Other evangelicals have made selective use of form-critical methods and principles of redaction to present solid exegesis of individual parts of the gospels, especially Robert Guelich (Wheaton, Illinois, Fuller, Hamburg), a "research pastor" in Minneapolis, on the Sermon on the Mount, and Robert Stein (Rutgers, Fuller, Andover Newton, Princeton Seminary), who teaches at Bethel Seminary in St. Paul, on the parables of Jesus.[14] Perhaps the most seminal New Testament work by contemporary evangelicals is being done by an American teaching in Canada and a Canadian employed in the United States, both of whom did doctoral studies in Great Britain. Richard Longenecker (Wheaton, Cambridge, Edinburgh), of Wycliffe College at the University of Toronto, is a careful student of Jewish Christianity, of exegetical practices in the New Testament world, and of the theology of Paul.[15] D. A. Carson (McGill, Central Baptist Seminary, Cambridge), who teaches at Trinity Seminary, has produced careful studies in Johannine theology, a fine commentary on Matthew, closely reasoned essays on redaction criticism, and path-breaking tools for studying the grammar of the Greek New Testament.[16]

Only a few evangelicals working in the Old Testament have reached the levels of these scholars, but a reasonable amount of good work is in progress. Until his untimely death in late summer 1985, Peter Craigie (Edinburgh, Durham, Aberdeen, McMaster), was dean of the faculty of humanities at the University of Calgary. He had led the way for his Old Testament peers with outstanding individual studies (such as on war in the Old Testament) and with several first-rate commentaries.[17] The dean of Trinity Seminary, Walter Kaiser (Wheaton, Brandeis), has prodded evangelicals to think synthetically about the Old Testament and has himself produced in several books a serious effort to construct both theology and ethics from the Old Testament around the theme of promise.[18] Other competent work by Americans evangelicals, which interacts self-consciously with modern criticism, is found in the appropriate volumes of the Word, New International Old Testament, and Tyndale commentary series.

Some evangelicals have also excelled in cognate studies. David Aune (Wheaton, Minnesota, Chicago), who teaches religious studies at St. Xavier College in Chicago, has produced carefully detailed interpretations of prophecy and eschatology in the larger world in which Christianity emerged.[19] And Edwin Yamauchi (Shelton, Brandeis), a professor of ancient history at Miami in Ohio, is a recognized expert on questions relating to the influence of Gnosticism upon the writing of the New Testament.[20]

In sum, these scholars and others who could be named are the fruit of an academic rebirth, as well as the seed for the next generation of evangelical scholarship.

FIRST IMPRESSIONS

An assessment of evangelical Bible scholarship must go far beyond the tabulation of graduate degrees, the recitation of *curricula vitae*, or a cataloging of the learned. Even these spare sources, however, make possible several preliminary conclusions about that scholarship and those who pursue it.

The most obvious fact is that American evangelicals still depend heavily upon the British, both for educational training and for partners in publication. This transatlantic bond has been a source of strength for over fifty years. It testifies to the value that can accrue when scholars from different nations pool their resources. In other religious activities American evangelicals have made great contributions to Great Britain, but in the specific area of Bible scholarship the debt which Americans owe to the British is considerable.

Almost no British evangelicals do doctoral work in the United States, but without access to the universities of the United Kingdom, American evangelicals would be deprived of a prime source of academic certification. British graduate training began to attract American evangelicals in the 1940s, and became even more important when F. F. Bruce, and then other evangelicals, obtained chairs at British universities. Twenty-eight of the eighty-eight IBR members with university doctorates who responded to a recent survey obtained them in Great Britain, seventeen in England, and eleven in Scotland. (Another six finished doctorates on the European continent and two in Canada.) Twelve of the authors in the *Word Biblical Commentary* teach in the United Kingdom, but a full half of its forty-six contributors did their final academic degrees there. Twenty-one of the fifty-three authors in the *Expositor's Bible Commentary* received their terminal graduate degrees in the United Kingdom. In sum, between one-fourth and one-half of the evangelical scholars on any particular biblical project are likely to have obtained final academic training in Great Britain.

The contribution of British-trained scholars to publication is just as pronounced. Table 5 shows to what extent the major commentary series depend upon British authors. Moreover, a majority of evangelicals who publish in the *Journal of Biblical Literature* or in *New Testament Studies* are British or have trained in Great Britain.[21] Without having precise figures, it is still almost certain that British authors like F. F. Bruce, I. H. Marshall, or the British-trained Australian Leon Morris account for more of the books which shape the judgments of American evangelical scholars than any American authors.[22]

The dependence upon British scholarship also has something to do with differences in professional placement. Far more British evangelicals are found in research universities, where a premium is placed on publication for academic peers, than in America, where evangelicals who conduct research in Scripture usually teach at seminaries or Christian colleges, where the greatest pressure is exerted to publish for the community at large. The difference shows up clearly among contributors to general projects, like the Baker *Evangelical Dictionary of Theology,* where 80 percent of the 235 contributors who are employed in America teach in seminaries or evangelical colleges, while only 10 percent are employed at universities. By contrast, of the fifty-one contributors who are employed outside the United States, mostly in Great Britain, 53 percent work in seminaries or evangelical colleges, 22 percent in universities. The contrast is even sharper for the specifically biblical projects. Of the twenty-seven contributors to the *Word Biblical Commentary* who teach in the United States, twenty-two (81 percent) are employed at seminaries or evangelical colleges, three (11 percent) at research universities. Again by contrast, ten of the nineteen British contributors, or 53 percent, teach at research universities. And roughly the same ratios hold for those who have written for the *Expositor's Bible Commentary*. (See Table 6.)

One possible conclusion from this comparison is that British evangelical scholarship has gone a further step in the direction of twentieth-century professionalization than the American. While Americans enjoy ready access to research universities for study, they have not yet won a place in these institutions as teachers. Reasons for this situation are complex, as are its implications, and both will be considered in the chapters which follow.

As well as providing for comparisons with the British, tabular data also tells us something about the internal makeup of the evangelical scholarly community. Perhaps most obviously, it is still an almost exclusively male preserve. Only one woman has written for a major commentary series (Joyce Baldwin, author of commentaries on Daniel, Esther, and Haggai/Zechariah/Malachi in the Tyndale *Old Testament* series). Only four or five are members of the IBR, and only four were enlisted to write for Baker's *Evangelical Dictionary of Theology* (of those four only one is a biblical scholar). In this regard the evangelicals do not differ dramatically from the larger academic community, but it is still a striking situation.[23]

Cumulative analysis of educational patterns and publishing careers also provides a sense of the networks that bind the evangelical scholars together. While boundaries remain fluid, some conclusions are possible. For one thing, Southern Baptists are now cooperating with Northern postfundamentalist evangelicals to a greater degree than before. One of the editors and several contributors to the *Word Biblical Commentary* teach at Southern Baptist institutions, where in previous projects it was difficult to find more than token Southern Baptist representation. A few other denominational tendencies are also worthy of notice. Members of the IBR, the most professional of the evangelical research societies, tend to be Baptists or Presbyterians. But among the IBR as well as more generally, evangelical scholars come from a large array of denominations, both mainline and independent, both old and new. While British Anglicans make extensive contributions to evangelical projects, almost no American Episcopalians contribute. Similarly,

TABLE 6
Academic Positions of Evangelical Scholars in the United States and Abroad

	Total	Seminary	Christian Colleges	University	Other
C. Henry's Symposia[a]					
U.S.	59	47 (79.7%)	5 (08.5)	3 (05.1)	4
Elsewhere[b]	26			14 (53.8)	12
Baker Dictionary[c]					
U.S.	235	124 (52.8)	63 (26.8)	23 (09.8)	25
Elsewhere	51			11 (21.6)	40
Expositor's Bible Commentary[d]					
U.S.	38	28 (73.7)	4 (10.5)	2 (05.3)	4
Elsewhere	15			9 (60.0)	6
Word Biblical Commentary[e]					
U.S.	27	18 (66.7)	4 (14.8)	3 (11.1)	2
Elsewhere	19			10 (52.6)	9
Institute for Biblical Research[f]					
U.S.	86	47 (54.7)	29 (33.7)	3 (03.5)	7
Elsewhere	16			8 (50.0)	8

(a) Authors in the series of volumes edited by Carl F. H. Henry under the general title *Contemporary Evangelical Thought*. Individual volumes were *Contemporary Evangelical Thought* (Great Neck, New York: Channel Press, 1957); *Revelation and the Bible* (Grand Rapids: Baker, 1958); *Basic Christian Doctrines* (New York: Holt, Rinehart and Winston, 1962); *Christian Faith and Modern Theology* (New York: Channel Press, 1964); *Jesus of Nazareth: Saviour and Lord* (Grand Rapids: Eerdmans, 1966); and *Fundamentals of the Faith* (Grand Rapids: Zondervan, 1969).
(b) "Elsewhere" most often means Canada or the United Kingdom.
(c) Authors for *Evangelical Dictionary of Theology*, edited by Walter A. Elwell (Grand Rapids: Baker, 1984).
(d) Authors for *The Expositor's Bible Commentary*, edited by Frank E. Gabelein and J. D. Douglas (Grand Rapids: Zondervan, 1979–).
(e) Authors for *The Word Biblical Commentary*, edited by David A. Hubbard and Glenn W. Barker (Waco, TX: Word, 1982–).
(f) These reflect results of a survey of members of the Institute for Biblical Research. See Appendix for further details.

after Carl Henry's success in enlisting Lutherans for evangelical causes, the Lutheran presence in publishing projects has declined. Only one of the ninety-nine authors in the *Word Biblical Commentary* and the *Expositor's Bible Commentary* is Lutheran. By contrast, the contribution of the Christian Reformed Church has remained an important factor from the mid-1950s to the present.

Schools of choice present some surprises. Almost as many evangelicals who write for the major publishing projects have somewhere along the way attended Harvard or Princeton Seminary as Wheaton or Fuller Seminary. Westminster and Gordon-Conwell seminaries join Wheaton and Fuller as the evangelical schools which have trained the most evangelical scholars active in the profession. Among the seminaries a major difference occurs in the training of faculty. At Asbury, Fuller, Gordon-Conwell, and Trinity Evangelical Divinity School, few of the teachers have graduated from the institutions in which they teach, while at the more conservative evangelical schools, the confessionally Reformed seminaries, as well as at the seminaries of the Southern Baptists, Adventists, and the Missouri Synod Lutherans, almost all of the faculty are graduates of the seminaries in which they teach or of clearly allied institutions. (See Table 1.)

It will be possible to tease other conclusions from numerical data as we move on. At this point, dutifully reinforced by a squadron of tables, it is safe to conclude that in many measurable features contemporary evangelical scholarship on the Scriptures enjoys a considerable good health. Now the compelling task is to describe evangelical beliefs concerning the Bible in relationship to scholarship, to take account of intramural conflicts, and to set these matters into a more meaningful historical context.

7. The Standpoints of Evangelical Scholarship

Canonical Scripture should always be interpreted on the basis that it is infallible and inerrant. However, in determining what the God-taught writer is asserting in each passage, we must pay the most careful attention to its claims and character as a human production. . . . Scripture is inerrant, not in the sense of being absolutely precise by modern standards, but in the sense of making good its claims and achieving that measure of focused truth at which its authors aimed.

INTERNATIONAL COUNCIL ON BIBLICAL INERRANCY, 1978

The recent and growing evangelical contribution to academic biblical study has tended to obscure a fundamental reality. The self-conscious evangelicals described in this book are seeking to play the academic game fairly, and the number of evangelicals recognized in the wider academic world now constitutes a significant subgroup among Bible scholars at large. Yet what it means to be an evangelical, in the way we are using the term here, still has more to do with beliefs about the Bible than with the practice of scholarship. Evangelical self-definition, that is, hinges upon a specific conception of Scripture more than upon a specific approach to research. Evangelical scholars are not professors who happen also to be conservative Protestants, but conservative Protestants who find themselves engaged in scholarship.

An examination of the standpoints of evangelical scholarship must, therefore, begin with convictions about Scripture, and with the (sometimes unstated) implications of those convictions. But this is not enough. Different groups of Christians have arrived at different answers on how to interpret the Bible. Evangelicals, for their part, have distinct convictions about that process as well, and these convictions also contribute to the evangelical perspective. By first defining attitudes toward the Bible and its interpretation, we are then in a position to describe evangelical standpoints toward scholarship. This chapter, in an effort to present a sharply etched picture, largely resists the temptation to illustrate its assertions.

The result may take on the qualities of an ideal type, sacrificing faithfulness to the complexities of lived reality in order to achieve some clarity. Whatever its limits, this procedure makes it possible to present more directly the argument that while evangelicals share general convictions about the Bible as well as distinctive attitudes toward who should interpret Scripture, these commonalities do not necessarily yield a common approach to scholarship.

IS THE BIBLE TRUE?

The most important conviction of evangelical scholars is that the Bible is true. Those who in America call themselves evangelicals usually affirm that truthfulness instinctively, simply, and unequivocally. Moreover, evangelicals hold that the Bible is true not just as religion but also as fact. While Scripture certainly portrays accurately the nature and dimensions of religious experience, it is also provides a true record of character (whether human or divine), cosmologies, historical actions, and states of personal being.

Traditionally, more than a few evangelicals have wanted to state this conviction with careful nuance. Many, as we shall see, have insisted that an affirmation of the Bible's truthfulness necessarily entails a dedication to its responsible interpretation. Many have also insisted that the proper focus of scriptural truth is its meaning for faith and practice, its revelation about the relationship between God and humanity, and its guidelines for righteous living. Such one in the nineteenth century was the Princeton theologian Charles Hodge, who concluded the chapter on Scripture in his *Systematic Theology* by stressing both the accessibility of the Bible to the church and the kind of truth Christians should expect to receive from the Bible:

The fact that all the true people of God in every age and in every part of the Church, in the exercise of their private judgment, in accordance with the simple rules [of interpretation] above stated, agree as to the meaning of Scripture in all things necessary either in faith or practice, is a decisive proof of the perspicuity of the Bible, and of the safety of allowing the people the enjoyment of the divine right of private judgment.[1]

Hodge, as it happens, also believed that the Bible was true about everything else, and so he spoke for many since his day as well. Some twentieth-century evangelicals, on the other hand, who affirm the Bible's truthfulness concerning faith and practice, are not as definite as Hodge on what they regard as incidental or secondary aspects of the Scriptures.[2] A still smaller group of evangelicals, both at the start of the twentieth century and today, would admit that the Bible contains a few random and unimportant errors, but go on to argue that these do not compromise the essential truth which the Scriptures impart. I. Howard Marshall, for example, has recently suggested that an evangelical who feels that Luke may have presented a mistaken chronology in Acts 5:33–39 might conclude that "here we have a genuine historical mistake, and that the presence of this and other mistakes demonstrates that our understanding of the truth of the Bible must allow for such things."[3]

At different times over the last century, evangelicals holding these various shadings of opinion have engaged one another in extensive and occasionally acrimonious debate. In fact, these intra-mural squabbles sometimes lead to such terrific fireworks that participants lose sight of the basic similarities of their positions. The differences among evangelicals over the nature of biblical truth touch upon serious concerns. And they reveal something important about the evangelical understanding of Scripture and its interpretation. But they have also sometimes led to misperceptions of larger realities. Evangelicals who affirm that the Bible is uniquely true with respect to divine-human relationships and either substantially or entirely true with respect to matters of fact in the external world make up a distinct group. In that affirmation they set themselves apart from those who deny that the Bible conveys cognitive truth, or from those who affirm that while the Bible is true, its truth is on the same order as that in other books. They are even quite different from those who argue that the Bible is uniquely true, but only as a record of religious experience or of divine-human encounter. As R. T. France has recently put it, "all who would wish to be included under this title [of evangelical] would agree to at least the following three propositions: (1) Special revelation is necessary for a true knowledge of God. (2) The Bible is the supreme and only sufficient locus of [or "means of apprehending"] such revelation. (3) The Bible is the inspired Word of God."[4] While many shades of evangelical opinion exist, especially on the relationship between biblical truthfulness as fact and as divine-human encounter, evangelical positions exhibit a greater unity than intra-evangelical debate sometimes suggests.

WHAT IS TRUTH?

Evangelical convictions about the Bible's truthfulness regularly involve a number of subsidiary convictions. When evangelicals say that the Bible is true, they are usually making a series of inter-related affirmations about the nature of the world, the character of religion, and the structure of epistemology. Some of these sub-sidiary affirmations have been the subject of intense evangelical attention during the last century, others have remained mostly beneath the surface. Evangelicals display different degrees of awareness about these issues. In addition, when they do pay atten-tion to them, they differ among themselves on whether it is better to demonstrate or presuppose these subsidiary affirmations. Three of the most important of these convictions deserve at least brief attention.

First is commitment to an open universe. Evangelicals believe in the reality of the transcendent and the possibility of the supernatu-ral. This conviction, which was an unquestioned part of Christian tradition more generally until the eighteenth century, has been in the forefront of evangelical concerns during this era of biblical criticism. Time and again the same note is heard: It is irresponsi-ble, academically as well as religiously, to rule out the supernatural when considering the Scriptures. One of the most consistent ob-jects of evangelical rebuttal in recent decades has been Rudolph Bultmann's assertion that "an historical fact which involves a res-urrection from the dead is utterly inconceivable."[5] Evangelicals look upon such utterances, or analogous ones championing the superiority of "scientific" over "primitive" world views, as intellec-tually bankrupt. They are confident that the supernatural is true —whether because of personal experience, religious authority, or arguments for the existence of God (which may range from those of Paul in Romans 1, through variations on Justin Martyr, Tertul-lian, Thomas Aquinas, John Locke, William Paley, or C. S. Lewis, to modern analytical statements negating atheistic conclusions). And so they insist that while students of Scripture may properly postpone direct consideration of the transcendent while working on specific biblical problems, they may never deny it or proceed as if its existence were irrelevant to an understanding of the Bible.

While this defense of supernaturalism has been prominent during the last century, evangelicals have not always been as self-conscious about other foundational convictions nor as active in describing and defending them. This is specifically the case for a second conviction entailed by the affirmation that the Bible is true. Evangelicals are "realists" in the sense that they believe that the world enjoys an independent existence apart from its perception by humans, that essence precedes existence, and that mind is capable of perceiving existence beyond itself with at least some accuracy. These beliefs, and kindred ones about the existence of a spiritual existence that encompasses the world of the senses, constitute a distinctly evangelical antimodernism. When evangelicals say the Bible is true, they have fairly specific ideas about what counts for truth. Most of these stand in opposition to principles which, to some extent or the other, have become conventions in Western academic life more generally.

Evangelicals, for example, are almost always pre-, anti-, or (in selected cases) post-Kantian. A few evangelicals may study Kant with profit, but almost none accept the Kantian conclusion that the human mind is the determining element of ontology and ethics. Evangelicals also reject historicism in the relativist or subjectivist senses of that term. They do not believe, with Carl Becker of a previous era or Hayden White today, that history-writing is thoroughly relative to the perspective of the historian or ultimately classifiable as a subspecies of imaginative literature. In addition, evangelicals reject conventionalism in science. To be sure, evangelicals, along with the American academic world as a whole, have read Thomas Kuhn's *The Structure of Scientific Revolutions* with profit and have made extensive use of his view that scientific knowledge depends upon social structures. Nonetheless, they usually do not share the extreme skepticism about the scientific enterprise which may be read out of Kuhn, or which is explicit in the works of theorists like Paul Feyerabend. Evangelical epistemology, in short, is normally far closer to nineteenth-century positivism, which loomed as such a threat to the faith, than to the postpositivistic science of the mid-twentieth century, which some evangelicals have used to create a breathing space for themselves over against the academic establishment.

Evangelicals, furthermore, oppose philosophical monism, of both idealist or materialist varieties. They do not believe in the relativizing effects of Hegel's dialectic, nor with Marx that our "very ideas are but the outgrowth of the conditions of . . . production and . . . property."[6] For evangelicals, mental and spiritual states have an independent reality which in some sense never changes. Finally, evangelicals are not psychological determinists. Whatever they may learn from Freud or Jung (and some are willing to learn a great deal), psychological explanations do not provide ultimate explanations for human actions or existence.

Evangelicals have not expended a great deal of concentrated effort in establishing their antimodernism. They have often assumed that the case for an open universe establishes also the weakness of modern world views. But this is only partly true. With significant exceptions, evangelicals have tended to rely upon common sense rebuttals of the various modernisms.[7] This in turn has led to a loss of clarity in debates between believers and nonbelievers as opposing sides regale each other with mutually unintelligible concepts. And it has led to an increase of suspicion among Christians. Few evangelicals have explored ways of simultaneously rejecting the basic perspectives of modern thinkers while incorporating their secondary insights into Christian frameworks. But when this has occurred, evangelicals who adopt selected features of modern thought sometimes berate other evangelicals for their obscurantism, while the others who suspect all modern thought look upon any attempt to employ it as heresy.

Two matters are important here for biblical scholarship. The first is that evangelical stances on these fundamental issues restrict the degree and quality of general academic cooperation. Nonevangelicals who define reality in modern terms can have at best limited tolerance for evangelicals who use modern insights selectively, and nearly none for those who regard modern thought—root and branch—as corrupt.

The second is that Bible scholarship, whether evangelical or not, has suffered from a lack of attention to foundational intellectual reasoning. Conclusions from modern thought do enter into arguments involving important biblical questions. Similarly, premodern philosophical concepts play an important role for evangelicals. Since questions of text, grammar, and translation, or of historical reconstruction from extrabiblical literature, require less extensive employment of such conclusions, these are usually the issues about which evangelicals and nonevangelical scholars have the most fruitful interchanges. But for larger critical issues, conclusions about the nature of human experience or the structure of reality are indispensable. When biblical scholars, who tolerate no shortcuts in matters relating to their expertise, nevertheless rely on philosophical conventions to advance their arguments about Scripture, the scholarly enterprise suffers. This is as true for evangelicals who rely instinctively on intellectual conventions of the eighteenth century as for secularists who employ modern conventions with the same apodictic confidence.[8]

A commitment to realism, as that term is used here, is a vital part of the evangelical understanding of truth. Where evangelicals themselves, or those who wish to grasp the nature of evangelical scholarship, merely take that realism for granted, confusion is the inevitable result.

Almost the same things may be said about a third conviction, the belief in the reliability of language. Although few evangelicals spend much time considering the question directly, they assume that language is a fit vehicle for communicating real information about real states of affairs. Or, as a position paper of the International Council on Biblical Inerrancy phrases it,

We affirm that God who made mankind in His image has used language as a means of revelation. We deny that human language is so limited by our creatureliness that it is rendered inadequate as a vehicle for divine revelation. We further deny that the corruption of human culture and language through sin has thwarted God's work of inspiration.[9]

In recent years, some evangelicals have recognized the need carefully to justify this conviction, but more generally it remains on the level of a widely shared presupposition.[10]

In sum, when evangelicals affirm the truthfulness of Scripture, they make an interrelated set of religious, philosophical, and linguistic affirmations. As evangelicals and other interested parties take greater care in examining the constituent facets of this claim about the Bible, evangelical scholarship will be sharpened and the cause of scholarship advanced.

WHAT IS THE BIBLE?

An additional preliminary question concerns the nature of the Bible itself.[11] All evangelicals believe the Scriptures are inspired by God and that they constitute divine revelation. Although some continue to press texts like 2 Timothy 3:16 and 2 Peter 1:21 in the effort to define exactly the nature of inspiration, evangelical scholars since A. A. Hodge and B. B. Warfield in the late nineteenth century have largely resisted this temptation. That God inspired Scripture is a fundamental datum. How it was done—through what combination of direct communication, extraordinary insight, tribal or oral histories, or use of documents—is much less important than that it occurred.

Evangelicals agree also that the Bible is the church's primary source of divine revelation. Scripture both is and contains the Word of God. Other questions may be open for much discussion —whether revelation of a secondary sort continues after Scripture; whether ecclesiastical tradition clarifies, augments, obscures, or is irrelevant to biblical revelation. But the main issue is fixed. God has chosen to reveal his character, his will for humankind, and his promise of salvation through the Scriptures. This is the ultimate reason for evangelical seriousness about biblical study.

Evangelicals, moreover, have usually considered the Bible's inspiration to be plenary and verbal. The entire Bible is a revelation from God. The words of Scripture themselves communicate that revelation. A never-ending round of discussion explores the problems and implications of revelation in such terms. What about textual variants? What about the New Testament use of the Old? What about the character of translations out of Greek and Hebrew? Within the last two centuries some efforts have been made to distinguish between verbal and plenary inspiration.[12] But most evangelical scholars continue to affirm that inspiration is both verbal and plenary, especially if they are allowed to say what they mean by the terms.

Something of the same can be said about two other labels evangelicals apply to Scripture, "infallibility" and "inerrancy." Since the term inerrancy has become the focus of much controversy and of considerable political maneuvering among evangelicals, it is not surprising that some have adopted it as a rallying cry while others denigrate it as a secondary matter. Although inerrancy usually has a more precise connotation than infallibility, both may be used in a general sense to affirm that God perfectly accomplishes his purposes through Scripture. J. I. Packer put it this way in *"Fundamentalism" and the Word of God:*

"Infallible" denotes the quality of never deceiving or misleading, and so means "wholly trustworthy and reliable"; "inerrant" means "wholly true." Scripture is termed infallible and inerrant to express the conviction that all its teaching is the utterance of God "who cannot lie," whose word, once spoken, abides for ever, and that therefore it may be trusted implicitly. . . . To assert biblical inerrancy and infallibility is just to confess faith in (i) the divine origin of the Bible and (ii) the truthfulness and trustworthiness of God.[13]

As meanings for inerrancy become more precise, consensus among evangelicals begins to break down. Yet whatever differences have existed on the use of these terms, most evangelicals affirm the general truth they were originally meant to preserve, that Scripture faithfully and authoritatively communicates God's message to humanity.

WHO INTERPRETS THE BIBLE?

One other important element shapes evangelical attitudes toward biblical scholarship, the question of "ownership" with regard to interpretation. All religious communities exhibit distinct patterns in interpreting sacred texts, but at least four elements are almost always present: (1) religious authority exercised by leaders; (2) technical wisdom from experts specially trained to study the holy writings; (3) popular acceptance or approval of interpretations; and (4) the interweaving of these various strands into a group's distinctive tradition of interpretation.

Crude as this schema is, it helps to differentiate among major patterns of twentieth-century biblical interpretation in the United States. If Catholic interpretation gives a preeminent place to religious authority, and if mainline or liberal Protestantism does the same for technical expertise, evangelical interpretation assigns first place to popular approval. Another way of putting these differences is to say that the magisterium for Catholics has been, at least officially, the church's teaching officers who, it is true, regularly solicit the counsel of scholars and acknowledge the sentiments of the people. Mainline Protestantism, on the other hand, has given magisterial authority to "scientific" study proceeding from university-level research, while attempting to adapt such learning to the needs of the pew and while recognizing the importance of popular leaders as mediators of the technical expertise. Evangelicals, by contrast, regularly speak of "the church" in its entirety as the magisterium. The most popular and influential leaders among evangelicals are those who have mastered the ability to sway mass audiences.[14] And while the evangelical community respects its scholars, it also expects them to communicate the results of research in a style that is both understandable and supports treasured beliefs.

The root of this evangelical bent toward democratic interpretation is the Reformation teaching on the priesthood of all believers. Although the Reformers were not themselves democratic, their doctrine of the spiritual priesthood as well as their promotion of vernacular Bibles pointed in a populist direction.[15] As a distinct evangelical tradition emerged in English-speaking areas during the centuries that followed the Reformation, practice reinforced principle. Puritans gravitated toward a congregational ecclesiology which made local groups of Christians responsible for their own church order. The eighteenth-century evangelical revivals advanced these developments. Although John Wesley was a conservative Tory politically, his Methodism encouraged a sense of great personal responsibility among the common members of classes and chapels. In America, one of the most distinctive things about the colonial Great Awakening was the way in which its leaders, like George Whitefield, spoke to the people on their own level. And in America the ideology of the Revolution, which colored virtually every aspect of society, pointed unequivocally in a democratic direction.

Modern conservative evangelicals are the lineal descendents of these earlier movements. They are also heirs of the nineteenth-century revival tradition, which in turn embodied the principles of the Reformation as these had been filtered through eighteenth-century revivals and the American Revolution.[16] In addition, evangelicals, as antimodernists, resisted at least some of the late nineteenth-century pressure to cede presumptive authority to the new class of university experts. The result is an expression of the Christian faith with a built-in preference for the popular. Such a faith, quite naturally, has immediate implications for the interpretation of the Bible.

Right from the beginning of debate over the new criticism, evangelicals protested the assumption that a select group of scholars had the right to dictate interpretations of Scripture. Sometimes this protest was made aphoristically, as when the British Congregationalist Joseph Parker asked, "Have we to await a communication from Tübingen, or a telegram from Oxford, before we can read the Bible?"[17] But it could also come as a considered judgment, as from Parker's fellow Congregationalist, John Kennedy, in an 1897 tract entitled *Old Testament Criticism and the Rights of the Unlearned.* While in science we must often trust experts, Kennedy wrote, "it cannot be too strongly insisted upon, that . . . the materials for forming a judgment on the most prominent religious problems of the day are within the reach of ordinary intelligence."[18]

An evangelical suspicion of the magisterial expert continues to the present. With evangelical scholars this suspicion does not degenerate into anti-intellectualism, but is rather part of the defense of traditional orthodoxies. Of many examples which could be cited, David Wells's recent polemic, in a discussion of modern christological deviations, forcefully restates the objection.

These views . . . are . . . indicative of broad tendencies in New Testament scholarship and raise difficulties for the church. Why is it that only now, two thousand years after the event, we are at last beginning to understand what Christianity is all about? But of course, by the word *we* what is in view is only an elite coterie of scholars. There are masses of Christians, all over the world, who have no ability to pick their way through the layers of literary tradition in Scripture and are quite incapable of digressing on the differences between *Historie* and *Geschichte.* Are we to suppose that the real interpretation of Jesus is alone accessible to a tiny minority in the church —its learned scholars—and that the remainder of Christian believers is excluded from such knowledge? To suppose such a thing is to subject the meaning of Scripture to a far more restrictive "tradition" than anything proposed by Rome in the sixteenth century and to invest our new magisterium—the coterie of learned scholars—with an authority more stifling and far-reaching than the Roman Catholic magisterium ever exercised. If God gave the Scriptures to the church for its nourishment, which he did, it will follow as an inevitable consequence that he did not intend those Scriptures to be co-opted by a magisterium either ecclesiastical or scholarly. On the contrary, his stated intention is that the believer might exercise his or her priestly obligation in reading and learning of him through his Word. The Scriptures must, therefore, be returned to the church.[19]

Scripture, for evangelicals, belongs preeminently to the communion of saints. While some may have special gifts in understanding the Bible, these gifts do not warrant a self-authenticating magisterium of exegetical science.[20]

Clearly, this propensity toward democracy is one of the factors nurturing the strong traditionalism of evangelicals. Evangelical faith does change (as it did, for example, in the shift from Jonathan Edwards's Calvinism to Charles Finney's Arminianism) and evangelicals do accept the authority of technical expertise in selected areas (as witnessed by the influence in the nineteenth century of evangelical pioneers in mass-market printing and in the twentieth by exploiters of broadcast media). But in matters of doctrine, especially the doctrine of Scripture, the authority of the people has been a conservative force.

The implications of this situation can be suggested by an example. It has always been the position of academic evangelicals that the meaning of Scripture is closely tied to the intent of the human author of any particular passage, and that established methods of philological, historical, and literary research must be employed to determine that intent.[21] Because of the popular traditionalism of evangelicalism as a whole, however, it has been harder for evangelical scholars to win acceptance for untraditional interpretations of Scripture than for scholars in other communions. Evangelicals who, for example, become convinced that Jonah was intended as a parable, or that the evangelists intended to include inspired reflections from the early church as part of the sayings of Jesus, find greater resistance to these views than their counterparts among mainline Protestants or, in more recent years, Roman Catholics. Part of that resistance stems from a suspicion that such views arise only when scholars give in to secularism. But part arises more simply from the fact that the evangelical community as a whole holds traditional views on these matters. To most evangelical scholars those traditional views deserve, as a matter of principle, considerable weight and serious consideration precisely because they are held by the community of faith as a whole.

The evangelical stance toward biblical study is traditional, therefore, not just for reasons having to do with textual or dogmatic matters narrowly conceived. A subtle blend of sixteenth-century Protestant ecclesiology and more recent American democracy also contributes to this perspective. Biblical study for evangelicals does not occur in an academic vacuum, nor can it be understood as a simple reflection of social and cultural deep structures. Rather, the effort to understand Scripture requires a process that includes, along with those who have special expertise, the whole people of God.[22]

SCHOLARSHIP AND A TRUTH-TELLING BIBLE

If we grant that evangelicals share similar convictions about the nature of the Bible, the nature of truth, and the ownership of interpretation, we might expect that a common standpoint would also exist on questions of scholarship. This, however, is not the case. Distinctive evangelical beliefs about the Bible, truth, and interpretation constitute more an intellectual subdivision than a single mansion of learning. Within that subdivision styles of housing differ very much among themselves, so much so in fact that some dwellings seem to resemble houses from other subdivisions more than those within their own. We turn now to a description of the different floorplans in the subdivision and to preliminary speculations on how they came to exist side by side.

One of the things that distinguishes evangelicals from fundamentalists is the evangelical insistence upon the value of scholarship from the wider world. As soon as evangelicals began to write about modern criticism, so soon did they protest their commitment to scholarship and their distaste for anti-intellectualism. To be sure, mystical approaches to Scripture continued to enjoy popularity among evangelicals at large. And the opinion that the Bible was a divine book given directly by God and hence that it was sacrilegious to probe it with critical questions also continued to flourish in the evangelical and fundamentalist populace. Thus it has always been common to read sentiments like that recorded in *The Pentecostal Herald* of March 1950:

To some men, it seems the Bible has become like buying a furnished building, sight unseen, tearing it down, separating and classifying its contents into their respective parts. To me the Word of God is more like a full honeycomb, overflowing with its own sweetness. I open each tiny cell separately, leisurely sampling, tasting and enjoying its delicious nectar to the fullest extent. . . . Tearing the Word of God into its component parts was never any pleasure to me, but rather a chore to be finished as soon as possible, so that I might go back to my feasting.[23]

And it is easy to come by literature, such as a recent pamphlet defending the King James Version, where criticism of all sort is ruled out:

The Bible is a supernatural Book. It is God's voice speaking, not only in the sense that the Word springs from Him, but from the standpoint also that it is expressed by Him in His own vocabulary. . . . The textual critics of our day, highly trained, called higher critics, are also saying, "Hath God said?" The higher, more lofty textual scholars have so falsely put together the knowledge they have gained that our generation now doubts if there is a Bible it can completely trust and say with assurance, "God hath said."[24]

But evangelical scholars, proclaiming the harmony, or at least the compatibility, of knowledge and faith, have never sanctioned such approaches. Rather, they have attempted to use the tools of learning in order to enhance the understanding of Scripture.

In the modern situation, however, many problems arise in the clash between evangelical beliefs about the Bible and the accepted results of critical scholarship. The Bible, evangelicals believe, is true, but nonevangelical scholars suggest that the Scriptures are sometimes inaccurate or naively primitive about historical and scientific matters; they contend that biblical writers occasionally approve actions which other parts of the Bible condemn as immoral; and they argue that countless passages, whether true or false, simply cannot bear the traditional interpretations that they had received.

This situation leads to a variety of evangelical responses. Committed in principle to both the truthfulness of Scripture and the value of scholarship, evangelicals must decide how the two are to coexist. That decision divides evangelicals into at least two major camps, with variations in each. Again, this division is artificial because living beings do not fall readily into orderly boxes. It is also artificial because theory and practice do not always converge. An evangelical scholar may make one theoretical profession and work according to some other standard. And the distinctions which follow also mask the fact that evangelicals of all varieties often work alike, especially where technical research can be used to extend, elucidate, deepen, expand, or refine accepted traditional interpretations of Scripture. Even with those caveats, distinctions among evangelicals are reasonably clear.[25]

The major division lies between those who tie the belief in biblical inspiration tightly to traditional interpretations and those for whom this bond is somewhat less secure. For the first, more traditionalist scholars, research is primarily useful as a way of protecting Scripture. It is necessary to carry on academic work because erroneous critical opinions must be rebutted and correct views of Scripture reinforced. This stance may be called "critical anti-criticism." It only superficially resembles what could be called "popular anti-criticism," or the anti-intellectual rejection of scholarship as inherently corrupting. Critical anti-critics make a commitment to scholarship, they sometimes achieve widespread recognition for linguistic or historical competence, and they are concerned about professional certification.

Critical anti-criticism as practiced by evangelicals depends upon the belief that the infallibility, or inerrancy, of the Bible is the epistemological keystone of Christianity itself. Should one aspect of Scripture come under suspicion, the whole Bible, along with its message of salvation, would be irreparably compromised. This belief in Scripture as the infallible Word of God, moreover, is considered the basis for traditional evangelical convictions about authorship, dating, literary transmission, and other critical questions. It is, in principle, conceivable that the results of sound research might overturn these convictions, but such research would have to be massively persuasive, and such a reversal would grievously damage the credibility of the Bible as a whole. Nigel Cameron has recently outlined the structure of this argument in an impressive essay on the interaction during the late nineteenth century between the practice of criticism and the belief in inspiration. The argument, as Cameron presents it, is somewhat complicated:

The Bible says "y," "y" being for some reason unlikely. Since it is always more likely that we should misinterpret Scripture than that Scripture should be wrong—on account of the fact that all our knowledge of God comes from Scripture alone, so a challenge to the veracity of any part of Scripture is a challenge to the authority of the whole, setting in jeopardy every other element of the revelation—presumably "y" is true nevertheless, unless the evidence should so overwhelm us as to cause us to abandon our faith in revelation.[26]

This conception of the relationship between research and biblical infallibility provides considerable motivation for scholarship. Research can both disperse apparent problems with the doctrine of inspiration and demonstrate that supposed errors in Scripture lack certain support from scholarly evidence. At the same time, this view clearly awards pride of place to the doctrine of infallibility. If research is not the servant of infallibility, it will become its destroyer.

Critical anti-critics divide among themselves not so much in principle as in practice. Some find their convictions a goad to active participation in the broader world of biblical scholarship. The inappropriate or prejudicial use of scholarship needs to be refuted, and so it is necessary to engage wholeheartedly in professional biblical work where so many false conclusions have been drawn on the basis of insubstantial or tainted evidence. Other critical anti-critics find the conventions of professional biblical scholarship too hostile. They turn instead to friendlier audiences. If prodigious labors and argumentation of recondite complexity are required to overturn even the smallest errors of the academic community, then it is better to point one's efforts toward evangelicals. The latter turn, therefore, to the journals of their own seminaries or denominations and to publishers who provide books for these constituencies. If the work which appears in such outlets does not sweep the academic world by storm, at least it provides evangelicals with secure and edifying conclusions.

Nonevangelicals, as well as evangelicals, sometimes underestimate the quantity of sturdy scholarship which appears as critical anti-criticism. It is often learned, careful, and forcefully logical within the boundaries set by conservative views of the Bible. Few, even evangelicals, would deny, however, that such work can also be parochial, selective, and question-begging. The best of this scholarship, as indeed much scholarship from before the rise of criticism, deserves a recognition it rarely receives.

The second major division of evangelical scholarship may be called "believing criticism." Individuals holding this position affirm that historical, textual, literary, and other forms of research (if they are not predicated on the denial of the supernatural) may legitimately produce conclusions that overturn traditional evangelical beliefs about the Bible. Moreover, such reversals need not necessarily undermine beliefs in the inspired or inerrant character of Scripture's revelatory truthfulness. It should be noted that evangelicals who practice this kind of "believing criticism" often also engage in critical anti-criticism. Like critical anti-critics they regularly put scholarship to use in defending traditional evangelical beliefs and in attacking the nontraditional conclusions of other scholars. But unlike the critical anti-critics, believing critics find insight as well as error in the larger world of biblical scholarship. They have benefited in numerous ways—not merely in textual or ancillary studies—from the scholarship of those who are not evangelicals. As a result they conclude that evangelical interpretations are, in principle, reformable. For these scholars the possibility exists that biblical inspiration is compatible with reinterpretation of venerable positions. And so scholarship, wherever it comes from, deserves serious considerations on its own merits.

The different orientations of critical anti-critics and believing critics leads to considerable contrast in the use of scholarly literature. A recent survey of members in the Evangelical Theological Society (ETS) and the Institute for Biblical Research (IBR) made this clear. While the distinction is not hard and fast, the ETS, a a society defined by its theological basis ("The Bible alone, and the Bible in its entirety, is the Word of God written, and is therefore inerrant in the autographs"), generally practices critical anti-criticism. The IBR, an organization established for Bible scholars in the professional world, leans in the direction of believing criticism. When respondents were asked to list the "academic books which have had the greatest impact on your scholarship . . . [even if you] do not . . . agree with these books," the results from the ETS were weighted heavily in the direction of evangelical theologians, several of whom have championed conservative views of inspiration (the individuals cited most frequently were, in order: Calvin, George Ladd, Carl Henry, Cornelius Van Til, C. S. Lewis, and Francis Schaeffer). Members of the IBR, by contrast, tended to list practicing Bible scholars (again, the most frequently cited, in order: Gerhard von Rad, George Ladd, Oscar Cullmann, Joachim Jeremias, John Bright, and Rudolf Bultmann).[27]

"Believing critics," as might be expected, take a more active part in the wider profession than critical anti-critics. In fact, most of the evangelicals who publish in the *Journal of Biblical Literature, New Testament Studies,* or similar periodicals do so from this stance. Again, to cite from the recent poll of the evangelical Bible scholars, 66 out of 102 members of the IBR had published in professional journals (or 64.7 percent), compared to 32 out of 191 members of the ETS (or 16.7 percent).[28]

It is important to recognize that believing criticism also appears in several varieties, ranging from expressions resembling critical anti-criticism to those resembling views of Christians who are not evangelicals. In the first instance, a believing critic may affirm that reversals of traditional views are possible, but in fact find that evidence does not require them. Several of the widely used evangelical Introductions adopt this stance, and it is a position argued cogently in many other places. This style of academic work differs from critical anti-criticism mostly by the sense that ultimate matters are not at stake in any particular question of research.

A second kind of believing criticism accepts the possibility of reversing traditional views and indeed argues that such reversals are justified by evidence from research. Evangelicals in this second group, however, go on to suggest that the reversals arise from a better understanding of biblical intent, gained through the exercise of scholarship, rather than the demonstration of errors. Criticism in these instances has become a friend, because it clarifies the obscure or corrects the mistaken. Academic proposals of this sort are often confusing to the evangelical community, especially for critical anti-critics, as the bare conclusion may not be different from the sort of reversal proposed by a non-evangelical. Believing critics of this second sort, however, regularly take pains to point out that the innovation is not intended as a detraction from high views of biblical infallibility, but rather as a better understanding of biblical intent. Other believing critics may contest the conclusions, but usually do so by questioning the use of evidence rather than the application of dogma. Our next chapter considers several recent examples of this sort.

A third type of believing critic concedes that reversals are possible, that they have indeed occurred, and that they may reveal minor mistakes in the biblical materials. Alternatively, such critics may defend critical conventions of the academic community that contradict evangelical traditions, but suggest that such matters are irrelevant to considerations of biblical inspiration. Questions in Old Testament criticism often arrive at this point. Evangelicals accept this or that critical conclusion and suggest that traditional evangelical reasons for rejecting that conclusion were inappropriate. Evangelical critics of this type regularly reflect some influence from neo-orthodox theologians or biblical scholars, and they may call certain evangelical formulations of inerrancy into question. They may even contest the whole evangelical concern for the question of error in the Bible. But on other important matters—belief in the truth-telling character of Scripture, its realistic interpretation, its substantial historicity, its ultimate authority—these critics align themselves with the evangelicals who are more conservative on critical matters. Representatives of this third variety of believing criticism were found fairly widely in Britain and the United States for about a third of a century after the onset of critical debates, they have never been entirely absent in Britain and they have appeared with more frequency on both sides of the Atlantic in the last twenty-five years.

A COMMUNITY OF FAITH AT WORK

What binds these scholars together—whether critical anti-critics or believing critics—is the assurance that evangelical beliefs about Scripture can coexist with the practice of academic research. Evangelicals go about that research for different purposes, and with different strategies, but it is nonetheless an important part of their self-identity. These different purposes, moreover, explain why from relatively common convictions about the Bible a variety of standpoints can emerge concerning scholarship.

At the end of the day, however, it is still evangelical conviction more than academic procedure that sets these scholars apart. When they, and the rest of the academic community, acknowledge this fundamental fact, progress can be made in interaction with others and in clarifying evangelical positions. This self-consciousness makes it possible to differentiate between questions, like the existence of pseudipigrapha in the New Testament, which are influenced by conceptions of inspiration, from those where point of view comes close to having no effect, like the discussion of some textual problems. But such self-consciousness also increases the likelihood that differences in world view may be treated as such and may be allowed their proper place in scholarly argumentation. For evangelicals to believe in a uniquely inspired Bible as well as for others to hold, say, radically evolutionary views about the development of religious consciousness are not conclusions from research. Yet such views have an obvious and crucial impact on arguments putting research to use. Those arguments will be made better, and the relative strength of opposing world views will come more clearly into focus, if Bible scholars understand and act upon the standpoints from which they do their work.

8. Contemporary Uncertainties

It is inevitable that interpretations will change and differ as we progress and disagree in our grasp of the literary form of the Bible. Such disagreement is not unhealthy, but rather a sign of life. . . . The danger is only when we forget that what we are studying is not *only* the words of men but the Word of God, and when we allow our human reason and conventions to be the arbiter of what may and may not be believed of that which we discover to be its intended meaning. When that happens among us, we have cause to be afraid for the future of evangelical belief. But what I want to say here is that the mere fact of disagreement does *not* mean that that stage has been reached, but is rather a natural and constructive aspect of a faithful evangelical attempt to do justice to the Word of God in the words of men.

R. T. FRANCE, "Evangelical Disagreements About the Bible," 1982

It is no surprise that given their different standpoints toward biblical scholarship, evangelicals often disagree among themselves. The Canadian theologian Clark Pinnock spoke truly when he said in 1976 that the evangelical resurgence since World War II has led to "an impressive, if unstable, alliance."[1] Yet disagreements among evangelical scholars on how to carry out scholarship are responsible for only some of the contemporary uncertainties. For one thing, these occasionally acrimonious debates among evangelical academics reflect even wider differences toward Scripture within the evangelical community at large. In addition, debates among evangelicals are not carried on in seclusion from discussions advanced by scholars who embrace other faiths, or none. The effort to regain standing in the academic world has been at least modestly successful. But as in all such struggles there are casualties.

The uncertainties which evangelicals currently face occur at a crucial juncture in their history. Leaders, both in the United States and Britain, who pioneered in the return to academic life are passing from the scene. In their wake, younger scholars are arising who regard both the requirements of the faith and the opportunities in the academy somewhat differently than the preceding generation. The very success of those who, during World War II and shortly thereafter, pushed evangelicals toward more serious academic work has created a fluid situation where boundaries are not as clear as they once had been.

The result is a series of related questions faced by those who, in their study of Scripture, would be both evangelical and academic. The first, which this chapter treats as an intramural question, is whether believing criticism, especially of the more creative sort, can and should succeed. A second is whether the superstructure of evangelical theology, taken in the most comprehensive sense of that term, is sufficient for understanding the nature of the Bible, for studying it as a historical and literary phenomenon, and for interpreting it responsibly. A third, which involves also the opinions of those outside the movement, is whether evangelical biblical work can *ever* expect a secure place in the wider academic world.

THE POTENTIAL OF BELIEVING CRITICISM

Evangelicals in the 1980s are being forced to face squarely an issue which at an earlier stage of the scholarly resurgence received only sporadic attention.[2] This question is whether a believing criticism, a scholarship that embodies more than marginal insights from the academic world as well as more than formal allegiance to evangelical views of the Bible, is in fact possible. The question bears especially hard on believing critics who actually propose new interpretations of Scripture, as opposed to those who merely admit that possibility. It is, moreover, not just an academic matter, for much more is involved than whether certain critical conclusions that once were suspect are now acceptable. The vitality of evangelical faith is also at stake, since some of the more compelling efforts to deepen, expand, apply, and affirm Christian doctrine and practice have come in recent decades from this same body of believing critics.

The emergence of an evangelical believing criticism is certainly one of the most significant developments in the recent history of American biblical scholarship, quite apart from its importance for the internal history of evangelicals. Practice usually preceded justification in the development of this criticism. But programmatic statements, like George Ladd's *The New Testament and Criticism* and, more recently, Carl Armerding's *The Old Testament and Criticism*, have also attempted to provide a general rationale.[3] Armerding, of Regent College in Vancouver, describes three general approaches to Scripture: (1) "traditional conservative," a view which may employ various academic tools but which comes predictably and inevitably to traditional conclusions because of the belief that Scripture is "totally the Word of God"; (2) "rational critical," which discounts the reality of God or revelation and regards the Old Testament as merely a human book reflecting the religious experience of Israel; and (3) "evangelical," which "sees the Bible as the Word of God in the words of men." This last view is the one Armerding advocates as a position preserving concepts of "special revelation" and "supernatural intervention," but at the same time accepting "the flow of history, the cause-and-effect relationships of human progress, and the literary forms in which these are expressed." Armerding admits that the attempt to do scholarship with both commitments leads to 'tension," especially given the nature of Old Testament criticism over the last 150 years. But he is willing to take the risk in order to be faithful to both divine revelation and its historical outworking.[4] His appeal for such a criticism, like similar efforts from others, is brief and introductory. While these have been helpful as pointers, the perspective of believing criticism receives fullest expression in the scholarship itself.

In recent years an increasing number of works that practice this kind of criticism have appeared in America. A genre of critical scholarship that has been well established in Britain since the 1940s, if not the 1880s, seems to be gaining a foothold among American evangelicals also. Believing critics whose works promote innovative views and then become the center of controversy, receive the greatest public attention. But they are not the most significant or the most representative. Nor is believing criticism always "progressive" in the sense of upsetting evangelical traditions. Rather, the one constant is the creative conjuncture of confidence in Scripture as the Word of God and dedication to the solid results of research wherever they are found. Most of the scholars mentioned in Chapters 5 and 6 practice this kind of work, and it is widely represented in the more academic evangelical commentaries. An indication of its extent is the fact that it even influences publications on the Old Testament, where evangelicals have found critical dilemmas much more unsettling than for the New.[5]

This believing criticism heralds a new maturity among evangelicals. It reveals first a willingness to consider God as the one who makes the practice of research possible, even if the results of that research jeopardize secondary preconceptions about the Bible. Evangelicals have long professed to believe in Common Grace, the principle that God communicates some truth to all humankind, Christian or not, through study of the natural world and of history. In the past, however, evangelical scholars have not entirely broken free from a docetic approach to Scripture, which treats the Bible as a magical book largely unrelated to the normal workings of the natural world, or from a gnosticism which acts as if the key to interpreting Scripture belonged exclusively to one's own sect. Such debilities have made it difficult for evangelicals to see how the professional study of the Bible could contribute to a better comprehension of its content. Believing critics, who address themselves to questions of literary form in the ancient world, examine historical and anthropological proposals concerning the setting of Scripture, and bring to bear modern theories of science, psychology, and sociology in their research, point to a different way by translating formal belief in Common Grace into productive study of the Scriptures.

Believing criticism also suggests that evangelicals may yet exercise a creative role in scholarship that, in America, has been mostly absent since the dawn of the critical age. Perceptive evangelical leaders have clearly seen the need for this kind of creativity in the general approach to the life of the mind. According to Fuller Seminary's Geoffrey Bromiley,

The real problem does not lie . . . in the relation of Evangelicalism as such to theological work but rather in a defensive mentality, a fixation on Liberal extravaganzas of speculation, which inhibits the freedom of action in the field. . . . The moment has arrived for a shift of the main enterprise to positive and constructive work . . . which will consider but not let itself be dominated by what others are doing."[6]

John R. W. Stott has echoed that appeal:

We need to encourage Christian scholars to go to the frontiers and engage in the debate, while at the same time retaining their active participation in the community of faith. . . . As part of their own integrity Christian scholars need both to preserve the tensions between openness and commitment, and to accept some measure of accountability to one another and responsibility for one another in the Body of Christ. In such a caring fellowship I think we might witness fewer casualties on the one hand and more theological creativity on the other.[7]

PERILS

An appreciation for Common Grace and a willingness to venture creatively in scholarship augur well, but only if difficulties in implementing a believing criticism do not overcome its potential. These difficulties are formidible and of several types. A first has to do with confusion in levels of discussion. This is a problem especially when academic arguments become the center of widespread public debate. It is a problem that may emerge in two ways. From an intellectual standpoint, there can be a failure to discriminate among types of academic discourse. Interested parties may pass too rapidly over the question of what a revisionist proposal entails —is it an argument redefining the nature of scriptural revelation, or is it an argument seeking to enhance the understanding of Scripture within an evangelical framework? This difficulty also emerges when evangelicals, whether academics or not, refuse to countenance the possibility that revision of any sort can take place in traditional interpretations of Scripture. Those who feel this way are bound to misperceive arguments that seek to incorporate new interpretations into the traditional framework.

A second difficulty for believing criticism is the immense diversity, both theologically and academically, among evangelicals. The groups and individuals making up the postwar evangelical movement unite on little except profession of a high view of Scripture and the need for divine assistance in salvation. Denominational traditions, cultural conventions, and fixtures of interpretation are all centrifugal forces. This situation is not eased by contemporary disagreements on what an infallible Bible means for daily living. Robert Johnston has phrased the situation dramatically:

that evangelicals, all claiming a common Biblical norm, are reaching contradictory theological formulations on many of the major issues they are addressing suggests the problematic nature of their present understanding of theological interpretation. To argue that the Bible is authoritative, but to be unable to come to anything like agreement on what it says (even with those who share an evangelical commitment), is self-defeating.[8]

Believing criticism, in other words, may require a breadth of tradition (to both value and restrain creative scholars), a stability of perspective (to provide revisionist proposals fair, but tough-minded, assessment), and a strength of community (to adjust corporately to change), which American evangelicalism does not possess.

The recent controversy over Robert Gundry's *Matthew: A Commentary on His Literary and Theological Art* (1981) illustrates the extent of these two problems. Gundry, a professor at Westmont College in California, had earlier published proficient technical studies, such as a treatment of Matthew's use of the Old Testament.[9] His 1981 work dealt directly with the implications of synoptic relationships, more specifically the reasons behind differences between accounts in Matthew and parallels in Mark, which Gundry accepted as the earlier gospel. According to Gundry, Matthew wrote his gospel to meet problems faced by the community of Jewish Christians as it entered the Greco-Roman world. In particular, Gundry felt that Matthew wanted to portray Jesus as a leader whose words and deeds identified him immediately as the divine Messiah. Therefore Matthew's deviation from Mark and from the hypothetical "Q," variations which Gundry analyzed exhaustively, could be explained by Matthew's theological intent.

The controversial aspect of the argument came when Gundry concluded that Matthew, in order to convey this theological message, ascribed nonhistorical actions to Jesus. As he put it,

Clearly, Matthew treats us to history mixed with elements that cannot be called historical in a modern sense. All history writing entails more or less editing of materials. But Matthew's editing often goes beyond the bounds we nowadays want a historian to respect. It does not stop at selecting certain data and dressing them up with considerable interpretation (let alone reporting in the relatively bare style found on the front page of a modern newspaper). Matthew's subtractions, additions, and revisions of order and phraseology often show changes in substance; i.e., they represent developments of the dominical tradition that result in different meanings and departures from the actuality of events.[10]

To show what this meant in one specific situation, Gundry concluded that the infancy narrative in Matthew was a recension of stories in Luke: Matthew transformed the visit of the shepherds into the visit of the Magi, the trip to Jerusalem into the flight to Egypt.

A further stage in Gundry's argument was the assertion that these nonhistorical elements would have been immediately understood as such by Matthew's readers, since the evangelist was writing his gospel according to the literary conventions of Jewish *midrash* and *haggadah*, literary genres in which embellishment of historical events was taken for granted. With this move Gundry felt he could both take advantage of modern redaction criticism on the gospels and sustain the evangelical tradition of biblical inerrancy. Redaction criticism gave him the tools to analyze Matthew's work. Inerrancy gave him a framework for asserting that the gospel was entirely true to the intent of its author and the understanding of its first-century readers. Gundry, in fact, closed his book with a lengthy "Theological Postscript" in order to point out how his advanced use of redaction criticism fit within the framework of biblical inerrancy.[11]

Many evangelical scholars treated Gundry's *Matthew* on its own terms as a serious effort to use modern critical tools for evangelical ends. Such ones responded, therefore, with an examination of Gundry's claim that Matthew intended to write in the style of *midrash* and *haggadah*. D. A. Carson put the issue this way:

It must first of all be pointed out that evangelicals will entirely miss the mark if they simply cry "Inerrancy!" and accuse Gundry of abandoning the camp. One may reasonably argue that Gundry is cutting a new swath, or that traditional formulations of the doctrine of Scripture should now be tightened up; but as such formulations stand, Gundry in no way contravenes them. Intelligent response to Gundry will have to wrestle with questions of literary genre, source criticism, redaction criticism, the significance of word statistics and the like. The doctrine of Scripture is relevant only insofar as the perspicuity of Scripture is at stake; and here, it must be remembered that Gundry has attempted to forestall criticism by addressing that matter himself.[12]

Carson himself attacked the assertion that Matthew was writing *midrash*, as did also several evangelicals writing for a project sponsored by the Tyndale Fellowship on the historical character of the gospels.[13] They vigorously argued the point that Gundry did not sufficiently demonstrate that Matthew in fact intended to write *midrash*. Therefore they concluded that while it is theoretically possible to conceive of a gospel where apparently historical events were meant to be taken as nonhistorical, the evidence that Matthew was doing this is not persuasive.

Other evangelicals concluded that Gundry's assertions concerning nonhistorical events in Matthew necessarily meant that he had abandoned evangelical confidence in an infallible Scripture, regardless of what Gundry himself thought. Concern on this score was especially prominent in the Evangelical Theological Society (ETS), whose members have always been deeply committed to the doctrine of biblical inerrancy.[14] Leading members of the ETS feared that Gundry's proposals would undermine confidence in the factuality of biblical history more generally. Thus, although the ETS defined itself simply by belief in biblical inerrancy, which Gundry affirmed in detail, concern remained. At its 1983 annual meeting in Dallas, the ETS first went on record (by a 119 to 36 vote) as "rejecting any position that states that Matthew or any other biblical writer materially altered and embellished historical tradition or departed from the actuality of events." It then voted (116 to 41) to request Gundry's resignation.[15]

Gundry, a believing critic, had attempted to join the affirmation of his faith to his practice of modern biblical scholarship. Some of his fellow evangelicals responded to his work on that level, while others read it as a statement concerning the doctrine of Scripture itself. The latter perception arose from a mingling of theological and interpretative categories as well as from the deeply imbedded traditionalism of evangelical opinions on critical questions. The episode as a whole showed both what strides evangelicals had made—to produce such a book and such sophisticated criticism of it—and yet how much further believing criticism had to go to secure its place as a legitimate exercise in its own right.

In spite of the turmoil over Gundry's book, the issues it posed were not as complex as those arising from the work of other scholars. Two additional difficulties which attend believing criticism are important here. One of these concerns the arguments used to advance revisionist views. As the whole history of the discipline attests, the biblical scholar, whether evangelical or not, requires skill in two areas—both the mastery of research and the ordering of research within larger intellectual contexts. Professional biblical scholars, however, receive the bulk of their training rather narrowly in areas emphasizing research. As a result they are rarely equipped to deal as skillfully with the contexts of research as with the particular research problems themselves. However much evangelical scholars are supposed to reflect commitment to dogma, it is rare when they show more skill than their nonevangelical colleagues in making plain the ramifications of narrow academic questions for larger matters of religious belief. Yet failure on this score is especially damaging for evangelical scholars, because their community combines high expectations in regard to the Bible's divine character with relatively little appreciation for the study of the Bible's human phenomena. Evangelicals scholars, as a consequence, need to take more pains, not less, in showing the relation of their research to larger issues of belief. Good research with plausible results may miscarry if the scholar does not spell out its implications with respect to dogma. This, to be sure, is less of a problem with work presented strictly for academic colleagues, but it is the rare evangelical who writes only for such an audience and not also for the church.

R. T. France, Principal of Wycliffe Hall Theological College, Oxford, in discussing disagreements over Scripture among British evangelicals, has well described this difficulty:

The professional scholars tend to press doggedly on with their researches without considering how their results are likely to affect the evangelical public. . . . There is need for care in presenting our material so that the non-specialist reader will not be misled. It is an exercise in communication, which is sadly not always the scholar's greatest aptitude. So unnecessary hostility is sometimes created towards new interpretations because they have not been presented with sufficient care and consideration for the natural reactions of the ordinary Christian.[16]

This kind of care and consideration, however, is essential if believing criticism is to flourish.

A last difficulty with believing criticism concerns theological content. It is always possible for such work to become a piously

veneered replica of naturalistic scholarship. The fears of the traditionalist evangelical community, in other words, are not entirely
groundless. Tools of biblical research are not themselves value-
free, and neither are the uses to which they are put. To take but
one example, some evangelicals have been relatively successful in
showing how redaction criticism can be used in concert with high
views of biblical inipration. Robert Gundry, for his part, made a
strong argument for this possibility, whatever one may conclude
about his actual success in practice. Other critics, however, do not
subject the conventions of redaction to scrutiny. They write as if
it were a foregone conclusion that incidents in the gospels sprang
exclusively from the theological imaginations of the evangelists.[17]
A world of difference separates two such approaches. The desire
to renew the evangelical study of Scripture by paying closer heed
to the conclusions of the academic world is worthy, especially in
light of the disregard for scholarship which has frequently characterized the American evangelical heritage. But to exploit that
scholarship without discrimination, however positive this may be
for professional participation, can also jeopardize the future of
believing criticism.

The complexities of these last two problems were evident in the
recent controversy over the work of J. Ramsey Michaels. In 1981
Michaels, who had taught at Gordon-Conwell Seminary for
twenty-five years, published *Servant and Son: Jesus in Parable and
Gospel.* This book analyzed Jesus' self-understanding through a
careful redactional reading of the gospels. As an effort to read the
synoptic gospels in conjunction with John and to bring a fresh
perspective to the life of Jesus, the book was entirely stimulating.
But it also raised perplexing questions concerning how the kind of
scholarship that the book presented fit into the framework of evangelical conviction. And it eventually led in 1983, after an intensive
internal debate, to Michael's resignation under fire from Gordon-
Conwell.

Part of the difficulty lay in Michael's way of exploiting nuances
in the gospel narratives to cast Jesus' self-consciousness into
sharper relief. I. Howard Marshall, for one, felt that this effort was
successful, since it left "scarcely an area where the author does not
have something to say. . . . He has . . . brought the figure of Jesus

to life in a new way."[18] But such single-minded attention to exegetical labor sometimes left larger issues dangling. Amid the flow
of interpretation, much of which could be appreciated without
hesitation, Michaels made some preliminary conclusions that cried
out for elaboration. Thus, when the gospel of John reports that the
Baptizer saw the extraordinary occurrences at Jesus' baptism, this
was probably not historical. When the Syro-Phoenician woman
asked Jesus to heal her daughter (Mark 7:24–30), Jesus had to be
shocked out of a conventional Jewish ethnocentrism which culpa-
bly regarded the Gentiles as "dogs." And when Jesus taught his
disciples the Lord's Prayer, "it is not so strange that he should also
pray for forgiveness. This is possible because he identified himself
fully and radically with his people in their sinfulness."[19]

The problem with such *obiter dicta* lay at two levels. More simply,
Michaels did not comment on the fact that these exegetical conclusions do not fit, or at least do not seem to fit, within an ordinary
evangelical framework. Biblical history, in the absence of overrid-
ing considerations, is historical. Jesus, though complete in his
humanity, lived without sin. Michaels seemed not to realize that his
fresh exegetical conclusions required positioning theologically
and hermeneutically. He did not offer, as Gundry had, a theoretical explanation for his conclusions. Arguments certainly are conceivable to show how redactional procedures could comport with
evangelical views, but Michaels did not advance them. The result
was uncertainty concerning what Michaels intended by his conclusions.

The second part of the problem was the stance of the institution.
Gordon-Conwell's basis of faith makes typically evangelical affirmations—that the Bible is "free from error" and that Jesus, who
united "divine and human nature" in one person, "lived a sinless
life." Its catalogue also indicates that the school is committed to
"openness toward truth and biblical insight wherever these are
found among current theologians and schools, balanced by an
impartial awareness of error where that is found" and to an encouragement of "high academic standards in relation to both ad-
missions and teaching, with a view to establishing a theological
center of acknowledged excellence."[20] The institution, however,
provided few clues concerning the implications of these affirma-

tions for biblical scholarship until Michaels's book was published. Michaels had taught similar things to his classes for many years, but so long as these were not made public, the seminary did not display urgency in defining coordinates of modern criticism. This, in turn, testified to the relative lack of concern for integrating professional scholarship, theological sophistication, and hermeneutical sensitivity, from which evangelicals as a whole have suffered.

By comparison with Gundry's *Matthew*, Michaels's *Servant and Son* probably evinced a more convincing exegesis. But by failing to discuss the implications of his work, as Gundry forthrightly attempted to do, Michaels left important questions unanswered. Again, to quote from Marshall's favorable review, "What is lacking from the book is any attempt to draw all the threads together and suggest what kind of picture of Jesus emerges from the whole discussion."[21] In the absence of such a synthesis, uncertainty as to what this book meant for an evangelical biblical scholarship was inevitable.

Practitioners of believing criticism, in sum, face two tasks. First is a question of scholarship: Are believing critics able to make convincing arguments to support their interpretations of the text? The second is a question of theory formation: Can believing critics demonstrate that their exegetical conclusions are compatible with larger evangelical convictions?[22] Both concerns, and their connection, are worthy of harder work from evangelical biblical scholars and more comprehensive understanding from the evangelical community at large.

Believing criticism encounters difficulties within the evangelical community because of the structure of that community and because of well-publicized conflict over specific issues. But these problems are not *sui generis*. They point, rather, to questions about the more general theological framework within which the scholarship proceeds. This is, quite naturally, something which concerns those who are not evangelicals, as we shall observe presently. It also, however, is a matter of no small discussion among evangelicals themselves. To those discussions, at once less focused yet more significant than controversies over individual books, we now turn.

THE THEOLOGICAL FRAMEWORK

To state this issue most broadly, a significant number of individuals within the movement have themselves asked whether evangelicals possess a strong enough intellectual base—involving not just individual doctrines, but theology in its most general sense—to support genuine biblical scholarship. Again, this issue arises in several forms, a number of which concern the traditional evangelical affirmations about scriptural inerrancy.

The frankest, most direct challenge at this point comes from those who want to substitute a better "high" view of Scripture for the one that has dominated conservative evangelicalism since its initial contacts with criticism. One of the reasons for making this substitution, though not necessarily the most important one, is to provide a better foundation for biblical scholarship. Two authors have recently made aggressive cases for this position, one as a practicing biblical scholar, the other as a philosophical theologian. James D. G. Dunn, a prolific British scholar who belongs to the Tyndale Fellowship and who has long associated with evangelicals, published in 1982 a lengthy essay on "The Authority of Scripture According to Scripture." This paper examined biblical testimony concerning Scripture itself and reflected on the nature of honest research. Dunn's conclusion was that the commonly accepted evangelical concept of biblical inerrancy was deficient. The traditional view, which Dunn ascribed to Warfield, is "exegetically improbable" because it overextends the implications of such crucial passages as 2 Timothy 3:16 and 2 Peter 1:20–21. It is also "hermeneutically defective" because its adherents fail to heed the meanings which biblical writers intended, "theologically dangerous" because it transforms a secondary concern about detailed factuality into a foundational precept of the faith, and "educationally disastrous" because it slides over the difficulties caused by a frank study of biblical phenomena.[23]

In stating his positive view of the matter, Dunn suggested that evangelicals follow the footsteps of biblical figures. He argued that Jesus used the Old Testament as if its passages were limited in their application by historical circumstances, with the result that the Scriptures' "authority as Word of God was relative to the particular situation to which they were addressed, for which they were intended to be the Word of God." The New Testament writers, furthermore, "were not concerned with the iota and dot level of a text in the way that Princeton theology so readily assumes." These pointers led Dunn to argue that the divinely inspired Scripture is relative to its historical circumstances. An "evangelical hermeneutic" will struggle to draw together the historically relative sense intended by the original authors with its similarly conditioned application in the present. This will, finally, lead to a realization that there is "a certain elusiveness in the Word of God in relation to any text" and hence to a greater dependence upon the Holy Spirit to communicate through Scripture the Word of God.[24]

Other evangelicals were not slow in responding, particularly to Dunn's willingness to accept an "elusiveness" in the Scriptures.[25] In addition, Dunn's emphasis on the relative character of biblical utterances is difficult to square with the evangelical belief—indeed, with the church's general insistence before the Enlightenment—that the Bible offers a normative, enduring Word from God. Dunn also may be faulted for judging evangelicals by their incautious contradictions, rather than by their most careful statements. Thus, on the supposed neglect by inerrantists of authorial intent, Dunn does have cause for complaint against the International Council on Biblical Inerrancy's 1982 position paper on hermeneutics. This document affirmed "that awareness of the literary categories, formal and stylistic, of the various parts of Scripture is essential for proper exegesis" (thus seeming to agree with Dunn), but also "that the biblical record of events, discourses and sayings, though presented in a variety of appropriate literary forms, corresponds to historical fact" (thus seeming the prejudge the question of authorial intent).[26] But Dunn really has nothing to say to more careful evangelical theologians like Warfield, who in 1880 grounded his view of biblical inspiration by noting how fatal it is to overlook "the prime question of the intention and profession of the writer."[27] Although Warfield's exegetical conclusions were usually conservative, he fully sanctioned the widest possible use of available scholarship to discover authorial intent, even if it called into question traditional evangelical interpretations of specific passages. In short, Dunn's work rightly calls attention to problems in the evangelical handling of Scripture and proposes an alternative which is more accommodating to the practice of biblical scholarship. If his proposal also has its weaknesses, they may serve as a propaedeutic to others who wrestle with the same questions.

Similar criticism of traditional evangelicals views and a proposal for a better way have appeared from William J. Abraham, an Irish Methodist who has taught in the United States for some years. In a two-pronged presentation, Abraham argued in *The Divine Inspiration of Holy Scripture* (1981) that traditional views of inerrancy always end by, in effect, denying the human character of Scripture and by treating it as if it were dictated directly by God. Traditional views are also overly deductive. Since they begin with the idea of inerrancy, they force exegesis into a predetermined mode which depreciates the human quality of the Bible. The latter part of this work and a subsequent book entitled *Divine Revelation and the Limits of Historical Criticism* (1982) made a positive statement. Sound philosophical reasoning does not stand in the way of believing that God intervened in history at the Incarnation, that Jesus was raised from the dead, or that God reveals himself personally through a divine speaking. The Bible, in its place, is inspired in the sense that great teachers inspire their pupils. Inspiration involves the communication of propositional truth, but also many other forms of communication. The Bible, therefore, may be regarded as divinely inspired, even if the text also always reflects the human character of God's "pupils," the biblical writers. This combination of divine and human provides for confidence in Scripture as the Word of God and in biblical criticism as a helpful means of understanding the text. As an afterword to the first volume, and in yet a third book, *The Coming Great Revival: Recovering the Full Evangelical Tradition* (1984), Abraham makes a plea for John Wesley's approach to the Bible. In so doing he indicates that for evangelicals always to frame questions about the nature of the Bible and of its interpretation in Calvinistic terms artificially truncates the benefits of the evangelical heritage.

Again, upholders of the traditional view have subjected Abraham's proposals to searching criticism.[28] It is by no means clear, for instance, that Warfield, James Orr, J. I. Packer, Carl Henry, Leon Morris, or other defenders of inerrancy are as methodologically naive or as wooden in their own biblical interpretation as Abraham suggests. These and others have, in fact, carefully exegeted the biblical statements about the nature of Scripture at the same time that they explore the apparent consequences of such exegesis for studying the rest of the Bible. In addition, a good bit of imprecision remains in Abraham's efforts to show how his positive description of divine speech differentiates his view from a carefully qualified affirmation of biblical inerrancy.

The work of Dunn and Abraham probably will not carry the day among evangelicals. Nor is it clear that it should. Nonetheless, they are both helpful goads in stimulating evangelicals toward more and better work. What is the exact character of the Bible? How may such a Bible be studied responsibly in an age of considerable advance concerning the literary, historical, and religious milieus of Scripture? Evangelicals who resist the proposals of Dunn and Abraham for a different conception of biblical scholarship owe it to themselves to show, as Donald Hagner put it in a different context, "that there *is* indeed a view of inerrancy that does not in principle repudiate a priori the methodologies and results of modern biblical scholarship."[29]

Questions raised by Abraham and Dunn treat narrowly the specific evangelical conception of the inerrancy of the Bible. Evangelicals in recent years have also queried theological issues of a more general sort. The most obvious of these is whether evangelicals possess a theology comprehensive enough actually to practice biblical scholarship, even granting a Bible without mistakes. More than one evangelical has pointed out that to attack naturalistic, evolutionary, or even neo-orthodox views of the Bible in defense of inerrancy is not the same as providing encouragement or guidelines for fruitful research.

Before the critical era, several varieties of Protestant theology—Lutheran, Reformed, Wesleyan—offered coordinates on a grand scale to assess general questions of learning and specific issues related to Scripture. The same sort of grounding existed among the evangelicals who first responded to criticism. B. B. Warfield, for instance, developed to considerable length a concept of *concursus* which he felt made it possible to study one and the same phenomenon from different, but coherent perspectives.[30] This principle encouraged Warfield to pursue seriously the authorial intent of the biblical writers. To engage in the historical study necessary for determining that intent was not superfluous or sacrilegious, but rather an intellectual and spiritual necessity. Through this means scholars could grasp the human meaning of Scripture, a meaning which, because of *concursus*, was the portal to its religious significance. *Concursus* also allowed Warfield, within his constitutional limits, a breathing space for the exercise of academic creativity. The concept, for instance, enabled him to adjust his Calvinism to a conservative form of evolution.[31] *Concursus* as Warfield developed it may have difficulties, and Warfield's inbred conservativism may have prevented him from exploring its implications thoroughly. But because it was a mature product of a more general theology—grounded in considerations of divine immanence and transcendence, linked to doctrines of both providence and grace—the concept had immediate and far-reaching implications for the exercise of an evangelical biblical scholarship.[32]

Since the fundamentalist-modernist controversies, however, evangelicals have usually lacked this kind of theological anchorage. Evangelical voices on both sides of the Atlantic have increasingly drawn attention to the striking absence of a secure theological framework for the study of Scripture. So Englishman David Wright: "One of our most urgent unfinished tasks is the elaboration of a satisfactory doctrine of Scripture for an era of biblical criticism. . . . In particular, we have to work out what it means to be faithful *at one and the same time both* to the doctrinal approach to Scripture as the Word of God *and* to the historical treatment of Scripture as the words of men."[33]

An even more striking appeal along the same lines has come from Bernard Ramm, one of the leaders with E. J. Carnell and Carl Henry in the postwar renewal of evangelical thought. Ramm's 1983 book, *After Fundamentalism,* called upon his fellow evangelicals to learn from Karl Barth how to be both genuinely Christian and genuinely honest about the "humanity" of Scripture. Ramm was especially distressed at the "obscurantism" which he felt had beset evangelical efforts to incorporate modern Western learning into the study of Scripture. Here was the primary problem, as Ramm saw it, complete with his own italics and an unflattering comparison to Barth:

*there is no genuine, valid working hypothesis for most evangelicals to interact with
the humanity of Scripture in general and biblical criticism in particular.* There are
only ad hoc or desultory attempts to resolve particular problems. Barth's
method of coming to terms with the humanity of the Scripture and biblical
criticism is at least a clearly stated program. . . . To date, evangelicals have
not announced such a clear working program. If Barth's paradigm does
not please them, they are still under obligation to propose a program that
does enable an evangelical to live creatively with evangelical theology and
biblical criticism.[34]

The historical record, both evangelical and more broadly Christian, suggests two things about Ramm's appeal. First, Christians
certainly have often done what he proposed. Whether it was
Augustine and Platonism, Thomas Aquinas and Aristotle, Luther
and nominalism, Wesley and eighteenth-century sentimentalism,
or Jonathan Edwards and Newtonianism, the history of the church
is filled with orthodox thinkers who have baptized (and transformed) apparently alien world views for the use of the church. But
history also reveals that the synthesis of any one era does not
remain intellectually or spiritually satisfying indefinitely, at least
without periodic readjustments requiring nearly as much creativity
as the original formulation. Ramm's appeal, therefore, does not
seek the impossible or the unorthodox, but it does call for the
exercise of creative theological energy on a very broad scale.

A final theoretical difficulty concerns hermeneutics, or sensitivity to interpretative contexts. Where heremeneutical naiveté prevails, evangelical criticism of whatever sort will receive less consideration than it deserves. Critics from the evangelical left and right,
who regularly upbraid their fellows for allowing cultural conventions to determine interpretations of Scripture, illustrate this
problem well. A common structure, for instance, joins the arguments of pacifist John Howard Yoder and theonomist Greg
Bahnsen.[35] They claim that evangelicals are so unself-consciously
committed to American cultural values—on the one hand recourse
to violence, on the other trust in participatory democracy—that
they cannot hear the words of Scripture which address such issues.
Whatever one thinks about the specific charges, the larger claim
implicit in these contentions is important. Evangelicalism, which
by its nature favors commitment over reflection, has not regularly
promoted sophisticated hermeneutics. While many elaborate sys-

tems are at hand for extracting meaning from the biblical text, few are available for understanding the interpretive constraints brought to the text, or more specifically the cultural presuppositions which often hide under the guise of commensensical interpretive techniques.

Once again, the problem does not lie in the potential of evangelical theology for encouraging self-conscious attention to hermeneutical matters. A tradition which includes, among others, Calvin and Johann Albrecht Bengel certainly has the resources. The more recent history of conservative evangelicals, however, has not as yet demonstrated the concern or the sophistication for such matters which are necessary for fully responsible study of the Bible. The problem calls for two tasks. The first is a crash program to study the important twentieth-century theoreticians of interpretation, from Max Weber to Paul Riceour. The second requires a careful exercise in discrimination to extract from this modern hermeneutical theory the elements that genuinely enhance the self-understanding of interpretation, while at the same time counteracting those which undermine Christian convictions.[36]

The democratic and activistic tendencies of modern evangelicalism work against the development of theoretical depth.[37] Evangelical biblical scholars nonetheless require just that sophistication if the great gains of recent years are to be more than seed cast by the side of the road. Questions about inerrancy, about the relationship between inerrancy and the human character of Scripture, about a theology rich enough to provide conceptual stability for criticism, and about hermeneutical self-consciousness are not the only issues at stake. But they define at least part of the agenda. It is not clear what the most satisfying answers to these issues will be, or where they will come from. They may arise from a neo-Reformed, a neo-Wesleyan, a neo-Lutheran, or some other creative reapplication of old formulas, or they may involve a new theoretical synthesis. The only lasting danger to evangelical biblical scholarship will be if no work is forthcoming on these issues of wide-ranging theological interest.

EVANGELICALS IN THE MARKETPLACE

The ongoing ambiguity of conservative scholarship in the larger academic world creates a third major uncertainty for evangelical Bible scholars. In light of the fundamentalist sectarianism that lies so recent in the evangelical past, no less than the secular triumphalism that has been so much a part of American universities for the last century, the question cannot be avoided: Does evangelical participation in the common world of biblical research have a future? This issue underlies the whole history of modern biblical criticism in the United States. And it is one which will receive increasing attention if the number of evangelical "believing critics" continues to increase in years to come.

The historical record, as well as conclusions from this evangelical observer of that history, suggest two closely related considerations. First is the reality of a great divide between students of the Bible. On many of the most important academic questions, it is simply inescapable that biblical scholars will divide between those who believe that Scripture is the unique Word of God, however thoroughly embodied in human history, and those for whom the Bible is fundamentally a human product, however infused with religious insight.[38] The second concerns the nature of this divide, for it is neither as absolute as partisans believe nor as insubstantial as the ecumenically minded hope. The divide, in other words, is semipermeable. It really does demarcate two different groups, but it also allows a considerable measure of free-flowing interchange.

The sturdiness of this divide should surprise no one. It will not go away with the wave of a wand, as those imply who appeal to the inductive method or to "the text itself" as a cure-all for stalemates. The divide is an ever-present reality, most especially when considering sore points of evangelical sensitivity. E. A. Speiser, for example, illustrated its presence in the introduction to his formidable commentary on Genesis: "Massive internal evidence," as he put it, had shown that Moses did not write the Pentateuch. Moreover, "the great majority of biblical scholars" concurred in this judgment which was, in turn, "the fundamental fact behind all recent progress in biblical study."[39] Implications for evangelical scholars of the Old Testament who, in spite of sometimes considerable learning still hold to a Mosaic provenance for the Pentateuch, could not be clearer.

The presence of this theological divide has inhibited productive biblical scholarship, but not fatally. Scholars on both sides have often illustrated the unfortunate consequences of allowing the divide to loom too large. Thus evangelicals who write off Julius Wellhausen's research as simply "evolutionary" or "Hegelian," as if this obviated the need to scrutinize Wellhausen's individual arguments on sources in the Pentateuch, are as short-sighted as nonevangelicals who discount arguments for the Pauline authorship of disputed letters as the mere product of "conservative motives [,] . . . traditional views on canonical authorship[,] and 'evangelical theology'."[40] To know that a scholar holds an evangelical view of biblical inspiration is useful, just as it is helpful to realize that someone thinks genuine scholarship depends upon "the historical-critical method."[41] But these bits of information reveal only where the scholar plows, not what skill is applied to the tilling nor what the harvest will be.

The early and recent history of biblical criticism in the United States, and its unfolding more generally in Britain, show that much can be achieved despite a division between evangelical and other scholars. Sometimes observers with higher goals in view speak disparagingly of the effort to work around such divides. So Robert Funk, in decrying the lack of specific attention by American biblical scholars to the nature of Scripture, has written ironic words about efforts to carry out "neutral" research: "Philological detail and certain ancillary disciplines, such as biblical archaeology, support scholarly 'objectivity,' while permitting one to evade the question of meaning. The scholar can present an evening of stereopticon slides on biblical sites without so much as touching on the question of religion."[42] But is this all bad? Assuming that they were aware of the larger questions, did it retard scholarship for William Henry Green and William Rainey Harper to aid each other in the study of Hebrew, or for contemporary scholars, of whatever persuasion, to exchange the results of research on the gnostic documents found at Nag Hammadi or on the Dead Sea Scrolls? To the contrary, it would appear as if cooperation on textual, archaeological, historical, and other ancillary matters had at least limited benefits for all concerned. In fact, it could even be that scholars who began to talk with each other on safe subjects like textual criticism or archaeology could establish a beachhead of trust and be in position to learn something additional from each other on the more divisive issues of biblical understanding.

If this rosy vision—the pursuit of a genuine liberality of scholarship—is to have a chance, evangelicals must work on at least three levels. First is the need for more self-conscious awareness of ideological, theoretical, or theological frameworks. Peter Craigie wrote shrewdly on this point by proposing that evangelicals abandon a defensive or apologetic posture in their work. To do so would allow them to perceive the realities of their discipline more clearly and to increase the chance of benefiting from the work of those on the other side of the divide. Craigie's remarks are even more apropos because they come in reference to the Old Testament, where divisions have been particularly deep:

Conservative biblical scholarship does not have primarily an apologetic role within contemporary biblical scholarship. Within the study of the Pentateuch, for example, the conservative role is not to establish this or that particular interpretation of the Pentateuch, over and against the current consensus held in the larger arena of biblical scholarship. Such a task, in my view, is essentially pointless, for it presupposes that the differences between the conservative and non-conservative views are based primarily on the interpretation of data as such. In my judgment, the difference lies elsewhere; the principal ground of difference lies in the theological or philosophical assumptions of the starting point. These assumptions, in turn, dictate which of the possible interpretations of the data is most appropriate. Thus, with respect to *apologia* and debate it should more appropriately be conducted in the areas of philosophy or theology, not with respect to the actual interpretation of the biblical data. And with respect to the practice of conservative scholarship, an awareness of the implications of different assumptions should introduce a more irenic attitude towards scholars with different assumptions, and consequently different interpretations of this or that set of biblical data.[43]

Knowing the boundaries, understanding what the divide prohibits and allows, is an essential first step.

A second task requires a catholic use of technical work to achieve more adventuresome theological syntheses within the evangelical framework. Simply to read safe scholars is merely to reproduce tired theology. Evangelicals whose works deepen insight, like Stein on the parables, Guelich on the Sermon on the Mount, Longenecker on exegesis within the New Testament, Kaiser in his Old Testament theology, are regularly those who mine a wide range of work while maintaining a firm grasp on evangelical principles. Just as it would be a poor philosopher who, even if disagreeing with Kant, did not benefit immensely from the effort to understand him, so it is the truly benighted evangelical who comes away from intensive work in, say, Bultmann, without more than a little to inspire evangelical faith. The way to more substantial evangelical work on Scripture calls for extensive, if discriminating, foraging in the scholarly world at large. Similar benefits could likewise accrue to nonevangelicals who took the effort to study evangelical scholars the same way.

A third level of work required for a better use of the current situation is the creative integration of detailed professional study, stimulating theological synthesis, and self-conscious hermeneutical sophistication. Technical research, theological conclusions, and the exercise of philosophical and cultural presuppositions simply do not proceed independently. Evangelicals who can keep all three in view put themselves in an ideal situation to contribute to both sides of the divide. Once again, James Barr is justified in castigating evangelicals who act as if the phenomena alone lead them to conservative conclusions.[44] Research in biblical facts is always part of theological and hermeneutical processes. To realize that, however, is not an excuse for sloppy research or careless thinking. It is rather a call for greater self-consciousness, more demanding discipline, more stringent argumentation—all to the end of clarifying the Scriptures as entities in themselves and as the norm for a believing community.

Evangelicals who carry on work at these levels should not expect to lay the academic world at their feet nor to advance without frustrating opposition. Some of the best evangelical books will continue to be panned by nonevangelicals who confuse ideology and scholarship.[45] At the same time the effort to write responsibly as scholars may earn the same evangelicals a measure of suspicion within their own community. Nonetheless, the way to sound evangelical research is clear. It must be technically competent, theologically informed, and hermeneutically self-conscious. Such work will never dominate the academic marketplace, at least as higher learning is presently constituted in the West. But it will receive at last some of the recognition that it deserves there, and will do so, moreover, while enhancing its contribution to the church.

The uncertainties of evangelical biblical scholarship involve a host of related academic and theological issues. Yet these matters, important as they are when considering biblical scholarship narrowly conceived, are only part of the story. The broader evangelical community, with its distinct traditions, interpretive conventions, and varied religious cultures—all having little to do with technical academic questions—also exerts a determinative influence. Evangelicals study the Bible first because they are evangelicals. To understand that fact makes it possible to see more clearly how scholarship and community intersect to define the past and to shape the future of evangelical study of Scripture.

9. Assessment and Projection

> It was Jacob Burckhardt, I believe, who said that the most important things in life do not get written about by historians simply because they are *too* close to people, too taken for granted. This may account for the absence of good histories dealing with American attitudes toward the Bible.
> MARTIN E. MARTY, *Humanizing America's Iconic Book*, 1982

Evangelical Bible scholarship over the last century has passed through several distinct phases. At the present, evangelicals are more active in the professional academic world than at any time since the very earliest days of American discussion concerning the new criticism of Scripture. No one can predict with certainty what path evangelical scholarship will take in the future. The preceding history does, however, suggest several things. First and most important, evangelical Bible scholarship is part of a larger story concerning the way evangelicals as a whole treat the Bible. It is also clear that evangelical students of the Old Testament face a different set of challenges than those who study the New. In addition, because the study of Scripture is both so intimately connected with the believing community and so much a part of the academic enterprise broadly conceived, the future of evangelical biblical scholarship involves several more comprehensive concerns. Evangelical Bible scholars face threats to their enterprise from their two communities of reference, the ecclesiastical and the academic. They also face the continuing challenge of attaining a full-orbed intellectual maturity to exploit the technical expertise so manifestly recovered within the past half-century.

SCHOLARSHIP AND COMMUNITY

A book like this one on evangelical Bible scholarship points up the need for a broader, more inclusive study of the general place of the Bible among American evangelicals. Beyond doubt, the Bible for many Americans is, as Martin Marty phrases it, an "icon" as well as an object of study.[1] With no American group is this more the case than with evangelicals. The evidence for this is so abundant on every hand that it almost escapes notice. Evangelicals are the major stimulus to the staggering number of Bibles sold each year in the United States (amounting to a $150 million annual business), some in finely wrought expensive editions, some as the cheapest of paperbacks. Evangelicals, by reputation and self-definition an antiliturgical folk, have nevertheless made a formulaic phrase, "the Bible says" (or its variants, like "my Bible says"), an all but essential part of the sermon. The iconic place of the Bible accounts for the fact that so many evangelicals profess belief in scriptural inerrancy, yet know little about the book's actual content.[2] It also helps explain why many different bodies of evangelicals continue to insist that they follow "the Bible alone" and are not influenced by historical or cultural conditioning, as they go their mutually exclusive ways in doctrine and practice. The Bible's iconic status explains its presence as a frequent gift to dignify educational promotions (both Sunday School and secular), marriages, and inductions into the military. It lies behind the occasionally bizarre reactions to efforts at introducing new translations, like the preacher who reportedly ignited a new copy of the Revised Standard Version with a blowtorch in his pulpit, while commenting that it was like the devil in being so hard to burn.[3] (Here it is worth recalling that although some evangelicals welcomed the appearance of the RSV, others denounced it in the sternest of language. Yet short years later some of the same ones who scorned the RSV became promoters of the *Living Bible,* a paraphrase which, for all its virtues in popular communication, could not compare with the RSV as a serious translation of the Scriptures.) In addition, it is the Bible as icon just as much as object of study which energizes evangelical political efforts to restore a Christian America or to promote other civic, economic, or social reforms.

All of these examples point to the fact that the academic study of Scripture is but one chapter in a larger, more complicated story. It is possible to understand certain things by studying one chapter in a long book, but that chapter can never be fully understood without perusing the whole volume. So it is with evangelical Bible scholarship. To study it in isolation from the history of the Bible in the community as a whole is merely to begin the task. As much as that larger story everywhere impinges upon academic study more narrowly defined, it is a tale that must be left for others to tell.[4]

THE CONTRASTING SITUATION FOR STUDYING THE TESTAMENTS

Nevertheless, there are still important things to conclude from a more limited attention to the academic study of Scripture. One of the most striking of these is the difference between evangelical scholarship on the Old Testament and on the New. Although the situation is changing, evangelical New Testament scholars still enjoy fuller participation in the larger academic world than their colleagues who study the Old Testament. Much of that difference can be attributed to the history sketched in this book. Evangelical or conservative New Testament scholars were more successful at an earlier date in providing a counterscholarship to radical European criticism. And they have continued to hold a more central place in the world of scholarship than evangelical students of the Old Testament. Part of the reason for this situation lies in the outstanding series of British New Testament scholars, from the Cambridge triumvirate through F. F. Bruce, who have paved the way for their American counterparts. Part lies in how firmly the newer critical orthodoxies concerning the Old Testament became entrenched in the university world.

The issue here is not one of expertise or of professional training. Many evangelical seminaries boast Old Testament scholars of prodigious learning, adept in the languages of the ancient world, sometimes with advanced degrees from the most prestigious graduate schools.[5] The issue rather concerns the stance of the evangelical community over against the critical consensus in Old Testament study. Modern criticism from the time of Wellhausen and his English-speaking popularizers struck hardest at precisely the aspects of the Old Testament which, by the turn of the century, had become increasingly important to evangelicals. These were the predictive element of prophecy and the historical character of creation. Modern Old Testament criticism, that is, relied self-consciously on theories of evolutionary development to revise traditional interpretations of the Old Testament just at the time that these theories were coming under most intense suspicion from evangelicals who were reasserting traditional interpretations. Unlike New Testament study, where the critical questions remained more localized—Did Paul write Ephesians or the pastorals? Which of Jesus' words came from himself and which came from the early church?—critical issues in the Old Testament depended heavily upon larger intellectual commitments. Evangelical scholars who argued against a late date for Daniel, a multiplicity of "Isaiahs," or the source theory of the Pentateuch found themselves confronting a concatenated series of high-order intellectual assertions. Alienation and disengagement was the result. Repelled by the intellectual framework, evangelical students of the Old Testament condemned the entire modern critical enterprise. Committed to that same intellectual framework, modern critical scholars found nothing of substance in the arguments of evangelicals. A standoff ensued, which made it very difficult for scholars on either side of the divide to see any value in insights from across the border.

While the disengagement between evangelicals and the wider world of scholarship continues to be sharper in the study of the Old Testament than of the New, changes are taking place. Evangelical work questioning critical conventions now seems more serious, partly because of apparent weaknesses in those conventions, partly because evangelicals show some willingness to accept limited aspects of the same conventions, and partly because evangelicals now are attempting more creative and synthetic interpretations of the Old Testament.

In addition, as the quotations from Everett Harrison in Chapter 5 suggest, some evangelicals appear willing to rethink the meaning of Jesus' words about the Old Testament. If the sayings of Jesus concerning "Moses," "the law," "David," and "the prophets" were not intended as literary answers to modern critical questions, some of the evangelical resistance to modern Old Testament criticism fades away. If, on the other hand, evangelicals conclude that these comments were meant as critical judgments, as Francis Patton and many evangelicals since his time have thought, then some form of standoff on the Old Testament will no doubt continue.

In any event, one of the most striking conclusions concerning the evangelical Bible scholarship of the last century is the manifest differences between study of the Old Testament and the New. Whether the situation alters enough to see the same kind of evangelical participation in scholarship of the Old Testament as of the New remains to be seen.

THE FULLNESS OF BIBLICAL REFLECTION

Evangelical biblical scholarship will not reach its potential if it remains concentrated on technical questions of research, or even on the contested areas of critical discussion. These are necessary but not sufficient building blocks for a full-orbed understanding of Scripture. Evangelicals who have become proficient in the use of critical tools and argument need also to become "meta-critics." They need to bring the fruits of biblical research into conjunction with theological, philosophical, historical, cultural, and even political and economic reasoning, in order to allow biblical work to flower in its fullness. At a minimum they need to realize what the British evangelical philosopher Paul Helm has seen clearly: "Basic issues in the interpretation of the New Testament are *theological* issues (or perhaps, better, metaphysical issues). . . . So for someone to say, 'I'm not interested in all this theology. Let's get back to the text of the New Testament' displays considerable naïvety."[6] Evangelicals have become mature in biblical scholarship. To this it remains to add broader, more creative, and more comprehensive intellectual maturity. For other academics, such comprehensive intellectual aspirations may be a luxury. For evangelicals, who claim that the Bible illumines all of life, it is a necessity. How is it possible to understand what the Bible communicates about the various spheres of existence without knowing the history, traditions, and inner workings of those spheres?

Ironically, the institutional form which has made it possible for evangelicals to mature as biblical scholars makes it more difficult to gain a broader intellectual maturity. Evangelical Bible scholarship in America has flourished in the seminary. Early in the debates over criticism, Princeton, Southern Baptist, and a few other seminaries paved the way for evangelicals. Then Westminster, and ethnic seminaries like Concordia and Calvin, held the conservative fort. More recently, a larger collection of evangelical seminaries have successfully promoted serious study of the Scriptures. The seminaries where evangelical scholars thrive are uniformly separated institutions, created as denominational schools with a narrow commission to serve the church or established as redoubts in which to protect orthodoxy from a hostile intellectual climate. This arrangement has given evangelical scholars a breathing space, a protected environment in which to develop expertise and self-confidence. Leaders of these institutions deserve most of the credit for the strengths of evangelical Bible scholarship. But the character of these institutions—separated from the universities, from mainline seminaries, and even from each other—has had its limitations.

The problem does not involve the quality of seminary faculties. It concerns rather the connections between biblical expertise and other forms of learning. The prominence of the seminary creates a situation in which experts in Scripture and theology work in different institutions from those who are trained in the wide range of academic subjects. Nothing exists in America like the universities of Britain and the Continent, where the most serious work in Bible and theology goes on right next to serious work in the other disciplines. In America, the threefold division of Christian liberal arts colleges, evangelical seminaries, and secular research universities has preserved many important values. Independent seminaries, for one important thing, are less likely to be corrupted by the secularism of a university than a divinity school attached to such a university. But a price has been paid.

As a result of these institutional divisions, there is little cross-fertilization in the United States between first-level evangelical Bible scholarship and first-level thinking in the arts and sciences. Evangelical seminaries enjoy capable biblical scholars, but these scholars have been isolated from comparably competent Christians in the liberal arts and comparably competent Christians and non-Christians in research universities. Professional societies bridge some of these gaps, but large chasms remain. Evangelical Bible scholarship thus loses the balance it could gain from advanced studies in, for example, astronomy, literary theory, and anthropology, and students in these fields lose the balance they need from experts in biblical and theological studies. Such a situation will continue, moreover, so long as the Christian colleges, the evangelical seminaries, and the research universities go their separate intellectual ways.

What is lost specifically is an ideal of Christian intellectual life in which biblical scholars and scholars from other disciplines work in constant relationship with each other. In such an ideal, scholars in Scripture would provide the others with fruits of their labor in biblical study and theological reflection. The others would offer Bible scholars interpretations of modern learning and creative ventures in applying the results of their labors to Christian teaching. Both would reflect on the foundational theological commitments and philosophical presuppositions that shape inquiry in every field.

Evangelicals have realized portions of this ideal, but only as individual scholars from diverse institutions establish informal networks among themselves. In general, however, the divided structures of evangelical thinking have nurtured divided mentalities, and attempts to integrate faith and wider worlds of learning are frustrated by the very successes of an approach which maintains several mutually distinct institutions of intellectual life.

Walter Ong, writing in 1959 before the *aggiornamento* of Vatican II revolutionized Roman Catholic seminary education, described a situation for his communion with many parallels to the lot of American evangelicals.

We must face the fact that today where original theological work is being done by Catholic theologians, it is where the theological faculty is part of a university—as at Innsbruck or Strasbourg or Louvain—operating and thinking at the intellectual fronts which a university keeps open, or where the theological faculty is inside a city which is a major university center —such as at Paris or Lyons or, until recently, at Zikawei in China—and in which contact with the intellectual front is not only inevitable but assiduously cultivated. In the United States we have failed to bring our theology into vital contact with our own university milieus, isolating our theology faculties from the university campus, with the result that even a place such as Austria, with a total population of some seven million, by no means all of them practicing Catholics, has been incomparably more productive theologically than we.[7]

Substitute "Britain" for "Austria," make one or two additional alterations, and Ong's words could describe American evangelicals.

The need is not for alternatives to the evangelical seminary. Such institutions are necessary, not only for pastoral training, but for their intellectual achievements as well. They are excellent places to work out theological issues within the framework of confessional convictions. And they provide helpful environments, liberated from the wearying demand for apologetical self-justification that is part of the university world.

The need is rather for additions to the evangelical seminary. Biblical study which is creative theologically, which pursues its tasks paying full attention to modern hermeneutical discussions, which seeks out insight from the liberal arts and sciences, and which responds to the needs of the world as well as to the church belongs in the world of the university. Some evangelicals talk about creating a research university where such study—at the same time both frankly Christian and intellectually unencumbered—could take place. More realistic is the possibility that evangelicals could be called to do their biblical work in the existing universities. For this to take place two things are necessary. The universities and university-connected divinity schools would first have to admit that an unreasoning prejudice against evangelical convictions has acted as a form of discrimination to keep evangelical Bible scholars off their faculties. In addition, evangelical Bible scholars would need the support of fellow evangelicals for the kind of creative work demanded by such a setting, and they would need to demonstrate both advanced academic skills and, more importantly, a sophisticated ability to combine evangelical convictions, critical expertise, and metacritical shrewdness. Evangelical scholars, positioned in the university but sustaining ongoing contact with colleagues in the evangelical seminaries, could point the way to the next stage of maturity in the evangelical study of Scripture.

FACING THE FUTURE

Whether or not that next stage arrives sooner, later, or never, there are still general predictions that can be made about the future of evangelical Bible scholarship. My conclusion is that it will survive as a significant force in the academic world and a vital resource for the church, and perhaps even assume an unanticipated influence, if the scholars can do several things: (1) speak out against the irresponsible biblical interpretations to which the evangelical tradition is heir; (2) resist the distinctly American pressure to equate a Protestant doctrine of the priesthood of all believ-

ers with democratic individualism; (3) go beyond strife over biblical inerrancy to creative synthetic theology based on the best biblical resources available; and (4) prosecute scholarship in the wider
world without falling prey to the secularism which is so much a part
of that world today.

The integrity of evangelical Bible scholarship depends in part
upon the willingness of academic leaders to discipline the interpretive excesses of the evangelical community. Professions of belief
in the inspiration and authority of the Bible are not enough. Evangelical scholars owe it to themselves, their churches, and the academic community to prune the lush but eccentric interpretations
that thrive among evangelical Bible-believers. Readings of Scripture based on arcane numerological tabulations, derived from
word studies in the King James Version, featuring flights of allegorical fantasy, advanced with transparent intent to justify social,
political, or economic hobby horses, or teased by legerdemain
from the apocalyptic visions of Ezekiel and Revelation—all should
be a scandal to the student of Scripture. And since these aberra-
tions appear most frequently among evangelicals, it is the duty of
evangelical scholars to correct them wherever possible.[8] Not to do
so offers critics of their scholarship an excuse for ignoring responsible evangelical work. Much more important, not to do so dishon-
ors the Scriptures.

Implicit in such an appeal for evangelical scholars to discipline
eccentric interpretations is a statement against democratic individualism. Although great pressure resists the thesis in America,
solid readings of Scripture simply do not arise democratically.
Protestant reformers, who promoted the doctrine of a believers'
priesthood, did not expect the people at large to have a determinative say in interpreting the Bible.[9] Nothing in the historic Protestant or Christian view of biblical inspiration, encourages the notion that technical questions about the Bible's meaning are to be
adjudicated by ballot. Early Protestants championed the cause of
Scripture's perspicuity, or clarity, but applied it to the central
teachings of salvation. This is where it belongs. Similarly, the
illumination of the Holy Spirit, which the Reformers also urged as
a necessity for understanding Scripture, involved the main convictions of the faith, the realities summarized in creeds and confes-
sions, not details of literary and critical judgment. The extensive

democratization of American life, for all its undeniable virtues, has had unfortunate consequences for the understanding of Scripture. Those who interpret the Bible authoritatively must know the Scriptures and their world academically. In 1658, John Lightfoot, a master of Cambridge University and member of the Westminster Assembly of Divines, wrote words as apposite now as then. Lightfoot recognized that to understand the words of the New Testament, it was necessary to set them in the appropriate Jewish setting. So he turned to the study of the Talmud, a work of exacting, arduous, and time-consuming labor.

For it is no matter what we can beat out concerning those manners of speech on the anvil of our own conceit, but what they signified among them in their ordinary sense and speech. . . . The almost unconquerable difficulty of the style, the frightful roughness of the language, and the amazing emptiness and sophistry of the matters handled [in the Talmud], do torture, vex, and tire them, that read them . . . so that the reader hath need of patience all along.[10]

The anvils of individual conceit have proliferated in America, and patience is at a premium. Nonetheless, to sustain a viable biblical scholarship, evangelicals must pursue the patient, learned way of Lightfoot, and renounce the allure of democratic criticism.

It will take a sublime mixture of courage and humility for evangelical Bible scholars to sustain such an enterprise. They must courageously defend patient, exacting scholarship in the face of those who use Scripture demagogically. And they must stand by while those who seek the lowest common denominator carry away honor, fame, and wealth.[11] At the same time, however, evangelical Bible scholars must take seriously the priesthood of all believers and the Holy Spirit's illumination of Scripture for all the faithful. The views of "simple" Bible-readers deserve the most careful attention, not because these readers can be guides to critical questions, but because through Scripture they apprehend the same ultimate realities before which even scholars must bow.

More strictly theological issues will also influence the future of evangelical Bible scholarship. Of these, the most visible is debate over biblical inerrancy. Properly to grasp the nature and implications of the Bible's authority is a legitimate and perennial task of the church. In recent years, however, evangelicals have expended so much energy on the subject of inerrancy that the practical and theological uses of Scripture seems to take second place. Evangelicals, to be sure, enjoy a rich heritage in the conviction that the Bible is an absolutely reliable authority. They also have a legitimate concern to protect that conviction in the twentieth century when the academic world gives it so little credence. Nonetheless, the seemingly unending round of efforts to defend and refine the concept of biblical errorlessness offers diminishing returns.

At least two strategies can move evangelicals beyond the formal concern for inerrancy to the material apprehension of the Bible. One, taken by a few evangelicals, is to conclude that it is not necessary to defend the errorless character of Scripture in order to rely upon its authority. In 1881, B. B. Warfield and A. A. Hodge concluded the opposite, that since "no organism can be stronger than its weakest part, . . . if error be found in any one element, or in any class of [biblical] statements, certainty as to any portion could rise no higher than belongs to that exercise of human reason to which it will be left to discriminate the infallible from the fallible."[12] Twenty years earlier, however, F. J. A. Hort had faced the same question and come to a slightly different conclusion. Hort felt that inconsequential mistakes in Scripture did not carry such dire consequences. As he put it in a letter to B. F. Westcott,

I do most fully recognise the special "Providence" which controlled the formation of the canonical books. . . . But I am not able to go as far as you in asserting the absolute infallibility of a canonical writing. I may see a certain fitness and probability in such a view, but I cannot set up an *a priori* assumption against the (supposed) results of criticism. . . . I shall rejoice on fuller investigation to find that imperfect knowledge is a sufficient explanation of *all* apparent errors, but I do not expect to be so fortunate. If I am ultimately driven to admit occasional errors, I shall be sorry; but it will not shake my conviction of the providential ordering of human elements in the Bible.[13]

Hort's conclusion—that the Bible may be authoritatively inspired even with inconsequential errors—was the foundation for his own productive study of the Bible, as it has been for other evangelicals since.

The other strategy is to embrace wholeheartedly a careful doctrine of inerrancy, but then to move beyond that starting point to other issues of pitch and moment. One of these is the hermeneutical question: How do we decide what an infallible Scripture teaches us? As J. I. Packer puts it, this has been the real crux of metacriticism for the last several decades: "The truth is that ever since Karl Barth linked his version of Reformation teaching on biblical authority with a method of interpretation that at key points led away from Reformation beliefs, hermeneutics has been the real heart of the debate about Scripture."[14] Another task might be the construction of an energetic evangelical theology, grounded on an inerrant Scripture, that genuinely comes to grip with both the magisterial theoretical questions (as posed by Einstein, Weber, Durkheim, Nietzsche, Heidegger, and the like) as well as the pressing practical exigencies (like urbanization, nuclear politics, and the lust for the material) of the twentieth century.

Either way—and the evangelical heritage suggests that the second has more potential than the first—evangelical scholars could move beyond the external examination of Scripture to an internal appropriation of its message.

Finally, the most pressing requirement for sustaining an evangelical biblical scholarship concerns the evangel. Evangelicals study the Bible because in it they read the words of life. Nothing threatens evangelical Bible scholarship more than a denial of that life. Or to put it more generally, than the secular denial of the gospel that prevails in so many forms in the modern world. This is a secularism which, in the university world, cavalierly dismisses the miraculous as a remnant of intellectual immaturity; which, within the community of evangelical scholars, transforms debates over Scripture into manipulative plays for power; and which, among evangelicals at large, waters down the scriptural story of human sin and divine grace to a soothing bromide of self-fulfillment and psychological ease. The secular impulse in all its forms sounds the death knell for appropriating Scripture. If evangelical Bible scholars are to flourish, they must be wise as serpents with respect to the world of thought, as innocent as doves with respect to the gospel.

Evangelicals today may be pleased with the record of biblical scholarship this book records. Bible scholars who are not evangelicals should realize that there is more than meets the eye from a cursory glance in the evangelical direction. It comports well with traditional evangelical belief to look forward confidently for further illumination to come from the Scriptures, both from those who hold evangelical convictions and those who do not. Such confidence rests not in human capacities to resolve dilemmas in criticism, but because of God's faithfulness who first brought Scripture into being and who through it continues to shine the light of his grace into a dark and sinful world.

10. Afterword

More than a decade has passed since I began research on the book that became *Between Faith and Criticism* and more than half a decade since I finished writing in 1985. While it is not possible to comment fully upon the extensive range of circumstances and events that have affected evangelical Bible scholarship during the intervening years, it may be appropriate at this time to say something about three areas directly touching the main concerns of the book. First, I would like to comment briefly on how response to the first edition has reinforced the basic stance from which I wrote. Second, it may also be worth pausing to note some of the activities in recent years that have continued trends described in the book. Third, and most important, it may be valuable to reflect at somewhat greater length on the larger interpretive contexts that have continued to play a vital role in evangelical study of Scripture.

THE STANCE OF THE BOOK

The range of reviews and personal correspondence that greeted *Between Faith and Criticism* was gratifying for several reasons. On a basic level, several critics helpfully pointed out subjects I had overlooked or relationships I had misunderstood, and so provided assistance to others who (I hope very soon) will carry the inquiries of the book much further. More important, however, were comments on the book's implicit stance. Some felt that its acceptance of traditional evangelical affirmations about Scripture prevented it from taking with due seriousness the modern critical challenges to those traditional views. From an opposing perspective, others held that kind words about the critical study of Scripture or recommendations to pursue a more self-conscious hermeneutic undercut traditional evangelical confidence in the full truthfulness of the Bible. I appreciated both kinds of comments, since together they reinforced an earlier intuition about the many perils that, at least in the present time, beset efforts to mediate between communities of faith, where the Bible is a sacred text simply to be received, and communities of secular scholarship, where the Bible is an ancient text aggressively to be explained.

The upshot from these divergent criticisms, however, was to make me even more deeply committed to the interpretive stance of the book. That stance combined two commitments that are both the product of specifically Christian reflection. On the one side, a heightened awareness of the genuine dangers of modern scholarly attitudes reinforced a pietistic conclusion. That conclusion may be stated as follows: It is more important than words can express to maintain the belief that the Bible tells the truth—and in some senses the entire truth—about God, the world of nature, the human condition, and the course of human history. While different believing communities express such a conviction in different ways, traditionally evangelical ways of stating it—in terms of verbal inspiration, infallibility, and inerrancy—seem ever more valuable to me, if they are carefully defined and qualified. Such convictions, with all that they imply about finding the way to Truth and Life, remain especially important in the contemporary period when the skeptical fashions of the academy debunk, and the subjective practices of the church undermine, the authority of a truth-telling, life-giving Scripture.

On the other side, a heightened awareness of the genuine value of modern scholarship has reinforced another Christian conclusion. It is the conviction that many of the instincts, assumptions, and practices of academic scholarship grow out of a covert trust in God and his work. Confidence in the capacity to know something about the past as well as in the mental exercises needed to pursue that knowledge both implicitly affirm a theistic view of history and rationality. While not underestimating the capacity of every interpreter to misapply, misunderstand, or misinterpret research about the Bible, it remains true that solid scholarship about Scripture— and from whatever source it comes—tells us something about conditions God had ordained, practices with words that God had made possible, conventions regarding texts that God had established among humans, and patterns of interpreting the past that God had enabled scholars to develop.[1] What such an affirmation means for the study of the Bible is that evangelicals quite properly need to cultivate a greater openness than has traditionally been the case toward new proposals from the secular academy about the historical contexts of Scripture, its literary genres, its parallels with other ancient Near Eastern literature, and its interpretation by a full range of hermeneutical strategies.

A combination of these two convictions underlay the writing of *Between Faith and Criticism*. Responses to the book have only solidified my belief that both are necessary to advance biblical scholarship.

ONGOING TRENDS

In the years since the publication of the book, many of the trends that it traced have continued. On the bright side of the picture, the capacity of evangelicals to retain traditional views of Scripture while yet pursuing scholarship in the academic sphere is even more pronounced. There is ongoing, and even increased, participation by evangelicals in the professional societies devoted to the study of Scripture. British evangelicals continue to produce path-breaking materials, both apologetic and technical.[2] The production of learned commentaries and other serious biblical literature continues without letup. Such works regularly appear as parts of ongoing series, but also as noteworthy monographs in their own right.[3] Old Testament scholarship is still more difficult for evangelicals than New Testament scholarship. Ever more radical arguments for the a-historical character of Old Testament narratives continue to exert considerable academic influence.[4] At the same time, however, evangelicals have been more active in pursuing their Old Testament work in the general academic marketplace.[5]

On the dark side, some of the same factors still prevail that have always created difficulties for evangelical Bible scholarship. Since intellectual sectarianism seems to be a constant in America, it is not surprising to see a continued profusion among evangelicals of quixotic eccentricities promoting crack-pot arguments that attack misplaced trust in modern textual criticism, expose the supposed catastrophes of modern translations, and pump the lurid details of end-times prophecy.

Sectarianism of another sort, this time from the academy, also afflicts the world of evangelical Bible scholars. A letter-writer commenting on the *New York Times*' review of Robert Alter and Frank

Kermode's widely discussed symposium, *The Literary Guide to the Bible* (Harvard University Press, 1987), made a point that could be reiterated for other aspects of American academic life:

> Elizabeth Struthers Malbon's review . . . shares with the book itself at least one major flaw. Missing from the book and ignored in the review are the conservative, evangelical scholars from many countries, churches, and theological nuances.
>
> They cannot be discounted as unworthy of an audience on the basis of ideology, since the same universities have granted doctorates to these as to scholars who appear in the book. The same publishers have released their work. They read papers at the same scholarly societies. There is no more distance between the positions of some evangelical scholars and some of those who wrote for the book than there is between the writers themselves.
>
> The editors are not wrong for not including at least one evangelical scholar, but they are incorrect for failing to acknowledge their choice.[6]

Thus, although evangelicals are producing more sophisticated work on Scripture, that work is often entirely discounted by large sections of the academic establishment.

One of the main reasons why evangelical Bible scholarship continues to be both encumbered with lunatic approaches and ignored in some strictly academic circles is historical. In the evangelical sub-culture the influence of early modern science (Bacon, Newton, Paley) remains strong, while in the university world modern and post-modern science (Darwin, Weber, Derrida) prevail. Evangelicals have regularly looked to England and Scotland for leads in biblical scholarship, while the university world has turned more instinctively to Germany. Where evangelicals continue to find their most basic constituency in the churches, university Bible scholars more consistently direct their efforts to other members of the intellectual elite. The lack of synchronization between the frameworks of evangelical scholars and the frameworks of the universities is not complete. But it has been, and probably will remain, a factor in the practical outworking of biblical scholarship.

INTERPRETIVE CONTEXTS

Such considerations of history draw attention to the larger interpretive contexts that shape the more general study of Scripture.

At the beginning of the last chapter in *Between Faith and Criticism*, I refer briefly to the intimate relationship between formal study and community values. This is a subject that deserves much more attention than it received in the first edition. It is a subject, moreover, that has been freshly illuminated by the ongoing sweep of current events as well as by a number of important recent publications.

Research in a number of areas is providing a growing amount of useful information on the contexts of evangelical Bible scholarship, information that sometimes illuminates by comparison and sometimes more directly. There have been, for example, a number of recent works on major figures from the turn of the twentieth century who also faced troubling questions about traditional commitments to Scripture. Marguerite Van Die's intellectual biography of an influential Canadian Methodist, Nathanael Burwash, describes the life of a "liberal evangelical" whose approach to Scripture marked him out as more conservative than American academic critics and more accommodating than American fundamentalists. A new study of Charles A. Briggs by Mark Massa has something of the same effect, for it reveals the complicated fate of someone who ended up far too liberal for conservatives and far too traditional for the new critics. Glenn Scorgie's theological biography of the Scottish Free Church leader, James Orr, describes a scholar who was closer to American conservatives than Briggs was, yet who nonetheless made several tactical adjustments to modern views of Scripture that remained suspect among American conservative evangelicals.[7] The help offered by these studies is indirect but important, for they show that the spectrum of options confronting late nineteenth-century traditionalists may have been broader than American evangelicals realized.

Other recent publications relate more directly to the ways in which community values influence appropriation of the Scriptures. Philip Barlow's study of the Mormons and Scripture shows how another group with strongly American values has put Scripture to use within a community with striking cultural parallels to evangelical communities.[8] John Merrill's essay on the use of Scripture by nineteenth-century temperance reformers provides an example of the recurring American process whereby movements of great contemporary urgency actually determine conclusions on what the Bible is thought to teach.[9] But the most impressive publishing on the general subject has come in a series of books sponsored by the

Society of Biblical Literature called "The Bible in American Culture." The six books in this series present a number of essays, rather than a single coherent perspective. Nonetheless, their treatment of subjects as diverse as the Bible's role in education, its manifold stimulation to the arts (both high and folk), and its influence on political and social thinkers constitute a great reservoir on the ways Americans have understood Scripture and put it to use.[10] As such, this work provides necessary background for studies of formal scholarship, because such scholarship always and everywhere sustains close connections with more general approaches to Scripture.

Another set of recent publications focuses more directly on the specific communities from which evangelical scholarship emerges. George Marsden's history of Fuller Seminary shows how a struggle between faithfulness to a theological tradition and efforts to gain present-day respect shaped this influential institution's attitudes toward both the Bible and scholarship. Similarly, Rudolph Nelson's biography of one of Fuller's early luminaries, E. J. Carnell, offers a more intense examination of the personal history of a leader who wanted to find a faith that was neither hamstrung by fundamentalistic biblical literalism nor undermined by liberal acceptance of modern criticism.[11] On another front, a number of thoughtful essays have probed uses of the term "evangelical." One of the accomplishments of those essays is to show that the broad mosaic of American evangelical churches includes emphases on Scripture that are more pietistic and less dogmatic, more intuitive and less doctrinal, than the best-known evangelical views.[12] A final set of works has illuminated broader aspects of evangelical experience. Helpful books by Randall Balmer, David Bebbington, Mark Ellingsen, Nathan Hatch, David Livingstone, and George Rawlyk are not directed specifically toward questions of modern biblical scholarship.[13] But in these studies, evangelical convictions about, attitudes toward, and practices with the Scriptures are a constant matter of discussion and interpretation. The cumulative result of these different works is to provide a more nuanced picture of evangelical communities and a greater sensitivity to the diversity of evangelical approaches to Scripture.

Important as these recent publications have been, events in church and academy have done even more to highlight the dense connections between community and scholars. Again, some of the most helpful events offer indirect, comparative insight. For example, struggles within the Roman Catholic Church to define the nature of authority touch regularly on Scripture. Catholic traditionalists do attempt to shore up support for an infallible Bible, but because the contested question of infallibility among Catholics is more the pope than Scripture, Catholic conservatives writing on the Bible do not end up saying the same thing as their conservative Protestant counterparts.[14] Some attention is paid, to be sure, to the kind of detailed exegetical questions that engage Protestants, but even more attention is directed to structures of interpretative authority. Evangelical Protestants do not agree that there is an apostolic magisterium charged with authoritative responsibility for interpreting the Bible, but they certainly should learn from their Catholic contemporaries that questions about the "who" of interpretive authority are every bit as vital as those concerning the "what" of interpretive conclusions. In other words, this contemporary situation might teach Protestant evangelicals an ironic lesson: if Catholics, with a theory of hierarchical interpretation, nonetheless can lapse into interpretive chaos, so evangelicals, with an interpretive theory of the priesthood of believers, nonetheless can vest a nearly papal authority in the interpretive pronouncements of exalted leaders.

Much closer to home is the struggle within the Southern Baptist Convention between "moderate" and "fundamentalist" factions.[15] In this Southern Baptist controversy, purely doctrinal issues (like the nature of biblical inspiration) and purely hermeneutical questions (like the degree to which the early chapters of Genesis are meant to be taken as a literal historical account) are certainly important. But so is also the timing of the controversy, which occurred precisely as the Southern Baptists were moving out of older, settled patterns in the South, or (to put it the other way around) when national cultural patterns were effacing what had formerly been a distinctly Southern way of life.

At least to a Yankee observer, debates within the Convention over biblical issues also seem to concern the pace of Southern Baptist integration into the rest of the nation. "Fundamentalists" seem more concerned about preserving an ecclesiastical ethos traditional to the South, "moderates" more interested in making the most of intellectual resources from the North. Debates within the Convention, however, are often short-circuited by focusing entirely on questions of biblical interpretation. In reality (again from an outsider's perspective), it would appear that all of the Southern Baptist contentions are simultaneously biblical plus something else. That is, not just whether to define the Bible as "inerrant" or "inspired," but whether to define the Bible as "inerrant" and resist the corruptions of Southern institutions by modern education or to define it as "inspired" and make use of a wide range of recent biblical scholarship from the Continent. A complication in the Southern Baptist controversy seems also to be an almost touching naivete about hermeneutical practice. "Moderates" feel vindicated in their exegesis if the Northern theological establishment supports their views; "fundamentalists" think their biblical interpretation is verified if an annual convention elects another "fundamentalist" president. But in evangelical theory, it is appropriate to be as suspicious about the interpretive power of an academic establishment or an annual convention as it is about the pope.

However misguided these few comments may be, the controversy among Southern Baptists does seem to underscore the reality that no examination of biblical scholarship is complete that does not also deal with the ecclesiastical and cultural circumstances in which exegesis, doctrinal formulation, hermeneutical practice, and biblical application take place.

Another circumstance with far-reaching implications for biblical scholarship is evangelical controversy over the role of women in the church. While evangelicals have debated this issue at regular intervals since at least the mid-nineteenth century, when revivalists like Charles Finney and Holiness teachers like Phoebe Palmer defended the propriety of women preaching and even female ordination, argument in the last two decades has become increasingly tied to scholarly questions of biblical interpretation. Traditionalists accuse their opponents of letting the spirit of the modern age determine exegetical results. Those who want to see women and men on an equal footing in the offices of the church respond by pointing to biblical and historical precedents for women's full participation, but they expend even more effort in showing how traditional interpretations of debated passages like 1 Corinthians 14:34–35 or 1 Timothy 2:10–15 arose from the cultural accidents of western history rather than from the original meaning of the texts themselves.[16]

For a historian of biblical scholarship who is also concerned about the integrity of evangelical profession, this debate is both fascinating and painful. It illustrates, first, how higher levels of academic certification can continue to coexist with the earlier evangelical bent toward democratic decision-making. In this debate the level of scholarly argument is very high but so is the quantity of political tub-thumping. Technical publications and high-level academic consultations vie with national interest groups, widely ballyhooed congresses, and not a little institutional in-fighting. This state of affairs flows naturally from the past, since evangelicalism has always been a democratic movement that tried somehow to cultivate the mind. Yet it also throws into sharper relief the fundamental historical tension within evangelicalism constituted by simultaneous confidence in technical, academic understanding of the Bible and a wholehearted trust in the will of the people.

Contention over women's roles also highlights the tight bond between general convictions and specific interpretations. On the range of questions raised by this debate it is becoming increasingly clear that there is no exegesis without presuppositions. Evangelicals who believe that the Bible in general teaches the progressive manifestation of a New Creation, who hold that the Bible's central purpose is to communicate new life in the Spirit, or who feel that developments in modern western society are at least potentially instructive to Christians, more easily find convincing those scholarly explanations that allow fuller scope for women's activities. On the other hand, those who believe that the Bible in general teaches a divinely ordained chain of command, who hold that the Bible offers a detailed blueprint of God's will for everyday life, or who feel that western society has entered into an apocalyptic decline, more easily find convincing those technical explanations that reinforce traditional male-female roles. But once evangelicals recognize that such general convictions predispose the outcome of exegesis,[17] then it is obvious that considerations of wide compass—culturally, socially, politically, psychologically—are an intrinsic part of all study of Scripture.

At the very least, then, the debate over the role of women in the church should heighten evangelical sensitivity to the broader contexts in which the Bible is studied and put to use. It will be cold comfort if such heightened awareness is merely a byproduct of a debate that ends in bitterness and a further splintering of an already excessively fragmented movement. Such awareness may, however, also be a way for evangelicals on different sides of this question to grasp the complexities at issue and, with that understanding, add full measures of charity and toleration to the particular urgencies of conviction.

A final recent circumstance that affects all questions of scholarship is the manifest politicization of the university.[18] Higher education has always been political, or ideological, even if Enlightenment notions of a magisterially neutral science once hid the full consequences of those politics and ideologies. But no longer. The open promotion in the university of liberationist, feminist, homosexual, and socialist agendas is sometimes matched by forthright defenses of more traditional ideologies. For biblical scholarship the result has been to undermine the ideal of neutrality. Evangelicals in the academy now may be attacked for lending aid, wittingly or unwittingly, to the tyrannies of patriarchialism, phallocentricism, and hierarchialism. But in such an environment, no consistent intellectual strategy can rule out of court the values that evangelicals consider appropriate as a basis for studying the Bible. Exegesis from someone who believes in the possibility of relationship with God is in principle no more or no less suspect than from someone who believes in the detestable evils of patriarchy. If the theological dispositions of evangelicals put them closer to the harassed defenders of older Enlightenment ideals (as I think they do), evangelical Bible scholars nevertheless should be able to take advantage of the current situation to promote a scholarship that fits not only the dictates of alien intellectuals, but also of their own faith.

Within this more ideological climate evangelical academics should take to heart occasional appeals from highly respected voices for a new scholarship of religious engagement. Penetrating reviews of Alter and Kermode's *Literary Guide to the Bible* from George Steiner and Donald Davie, for example, both commented on the ultimate sterility when a book that has meant eternal life to so many people for so many generations is treated as if it were a bit of arcane esoterica relevant only to scholars who have outgrown the need for religion.[19] In similar fashion, David Brion Davis recently chastised the more than one hundred authors of *Scribner's Encyclopedia of the American Religious Experience* for writing as if their subjects were of scant concern to the core of their beings.[20] If scholars of such substance call for a distinctly religious approach to religious texts and experiences (albeit without lapsing into atavistic anti-intellectualism), it suggests that the academic climate is changing. Now may be the time for evangelicals to raise their sights higher than merely borrowing, using, and applying scholarship from the academy at large. Now may be the time to draw upon ongoing vitality in the churches and the creative confusion of the academy to construct distinctly evangelical approaches to the study of Scripture. As in previous ages when Augustine exploited Plato and Thomas Aquinas drew on Aristotle for distinctly Christian purposes, so perhaps the time has come for evangelicals to plunder the well-burnished riches of the Enlightenment and the newer treasures of modernity to furnish a house of learning made with their own hands.

In the end, a historian can only guess about the future. From one angle of vision, there are enough unfavorable signs to forecast hard days for the evangelical study of the Bible. It is possible to imagine greater intellectual and spiritual confusion flowing from evangelicals' tangled allegiances to academic respectability, cultural fashion, and hereditary sectarian shibboleths. The distractions of "modernity" are calling into doubt the capacities of all Americans, including evangelicals, to think solidly about any issue at all. Intransigence about any changes in biblical interpretation seems on the rise among those who defend tradition merely because it is traditional. Persistent longings for academic position and intellectual respect tempt others to temporize on all manner of foundational commitments. The evangelical populist strain threatens constantly to surge into tyrannies of the majority.

From another angle, however, it is possible to imagine a brighter intellectual and spiritual day arising from an alliance of deep Christian conviction, self-critical but loyal attachment to evangelical traditions, and discriminating use of contemporary scholarly resources. Perhaps from unjustified personal predilection, or maybe from a hint of grace, I find myself more optimistic about evangelical biblical scholarship now than when I first began to work on *Between Faith and Criticism*. In the intervening years I have been the recipient of intellectual insight and Christian charity from Southern Baptist "moderates" and Southern Baptist "fundamentalists," from evangelicals who defend the ordination of women and those who oppose it. I have been nurtured in faith by reading the biblical writings of scholars from evangelical strongholds like Regent College and Gordon-Conwell, Trinity, Westminster, Asbury, and Fuller seminaries. Some of this work has been internally contradictory, and not all of it has been irrefutable. But it has been solid, and to one not actively engaged in the professional study of the Bible, the commonalities seem much larger than the differences. In wider circles, moreover, I have sampled biblical writers from the religion department of Abilene Christian, from the Yale Divinity School, from the Vatican, and from students of F. F. Bruce scattered all over the world who, despite differences that are not trivial, still were united in finding Scripture the source of insight, instruction, direction, encouragement, and life.

But most of all I am encouraged to look for a better evangelical Bible scholarship because I have been privileged to glimpse with slightly greater clarity the wonders of Scripture itself. Week by week, in church and Bible study, the same couple to whom *Between Faith and Criticism* was dedicated have continued to minister the Scriptures to my family and myself with clarity, warmth, and compassion. Week by week, that ministry, braced by careful study but inspired even more by patient godliness, has revealed the Bible as a living book pointing beyond itself to a holy and loving God. That revelation is the final reason for thinking that "evangelical" scholarship, scholarship arising from "the gospel" displayed in Scripture, can only get better and better, no matter what the current conditions or what those of us who are today known as evangelicals try to do.

Appendix: Survey of Evangelical Bible Scholars

On February 15, 1984, I mailed a twenty-question survey to members of three evangelical professional organizations: the Evangelical Theological Society (hereafter ETS), the Institute for Biblical Research (IBR), and the Wesleyan Theological Society (WTS). Shortly before that date, secretaries of the respective organizations had graciously made available current membership lists (respectively, Simon J. Kistemaker, Gerald Hawthorne, and Wayne E. Caldwell). (For information on these groups, see Chapter 5, pages 105–106.)

The survey was sent to all 148 members of the IBR, to 223 randomly selected members of the ETS (1 out of 7 from a total membership of 1566), and to 211 randomly selected members of the WTS (1 out of 6 from a total membership of 1271). Because names were randomly selected, two surveys were inadvertently sent to one person who was a member of both WTS and IBR, and two surveys were sent to each of four people who were members of ETS and IBR. This meant that surveys went out to a total of 577 individuals.

Questions on the survey dealt with matters of demography, educational preparation, preferred Bible translations, the influence of others on academic work, professional activity in Bible scholarship, and similar matters. The surveys were returned anonymously.

Some of the results from the survey are mentioned in the chapters of this book. This appendix presents fuller summaries of the questionnaire's findings.

Results are presented in two general categories under each area of interest. First are gross totals for the three societies. Second, for many of the variables, I have supplied a more detailed breakdown for those who are members of just the ETS, just the IBR, and of both groups. As it happens, the members of the ETS and IBR are more active in professional scholarship than those of the WTS. In addition, the networks found in the ETS and IBR draw in the variety of evangelicals who are the main focus of this book. Finally, contrasts among the members of the IBR (an evangelical group organized around professional concerns), members of the ETS (organized around theological concerns), and those in both—especially educational preparation and influence from other scholars—show in greater detail the wide range of interests among evangelical Bible scholars in these organizations as well as some of the reasons for intramural differences.

At a later date, I hope to develop more fully some of the implications of the information returned in the survey. For now, this partially digested summary will be useful in fleshing out the picture of contemporary evangelical scholarship sketched in this book.

Figures in parentheses, which are supplied for some of the results, are percentages.

I. SURVEY INFORMATION

A. QUESTIONNAIRES DISTRIBUTED*

To members of the ETS	223
To members of the IBR	148
To members of the WTS	211
Total number surveyed	577

B. QUESTIONNAIRES RETURNED

Members of only the ETS	136
Members of only the IBR	58
Members of only the WTS	78
Members of both ETS and IBR	40
Members of both ETS and WTS	13

---

* Adjustment: In one case a member of the WTS who was also a member of the IBR received two surveys. In four cases members of the ETS who were also members of the IBR received two surveys each.

Members of both IBR and WTS	2
Members of ETS, IBR, and WTS	2
Total returned	329

C. Questionnaires Returned from the Three Societies (gross totals)

Members of ETS	191
Members of IBR	102
Members of WTS	95
Total (including duplications)	388

D. Questionnaires Returned from ETS and IBR Members

Members of only the ETS	149
Members of only the IBR	60
Members of both ETS and IBR	42
Total	251

II. DEMOGRAPHIC AND DENOMINATIONAL INFORMATION

A. Sex all ETS, IBR, WTS Members*

	ETS	IBR	WTS
Male	191	100	92
Female	0	2	2

B. Sex ETS, IBR, ETS and IBR

	Just ETS	Just IBR	Both ETS/IBR
Male	149	58	42
Female	0	2	0

C. Age (as of February 1984) all ETS, IBR, WTS Members

	ETS	IBR	WTS
20–29	22	1	16

*In this and other tables, totals for each group sometimes fall below numbers of questionnaires returned, because some answers were omitted.

	ETS	IBR	WTS
30–39	64	19	22
40–49	43	34	23
50–59	41	35	19
60–69	20	10	9
70+	1	3	6
Mean	43.0	48.5	44.7

D. AGE (AS OF FEBRUARY 1984) ETS, IBR, ETS AND IBR

	Just ETS	Just IBR	Both ETS/IBR
Mean	41.7	50.0	47.9

E. CITIZENSHIP ALL ETS, IBR, WTS MEMBERS

	ETS	IBR	WTS
United States	170 (89.5)	86 (85.1)	85 (89.5)
Canada	18	11	6
Elsewhere	2	4	4

F. CITIZENSHIP ETS, IBR, ETS AND IBR

	Just ETS	Just IBR	Both ETS/IBR
United States	136 (91.3)	52 (86.7)	34 (82.9)
Canada	12	5	6
Elsewhere	1	3	1

G. TYPE OF EMPLOYMENT ALL ETS, IBR, WTS MEMBERS

	ETS	IBR	WTS
Seminary	68 (35.6)	51 (50.0)	15 (15.8)
Other education	59 (30.9)	43 (42.2)	18 (18.9)
Church or Christian	52 (27.2)	8 (07.8)	57 (60.0)
Other	12 (06.3)	0	5 (05.3)

H. TYPE OF EMPLOYMENT ETS, IBR, ETS AND IBR

	Just ETS	Just IBR	Both ETS/IBR
Seminary	46 (30.9)	29 (48.3)	22 (52.4)
Other education	40 (26.8)	24 (40.0)	19 (45.2)

	Just ETS	Just IBR	Both ETS/IBR
Church or Christian	51 (34.2)	7 (11.7)	1 (02.4)
Other	12 (08.1)	0	0

I. WHETHER PLACE OF EMPLOYMENT IS CHRISTIAN OR SECULAR, ALL ETS, IBR, WTS MEMBERS

	ETS	IBR	WTS
Christian	172 (90.1)	95 (93.1)	90 (94.7)
Secular	19	7	5

J. WHETHER PLACE OF EMPLOYMENT IS CHRISTIAN OR SECULAR, ETS, IBR, ETS AND IBR

	Just ETS	Just IBR	Both ETS/IBR
Christian	131 (87.9)	54 (90.0)	41 (97.6)
Secular	18	6	1

K. DENOMINATIONAL AFFILIATION ALL ETS, IBR, WTS MEMBERS*

	ETS (n = 191)	IBR (n = 102)	WTS (n = 95)
Baptist	59 (30.9)	29 (28.4)	0
[SBC]	[12]	[7]	
[GARB]	[11]	[3]	
[BGC]	[8]	[4]	
[CB]	[7]		
[AB]	[7]	[6]	
[Canadian]	[8]	[4]	
Presbyterian/Ref.	35 (18.3)	30 (29.4)	0
[PCA]	[18]	[7]	
[PCUSA]	[4]	[11]	
[CRC]	[4]	[7]	

*Abbreviations: SBC = Southern Baptist Convention, GARB = General Association of Regular Baptists, BGC = Baptist General Conference, CB = Conservative Baptists, AB = American Baptists, PCA = Presbyterian Church of America, PCUSA = Presbyterian Church of the United States of America, CRC = Christian Reformed Church, UM = United Methodists, EFC = Evangelical Free Church, Ev. Cov. = Evangelical Covenant Church, Restorationist = Church of Christ or Christian Church, CMA = Christian and Missionary Alliance

	ETS (n = 191)	IBR (n = 102)	WTS (n = 95)
Nazarene	3 (01.6)	0	28 (29.5)
Meth./Wesleyan	11 (05.8)	6 (05.9)	47 (49.5)
[Free]	[4]	[3]	[17]
[Wesleyan Ch.]	[4]		[16]
[UM]	[2]	[3]	[12]
Nondenom./Ind.	28 (14.7)	4 (03.9)	1 (01.1)
EFC/Ev. Cov.	9	5	
Restorationist	8	3	2
CMA	8		3
Brethren	5		2
Plymouth Brethren	5	7	
Mennonite	4	3	
Evangelical Church			4
Friends	1	1	3
Episcopal/Anglican	2	6	
Assemblies of God	3	2	
Advent Christian	3	2	
Church of God	2		3
Lutheran	2	2	
Others	3	2	2

L. ACADEMIC SPECIALTY, ALL ETS, IBR, WTS MEMBERS

	ETS	IBR	WTS
New Testament	66 (34.7)	67 (65.7)	28 (29.5)
Old Testament	39 (20.5)	29 (28.4)	5 (05.3)
Theology	40	2	24
Other	45	4	38

M. ACADEMIC SPECIALTY, ETS, IBR, ETS AND IBR

	Just ETS	Just IBR	Both ETS/IBR
New Testament	38 (25.7)	39 (65.0)	28 (66.7)
Old Testament	25 (16.9)	15 (25.0)	14 (33.3)
Theology	40	2	
Other	45	4	

III. COLLEGES, UNIVERSITIES, AND SEMINARIES FROM WHICH GRADUATED

A. SCHOOLS ATTENDED (FOR ANY DEGREE), ALL ETS, IBR, WTS MEMBERS (TOP 15 PLUS TIES)

ETS	IBR	WTS
Wheaton College 32	Wheaton College 18	Asbury Seminary 23
Dallas Seminary 24	Princeton Seminary 15	Nazarene Theological Seminary 18
Trinity Seminary 20	Fuller Seminary 12	Marion College 10
Grace Seminary 16	Harvard 10	Olivet Nazarene College 7
Westminster Seminary 15	Trinity Seminary 10	Anderson College 5
Princeton Seminary 10	Westminster Seminary 8	Princeton Seminary 5
Fuller Seminary 9	Gordon-Conwell Seminary 8	Trevecca Nazerene College 5
Northern Baptist Seminary 7	Manchester 7	Western Evangelical Seminary 5
Gordon-Conwell Seminary 6	Brandeis 6	Drew 4
Western Conservative Baptist Seminary 5	Calvin College 6	Greenville College 4
Talbot Seminary 5	Calvin Seminary 6	Asbury College 3
Harvard 5	Alberdeen 6	Houghton College 3
Aberdeen 5	Union Seminary (VA) 6	Nazarene Bible College 3
Harding 4	Cambridge 5	Ohio State 3
Houghton College 4	St. Andrews 4	
Trinity College 4	Southwest Baptist Seminary 4	
Union Seminary (VA) 4		

B. SCHOOLS ATTENDED (FOR ANY DEGREE), ETS, IBR, ETS AND IBR (TOP 10 PLUS TIES)

Just ETS	Just IBR	Both ETS/IBR
Dallas Seminary 22	Princeton Seminary 11	Wheaton College 12
Wheaton College 20	Fuller Seminary 9	Gordon-Conwell Seminay 6
Grace Seminary 16	Wheaton College 6	Harvard 5
Trinity Seminary 15	Calvin College 5	Trinity Seminary 5
Westminster Seminary 10	Harvard 5	Westminster Seminary 5
Fuller Seminary 6	Trinity Seminary 5	Aberdeen 4
Northern Baptist Seminary 6	Calvin Seminary 4	Princeton Seminary 4
Princeton Seminary 6	Manchester 4	Union Seminary (VA) 4
	St. Andrews 4	

Just ETS	Just IBR	Both ETS/IBR
Talbot Seminary 5	Brandeis 3	Brandeis 3
Western Conservative	Cambridge 3	Fuller Seminary 3
Baptist Seminary 3	Princeton 3	Manchester 3
	Southwest Baptist	
	Seminary 3	
	University of Southern	
	California 3	
	Westminster Seminary 3	

IV. BIBLE TRANSLATIONS REGULARLY USED

A. FOR FAMILY USE, ALL ETS, IBR, WTS MEMBERS (IN THIS AND NEXT TWO TABLES, PERCENTAGES TOTAL MORE THAN 100 BECAUSE SOME CHECKED MORE THAN ONE VERSION.)

	ETS	IBR	WTS
King James	18 (09.4)	2 (02.0)	21 (22.1)
New American Standard	36 (18.8)	8 (07.8)	14 (14.7)
New International Version	128 (67.0)	60 (58.8)	52 (54.7)
Revised Standard Version	23 (12.0)	40 (39.2)	16 (16.8)
Others	21 (11.0)	10 (09.8)	28 (29.5)

B. FOR STUDY, ALL ETS, IBR, WTS MEMBERS

	ETS	IBR	WTS
King James	4 (02.1)	0 (00.0)	8 (08.4)
New American Standard	97 (50.8)	26 (25.5)	35 (36.8)
New International Version	69 (36.1)	28 (27.5)	36 (37.9)
Revised Standard Version	41 (21.5)	59 (57.8)	33 (34.7)
Others	32 (16.8)	14 (13.7)	20 (21.1)

C. FOR STUDY, ETS, IBR, ETS AND IBR

	Just ETS	Just IBR	Both ETS/IBR
King James	4 (02.7)	0 (00.0)	0 (00.0)
New American Standard	79 (53.0)	8 (13.3)	18 (42.9)
New International Version	52 (34.9)	11 (18.3)	17 (40.5)
Revised Standard Version	23 (15.4)	41 (68.3)	18 (42.9)
Others	28 (18.8)	10 (16.7)	4 (09.6)

V. MEASURES OF PROFESSIONALIZATION

A. EARNED DOCTORATES, ALL ETS, IBR, WTS MEMBERS

	ETS (n = 190)	IBR (n = 102)	WTS (n = 94)
University doctorate	65 (34.2)	86 (84.3)	19 (20.2)
Seminary doctorate	33 (17.4)	10 (09.8)	1 (01.1)
No doctorate	92 (48.4)	6 (05.9)	74 (78.7)

B. EARNED DOCTORATES, ETS, IBR, ETS AND IBR

	Just ETS	Just IBR	Both ETS/IBR
University doctorate	28 (18.9)	49 (81.7)	37 (88.1)
Seminary doctorate	28 (18.9)	5 (08.3)	5 (11.9)
No doctorate	92 (62.2)	6 (10.0)	0 (00.0)

C. OTHER PROFESSIONAL MEMBERSHIPS, ALL ETS, IBR, WTS MEMBERS*

	ETS	IBR	WTS
Evangelical organizations	16 (08.3)	2 (01.9)	4 (04.2)
Professional groups	79 (41.4)	79 (77.5)	15 (15.8)
None	96 (50.3)	21 (20.6)	76 (80.0)

D. OTHER PROFESSIONAL MEMBERSHIPS, ETS, IBR, ETS AND IBR

	Just ETS	Just IBR	Both ETS/IBR
Evangelical organizations	14	0	2
Professional groups	48 (32.2)	48 (80.0)	31 (73.8)
None	87	12	9

*In this and the next table, "evangelical organization" means that the respondent belonged to only other evangelical or denominational societies. Some in the category "professional groups" also belonged to other denominational or denominational societies.

E. Authorship of Journal Articles, all ETS, IBR, WTS Members*

	ETS	IBR	WTS
Evangelical	95	32	26
Professional	32 (16.8)	66 (64.7)	6 (06.3)
None	64 (33.5)	4 (03.9)	63 (66.3)

F. Authorship of Journal Articles, ETS, IBR, ETS and IBR

	Just ETS	Just IBR	Both ETS/IBR
Evangelical	73	10	22
Professional	13 (08.7)	47 (78.3)	19 (45.2)
None	63 (42.3)	3 (05.0)	1 (02.4)

G. Authorship of Books, all ETS, IBR, WTS Members†

	ETS	IBR	WTS
Evangelical	56	34	12
Professional	15 (07.9)	38 (37.3)	4 (4.2)
None	120 (62.8)	30 (29.4)	79 (83.2)

H. Authorship of Books, ETS, IBR, ETS and IBR

	Just ETS	Just IBR	Both ETS/IBR
Evangelical	36	14	20
Professional	5 (03.4)	28 (46.7)	10 (23.8)
None	108 (72.5)	18 (30.0)	12 (28.6)

*In this and the following table, "evangelical" means articles published only in evangelical or denominational journals. The "professional" category includes both those who have published only in professional journals as well as those who have published in both professional and evangelical or denominational journals.

†In this and the next table, categories designate the same as for tables [E] and [F].)

VI. PERSONAL INFLUENCE ON SCHOLARS

A. INDIVIDUALS CITED AS MOST INFLUENTIAL, ALL ETS, IBR, WTS MEMBERS*

ETS (n = 191)	IBR (n = 102)	WTS (n = 95)
John Calvin 29	George Ladd 20	H. Orton Wiley 25
George Ladd 23	F. F. Bruce 13	John Wesley 19
Francis Schaeffer 16	Gerhard von Rad 13	C. S. Lewis 8
Cornelius Van Til 16	John Bright 11	Mildred B. Wynkoop 8
F. F. Bruce 14	Oscar Cullmann 11	John Bright 6
C. S. Lewis 14	Joachim Jeremias 11	Francis Schaeffer 6
Louis Berkhof 13	Herman Ridderbos 10	Karl Barth 5
Carl Henry 13	Karl Barth 9	Dietrich Bonhoeffer 5
Charles Hodge 13	Rudolf Bultmann 9	Sören Kierkegaard 5
Walter Kaiser 13	Donald Guthrie 9	Bruce Metzger 5
Herman Ridderbos 11	John Calvin 7	H. Richard Niebuhr 5
Donald Guthrie 10	Brevard Childs 7	Paul Tillich 5
James Barr 9	C. H. Dodd 7	George A. Turner 5
B. B. Warfield 9	James Barr 6	
	Walther Eichrodt 6	
	C. F. D. Moule 6	

*Results in this and the next table came in response to the following question: 'Please list the three individuals, living or dead, who have exerted the dominant influence on your scholarly work. You do not have to share the conclusions of these individuals but they should be the ones whose work influences you the most."

B. Individuals Cited as Most Influential, ETS, IBR, ETS and IBR

Just ETS (n = 149)	Just IBR (n = 60)	Both ETS/IBR (n = 42)
John Calvin 25	George Ladd 13	F. F. Bruce 7
George Ladd 16	Gerhard von Rad 13	George Ladd 7
Cornelius Van Til 15	Oscar Cullmann 11	Donald Guthrie 6
C. S. Lewis 14	Joachim Jeremias 10	Louis Berkhof 4
Francis Schaeffer 14	John Bright 9	John Calvin 4
Carl Henry 13	Rudolf Bultmann 9	C. H. Dodd 4
Walter Kaiser 13	Karl Barth 8	I. Howard Marshall 4
Charles Hodge 11	F. F. Bruce 6	Herman Ridderbos 4
Louis Berkhof 9	Herman Ridderbos 6	Brevard Childs 3
B. B. Warfield 8	C. F. D. Moule 5	Walther Eichrodt 3
Karl Barth 7	George Wright 5	John Murray 3
James Barr 7	James Barr 4	Geerhardus Vos 3
F. F. Bruce 7	Brevard Childs 4	
Norman Geisler 7	W. G. Kümmel 4	
Donald Guthrie 7		
Herman Ridderbos 7		

C. Authors Cited as Most Influential, all ETS, IBR, WTS Members*

ETS (n = 191)	IBR (n = 102)	WTS (n = 95)
John Calvin 33	George Ladd 22	H. Orton Wiley 23
George Ladd 27	John Bright 13	John Wesley 17
Francis Schaeffer 16	F. F. Bruce 13	Mildred B. Wynkoop 8
Cornelius Van Til 16	Joachim Jeremias 13	C. S. Lewis 7
Carl Henry 15	Gerhard von Rad 13	W. T. Purkiser 6
F. F. Bruce 14	Oscar Cullmann 12	John Bright 5

*Results in this and the next three tables came in response to the following question: "List the five academic books which have had the greatest impact on your own scholarship or the direction of your academic work. Again, you do not have to agree with these books, but they should be ones that exerted a formative influence on your work in biblical studies or theology."

ETS (n = 191)	IBR (n = 102)	WTS (n = 95)
C. S. Lewis 14	Herman Ridderbos 11	Karl Barth 5
Louis Berkhof 13	John Calvin 9	Dietrich Bonhoeffer 4
Walter Kaiser 13	Karl Barth 8	Adam Clarke 4
Herman Ridderbos 12	Rudolf Bultmann 8	Donald Guthrie 4
James Barr 10	Brevard Childs 7	Sören Kierkegaard 4
Charles Hodge 10	Walther Eichrodt 7	George Ladd 4
B. B. Warfield 10	R. K. Harrison 7	J. Gresham Machen 4
Karl Barth 9	C. F. D. Moule 7	Bruce Metzger 4
John Bright 9	Donald Guthrie 6	H. Richard Niebuhr 4
Geerhardus Vos 9	Geerhardus Vos 6	Francis Schaeffer 4
	James Barr 6	Paul Tillich 4
		George Allen Turner 4

D. Authors Cited as Most Influential, ETS, IBR, ETS/IBR

Just ETS (n = 149)	Just IBR (n = 60)	Both ETS/IBR (n = 42)
John Calvin 27	Gerhard von Rad 13	George Ladd 11
George Ladd 16	Oscar Cullmann 11	F. F. Bruce 7
Carl Henry 15	George Ladd 11	John Calvin 6
Cornelius Van Til 15	Joachim Jeremias 10	Herman Ridderbos 5
C. S. Lewis 14	John Bright 9	Louis Berkhof 4
Francis Schaeffer 14	Rudolf Bultmann 7	John Bright 4
Walter Kaiser 13	Karl Barth 6	Walther Eichrodt 4
Louis Berkhof 9	F. F. Bruce 6	I. Howard Marshall 4
Charles Hodge 8	Herman Ridderbos 6	F. I. Anderson 3
B. B. Warfield 8	C. F. D. Moule 5	James Barr 3
James Barr 7	G. E. Wright 5	Brevard Childs 3
Karl Barth 7		C. H. Dodd 3
F. F. Bruce 7		Donald Guthrie 3
Herman Ridderbos 7		R. K. Harrison 3
		Joachim Jeremias 3
		John Murray 3
		Stephen Neill 3
		Geerhardus Vos 3

E. Individual Books Cited as Most Influential, all ETS, IBR, WTS Members

ETS (n = 191)

John Calvin, *Institutes of the Christian Religion*   32

George Ladd, *A Theology of the New Testament*   18

Louis Berkhof, *Systematic Theology*   19

G. Kittel, *Theological Dictionary of the New Testament*   10

Cornelius Van Til, *The Defense of the Faith*   10

C. S. Lewis, *Mere Christianity*

Francis Schaeffer, *The God Who Is There*

James Barr, *The Semantics of Biblical Language*

Charles Hodge, *Systematic Theology*

Walter Kaiser, *Toward an Old Testament Theology*

Herman Ridderbos, *Paul: An Outline of His Theology*

Geerhardus Vos, *Biblical Theology*

Karl Barth, *Church Dogmatics*

R. K. Harrison, *Introduction to the Old Testament*

Carl Henry, *God, Revlation, and Authority*

B. B. Warfield, *The Inspiration and Authority of the Bible*

IBR (n = 102)

George Ladd, *A Theology of the New Testament*   10

John Calvin, *Institutes of the Christian Religion*

Oscar Cullmann, *Christ and Time*

Gerhard von Rad, *Old Testament Theology*

John Bright, *A History of Israel*

Walther Eichrodt, *Theology of the Old Testament*

R. K. Harrison, *Introduction to the Old Testament*

Joachim Jeremias, *The Parables of Jesus*

Herman Ridderbos, *Paul: An Outline of His Theology*

Karl Barth, *Church Dogmatics*

C. F. D. Moule, *The Birth of the New Testament*

Raymond Brown, *The Gospel According to John*

F. F. Bruce, *Acts* (Greek Text)

Brevard Childs, *Introduction to the Old Testament as Scripture*

C. E. B. Cranfield, *Romans*	5
George Ladd, *The New Testament and Criticism*	5
Stephen Neill, *The Interpretation of the New Testament 1861–1961*	5

WTS (n = 95)

H. Orton Wiley, *Christian Theology*	21
John Wesley, *Works*	9
John Wesley, *Standard Sermons*	6
Mildred Bangs Wynkoop, *A Theology of Love*	6
C. S. Lewis, *Mere Christianity*	5
H. Richard Niebuhr, *Christ and Culture*	4
Purkiser, Taylor, and Taylor, *God, Man, and Salvation*	4
Karl Barth, *Church Dogmatics*	3
John Bright, *A History of Israel*	3
Colin Brown, *New International Dictionary of N.T. Theology*	3
Rudolf Bultmann, *Theology of the New Testament*	3
Adam Clarke, *Commentaries*	3
George Ladd, *A Theology of the New Testament*	3
Bruce Metzger, *The Text of the New Testament*	3
Leon Morris, *The Apostolic Preaching of the Cross*	3
Herman Ridderbos, *Paul: An Outline of His Theology*	3
James Sire, *The Universe Next Door*	3
Paul Tillich, *Systematic Theology*	3
George Allen Turner, *The Vision That Transforms*	3
Gerhard von Rad, *Old Testament Theology*	3
B. B. Warfield, *The Inspiration and Authority of the Bible*	3

F. INDIVIDUAL BOOKS CITED AS MOST INFLUENTIAL, ETS, IBR, ETS AND IBR

Just ETS (n = 149)

John Calvin, *Institutes of the Christian Religion*	26
George Ladd, *A Theology of the New Testament*	12
Cornelius Van Til, *The Defense of the Faith*	10
Louis Berkhof, *Systematic Theology*	9
C. S. Lewis, *Mere Christianity*	9
Walter Kaiser, *Toward an Old Testament Theology*	8

G. Kittel, *Theological Dictionary of the New Testament*	8
Francis Schaeffer, *The God Who Is There*	8
Carl Henry, *God, Revelation, and Authority*	7
G. C. Berkouwewr, *Studies in Dogmatics*	6
Charles Hodge, *Systematic Theology*	6
A. H. Strong, *Systematic Theology*	6
Geerhardus Vos, *Biblical theology*	6

Just IBR (n = 60)

Gerhard von Rad, *Old Testament Theology*	9
Oscar Cullmann, *Christ and Time*	8
Joachim Jeremias, *The Parables of Jesus*	6
John Bright, *A History of Israel*	5
Karl Barth, *Church Dogmatics*	4
Raymond Brown, *The Gospel According to John*	4
Rudolf Bultmann, *Theology of the New Testament*	4
R. K. Harrison, *Introduction to the Old Testament*	4
Joachim Jeremias, *New Testament Theology*	4
George Ladd, *A Theology of the New Testament*	4
C. F. D. Moule, *The Birth of the New Testament*	4
Herman Ridderbos, *Paul: An Outline of His Theology*	4

Both ETS/IBR (n = 42)

John Calvin, *Institutes of the Christian Religion*	6
George Ladd, *A Theology of the New Testament*	6
Louis Berkhof, *Systematic Theology*	4
Walther Eichrodt, *Old Testament Theology*	4
James Barr, *The Semantics of Biblical Language*	3
John Bright, *A History of Israel*	3
F. F. Bruce, *Acts* (Greek Text)	3
R. K. Harrison, *Introduction to the Old Testament*	3
I. H. Marshall, *New Testament Interpretation*	3
Stephen Neill, *The Interpretation of the New Testament*	3
Herman Ridderbos, *Paul: An Outline of His Theology*	3

Notes

1. INTRODUCTION

Epigraph: 2 Timothy 3:16, Authorized Version.

1. Christopher Hill, *Economic Problems of the Church, from Archbishop Whitgift to the Long Parliament* (Oxford: Clarendon Press, 1956), xii.
2. "Evangelical Christianity in the United States: National Parallel Surveys of General Public and Clergy," conducted for *Christianity Today* by the Gallup Organization, Inc., and the Princeton Religion Research Center (Princeton, NJ: Gallup, n.d. [1979]), 27, 35, 45.
3. Donald A. Hagner, "What Is Distinctive about 'Evangelical' Scholarship?" *TSF Bulletin* (January–February 1984): 5.
4. To cite just one example, the Appendix to this book, which reports on a poll of members of the Evangelical Theological Society, the Institute for Biblical Research, and the Wesleyan Theological Society, shows how relatively few institutional, personal, and denominational connections link members of the Evangelical Theological Society and those of the Wesleyan Theological Society. Yet both groups, by a theological definition, are clearly "evangelical."
5. Other recent books that study roughly this same group, though sometimes employing more normative and theological definitions, include Ernest Sandeen, *The Roots of Fundamentalism: British and American Millenarianism, 1800–1930* (Chicago: University of Chicago Press, 1970); David F. Wells and John D. Woodbridge, eds., *The Evangelicals: What They Believe, Who They Are, Where They Are Changing*, expanded ed. (Grand Rapids: Baker, 1977); John D. Woodbridge, Mark A. Noll, and Nathan O. Hatch, *The Gospel in America: Themes in the Story of America's Evangelicals* (Grand Rapids: Zondervan, 1979); George M. Marsden, *Fundamentalism and American Culture: The Shaping of Twentieth-Century Evangelicalism 1870–1925* (New York: Oxford, 1980); Robert Booth Fowler, *A New Engagement: Evangelical Political Thought, 1966–1976* (Grand Rapids: Eerdmans, 1982); James Davison Hunter, *American Evangelicalism: Conservative Religion and the Quandary of Modernity* (New Brunswick: Rutgers University Press, 1983); and George Marsden, ed., *Evangelicalism and Modern America* (Grand Rapids: Eerdmans, 1984).
6. Marsden, "The Evangelical Denomination," in *Evangelicalism and Modern America*, xiii–xiv.
7. Benjamin B. Warfield, " 'It Says:' 'Scripture Says:' 'God Says'," in *The Works of Benjamin B. Warfield, Vol. I: Revelation and Inspiration* (New York: Oxford, 1927 [reprinted Grand Rapids: Baker, 1981]), 283.

2. RESPONSE TO CRITICISM: 1880–1900

Epigraph: A. A. Hodge and B. B. Warfield, "Inspiration," *Presbyterian Review* 2 (April 1881): 260.

1. For an overview concerning American perception of Scripture before the onset of criticism, see Nathan O. Hatch, "*Sola Scriptura* and *Novus Ordo Seclorum,*" and George M. Marsden, "Everyone One's Own Interpreter? The Bible, Science, and Authority in Mid-Nineteenth-Century America," in *The Bible in America: Essays in Cultural History,* edited by Hatch and Mark A. Noll (New York: Oxford University Press, 1982), 59–78, 79–100.

2. For a convenient summary, see Alan Richardson, "The Rise of Modern Biblical Scholarship and Recent Discussions of the Authority of the Bible," in *The Cambridge History of the Bible, Vol. III: The West from the Reformation to the Present Day,* edited by S. L. Greenslade (Cambridge: Cambridge University Press, 1963), 294–318.

3. See Laurence R. Veysey, *The Emergence of the American University* (Chicago: University of Chicago Press, 1965); and for the special effects on Protestant conservatives, George M. Marsden, "The Collapse of American Evangelical Academia," in *Faith and Rationality: Reason and Belief in God,* edited by Alvin Plantinga and Nicholas Wolterstorff (Notre Dame: University of Notre Dame Press, 1983), 219–64.

4. Carl Becker, *Cornell University: Founders and Founding* (Ithaca: Cornell University Press, 1943), 156.

5. Grant Wacker, "The Demise of Biblical Civilization," in Hatch and Noll, *The Bible in America,* 125.

6. A fine summary is offered by Jerry Wayne Brown, *The Rise of Biblical Criticism in America, 1800–1870: The New England Scholars* (Middletown, CT: Wesleyan University Press, 1969).

7. Samuel Stanhope Smith, *An Essay on the Causes of the Variety of Complexion and Figure in the Human Species* (2d ed., 1810), with an illuminating introduction by Winthrop D. Jordan on Smith's use of science to support orthodoxy (Cambridge: Harvard University Press, 1965); Timothy Dwight, *Theology Explained and Defended in a Series of Sermons . . . ,* edited by Sereno F. Dwight (Edinburgh, 1831), xxiii–xxiv, 399–400; Mark A. Noll, "The Founding of Princeton Seminary," *Westminster Theological Journal 42* (Fall 1979): 72–110; and more generally, Natalie A. Naylor, "The Theological Seminary in the Configuration of American Higher Education: The Ante-Bellum Years," *History of Education Quarterly 17* (Spring 1977): 17–30.

8. For an indication of the breadth of that consensus, see Randall H. Balmer, "The Princetonians and Scripture: A Reconsideration," *Westminster Theological Journal 44* (Spring 1982): 352–65.

9. See especially Theodore Dwight Bozeman, *Protestants in an Age of Science: The Baconian Ideal and Antebellum American Religious Thought* (Chapel Hill: University of North Carolina Press, 1977); and also the literature cited in Mark A. Noll, "Common Sense Traditions and American Evangelical Thought," *American Quarterly 37* (Summer 1985): 216–38.

10. For general accounts, see Lefferts A. Loetscher, *The Broadening Church: A Study of Theological Issues in the Presbyterian Church since 1869* (Philadelphia: University of Pennsylvania Press, 1957), 29–37; and Ira W. Brown, "The Higher Criticism Comes to America," *Journal of the Presbyterian Historical Society 38* (December 1960): 198–99.

11. See the conservative Francis L. Patton's acknowledgment of this in "The Dogmatic Aspect of Pentateuchal Criticism," *Presbyterian Review 4* (April 1883): 361, where Patton expresses his concern not so much about criticism that questions the supernatural, but about "evangelical criticism" held by

those who believe that Christ died to save sinners, who "in other words . . . believe the gospel." A. A. Hodge and B. B. Warfield expressed something of the same when they said that the question lay "between the more strict and the more lax views of Inspiration maintained by *believing* scholars" (my emphasis); "Inspiration," *Presbyterian Review* 2 (April 1881): 236.

12. See W. Neil, "The Criticism and Theological Use of the Bible 1700–1950," in Greenslade, *The Cambridge History of the Bible,* III, 287–88; Ronald Nelson, "Higher Criticism and the Westminster Confession: The Case of William Robertson Smith," *Christian Scholar's Review* 8 (1978): 199–216; and Warner M. Bailey, "William Robertson Smith," *Journal of Presbyterian History 51* (1973): 285–308.

13. Loetscher, *Broadening Church,* 29–30.

14. Charles A. Briggs, "A Critical Study of the Higher Criticism with Special Reference to the Pentateuch," *Presbyterian Review 4* (January 1883): 69.

15. The order in which they appeared in the *Presbyterian Review* was as follows: Charles A. Briggs, "Critical Theories of the Sacred Scriptures in Relation to Their Inspiration," 2 (July 1881): 550–79; Henry Preserved Smith, "The Critical Theories of Julius Wellhausen," *3* (April 1882): 357–88; Samuel I. Curtiss, "Delitzsch on the Origin and Composition of the Pentateuch," *3* (July 1882): 553–88; Charles A. Briggs, "A Critical Study of the Higher Criticism with Special Reference to the Pentateuch" *4* (January 1883): 69–130.

16. Curtiss, "Delitzsch on the Pentateuch," 588; Briggs, "Critical Study of the Higher Criticism," 130.

17. Preserved Smith, "Critical Theories of Wellhausen," 371.

18. Briggs, "Critical Theories," 555, 552.

19. Ibid., 558.

20. Preserved Smith, "Critical Theories of Wellhausen," 386; and for an almost identical affirmation, Briggs, "Critical Theories," 557.

21. Curtiss, "Delitzsch on the Pentateuch," 573–74.

22. Briggs, "Critical Theories," 557; and for very similar statements, Preserved Smith, "Critical Theories of Wellhausen," 374 n; and Briggs, "Critical Study of the Higher Criticism," 99.

23. Here is the order in which they appeared in the *Presbyterian Review:* Hodge and Warfield, "Inspiration" 2 (April 1881): 225–60; Green, "Professor W. Robertson Smith on the Pentateuch" *3* (January 1882): 108–56; Beecher, "The Logical Methods of Professor Kuenen" *3* (October 1882): 701–31; Patton, "The Dogmatic Aspects of Pentateuchal Criticism" *4* (April 1883): 341–410.

24. Hodge and Warfield, "Inspiration," 237.

25. Beecher, "Methods of Kuenen," 731; Hodge and Warfield, "Inspiration," 243. See ibid., 244, for the determination to first present the doctrine before examining the phenomena critically.

26. Green, "Robertson Smith on the Pentateuch," 111; Beecher, "Methods of Kuenen," 705. For a statement about the values of a proper criticism, see also Patton, "Dogmatic Aspects of Pentateuchal Criticism," 344.

27. Hodge and Warfield, "Inspiration," 238.

28. Briggs, "Critical Theories," 552, 559–79; Briggs, "Critical Study of the Higher Criticism," 70–74, and *passim.*

29. Patton, "Dogmatic Aspects of Pentateuchal Criticism," 346–47, 362–64, 396–400. This debate over the church's historical position has recently been given

an uncanny reprise in works by Jack B. Rogers and Donald K. McKim, *The Authority and Interpretation of the Bible: An Historical Approach* (San Francisco: Harper & Row, 1979), and John D. Woodbridge, *Biblical Authority: A Critique of the Rogers-McKim Proposal* (Grand Rapids: Zondervan, 1982). As in the earlier exchange, the more conservative position seems clearly stronger in the exact matter under consideration. Briggs and Rogers/McKim may be correct that the older statements did not mean to affirm exactly what Patton and Woodbridge did about the Bible's detailed inerrancy, but it is impossible to make the older spokesmen say anything which could sanction the revolutionary new views proposed to Americans in the nineteenth century. Woodbridge is especially helpful in showing that conservatives on the Continent had been dealing with critical views of one sort or another for nearly two centuries before they burst on the American scene; hence, there was no need to swoon before the supposedly assured results of "modern" scholarship. On the other side of the issue, the conservative case may not be as strong as it appears if the information and interpretations of the modern era pose problems concerning Scripture that preceding generations had not faced. In that case, neither side carries the day by providing answers from church history for questions which took on a new shape in the critical era.

30. Patton, "Dogmatic Aspects of Pentateuchal Criticism," 379; Green, "Robertson Smith on the Pentateuch," 122, with similar sentiments on 119.
31. Beecher, "Methods of Kuenen," 707, 729–30.
32. Green, "Robertson Smith on the Pentateuch," 109.
33. Preserved Smith, "Critical Theories of Wellhausen," 370.
34. Beecher, "Methods of Kuenen," 705–07.
35. Hodge and Warfield, "Inspiration," 242.
36. Patton, "Dogmatic Aspects of Pentateuchal Criticism," 396.
37. Green, "Robertson Smith on the Pentateuch," 156.
38. Hodge and Warfield, "Inspiration," 241. For a good discussion of Jowett and *Essays and Reviews*, see Owen Chadwick, *The Victorian Church: Part II*, 2d ed. (London: A. & C. Black, 1972), 177.
39. Hodge and Warfield, "Inspiration," 242.
40. Green, "Primeval Chronology," *Bibliotheca Sacra 47* (April 1890): 285–303; Warfield, "Calvin's Doctrine of the Creation," *Princeton Theological Review 13* (April 1915), as found in Benjamin B. Warfield, *The Works of Benjamin B. Warfield, Vol. V: Calvin and Calvinism* (New York: Oxford University Press, 1931), 287–349, especially 299–306. Beecher, "The Literary Form of the Biblical History of Ruth and Judges," *Journal of Biblical Literature 4* (1884): 3–28; and "The Historical Situation in Joel and Obadiah," *Journal of Biblical Literature 8* (1888): 14–40.
41. Hodge and Warfield, "Inspiration," 241.
42. Beecher, "Methods of Kuenen," 704.
43. Patton, "Dogmatic Aspects of Pentateuchal Criticism," 402, 410.
44. Hodge and Warfield, "Inspiration," 237–38.
45. See number 6 in text above, page 24.
46. Ira Brown, "The Higher Criticism Comes to America," 203; Norman H. Maring, "Baptists and Changing Views of the Bible, 1865–1918 (Part II)," *Foundations 1* (October 1958): 30; and more generally Daniel Day Williams, *The Andover Liberals: A Study in American Theology* (New York: Columbia University Press, 1941).

47. Maring, "Baptists and Changing Views of the Bible, 1865–1918 (Part I)," *Foundations 1* (July 1958): 63–64.
48. Ibid., 64; Maring, "Baptists and the Bible (Part II)," 45–47.
49. Ira Brown, "The Higher Criticism Comes to America," 205.
50. Loetscher, *Broadening Church*, 48–74.
51. Ibid., 38–39.
52. Quoted in ibid., 50.
53. Talbot W. Chambers, "The Inaugural Address of Professor Briggs," *Presbyterian and Reformed Review* 2 (July 1891): 493.
54. One can only wonder, however, if the long-term results of the trials were propitious for the conservative cause. On this matter, G. Ernest Wright once observed, "As was the case in Scotland [with W. Robertson Smith], the trials [of Briggs and Preserved Smith] did more than anything else could possibly have done to further the new views in this country"; Wright, "The Study of the Old Testament," in *Protestant Thought in the Twentieth Century: Whence and Whither?* edited by Arnold S. Nash (New York: Macmillan, 1951), 19.
55. See, for example, the essays on "The Inerrancy of the Original Autographs" (1893) and "The Divine and Human in the Bible" (1894), anthologized in *The Princeton Theology 1812–1921*, edited by Mark A. Noll (Grand Rapids: Baker, 1983), 268–79.
56. Ernest W. Saunders, *Searching the Scriptures: A History of the Society of Biblical Literature, 1880–1980* (Chico, CA: Scholars Press, 1982), 11, with list of SBL presidents, 117–18. The informative work of Professor Olbricht of Abilene Christian University is found in several unpublished papers, including "The Society of Biblical Literature: The Founding Fathers," "The First Ten Years of *The Journal of Biblical Literature:* An Analysis of Content," and "Biblical Primitivism in American Biblical Scholarship, 1630–1870."
57. *Journal of Biblical Literature* 20 (1901): xv; Chadwick, *Victorian Church: Part Two*, 102.
58. For an overview of Green's career and a helpful bibliography, see "The Jubilee of Prof. William Henry Green," *Presbyterian and Reformed Review* 7 (July 1896): 507–21.
59. See the essays in *Hebraica* on "The Pentateuchal Question" by Harper: 5 (1888–1889): 18–73, 243–91; 6 (1889–1890): 1–48, 241–95; and by Green: 5 (1889): 137–89; 6 (1890): 109–38, 161–211; and 7 (1890–1891): 1–38, 104–42. A number of substantial essays by Green on the Pentateuch appeared in the *Presbyterian and Reformed Review* 4–5 (1893–1894), including "Briggs' Higher Criticism of the Hexateuch," "Critical Views Respecting the Mosaic Tabernacle," "Klostermann on the Pentateuch," "Moses of the Critics," and "Sons of God and Daughters of Men."
60. William Henry Green, "The Pentateuchal Question," *Hebraica* 5 (1889): 137.
61. The *Presbyterian and Reformed Review* and *Bibliotheca Sacra*, among other publications, regularly carried essays of this nature.
62. J. Estill Jones, "The New Testament and Southern [Seminary]," *Review and Expositor 82* (Winter 1985): 21–29, with quotation on 22.
63. See Floyd F. Filson, "The Study of the New Testament," in *Protestant Thought in the Twentieth Century 52*; Merrill M. Parvis, "New Testament Criticism in the World-War Periods," in *The Study of the Bible Today and Tomorrow*, edited by Harold R. Willoughby (Chicago: University of Chicago Press, 1947), 55.

232 / NOTES TO PAGES 32-36

3. DECLINE: 1900–1935

Epigraph: W. H. Griffith Thomas, "Old Testament Criticism and New Testament Christianity," in *The Fundamentals,* four vols. (Grand Rapids: Baker, 1972 [from 1917 four-vol. edition issued by the Bible Institute of Los Angeles; orig. 1910–1915]), I, 133.

1. Robert W. Funk, "The Watershed of the American Biblical Tradition: The Chicago School, First Phase, 1892–1920," *Journal of Biblical Literature* 95 (1976): 7.

2. Where the population of the United States increased slightly more than three times from 1870 to 1930, the number of college degrees increased twenty-threefold, faculty twenty-sixfold, and student enrollment twenty-ninefold. Figures are from *Historical Statistics of the United States: Colonial Times to 1957* (Washington, D.C.: Bureau of the Census, 1960), 210–12. For general accounts of the widespread changes in Western higher education during this period, see Fritz K. Ringer, *Education and Society in Modern Europe* (Bloomington: Indiana University Press, 1979); and A. J. Engel, *From Clergymen to Don: The Rise of the Academic Profession in Nineteenth-Century Oxford* (Oxford: Clarendon Press, 1983).

3. G. Ernest Wright, "The Study of the Old Testament," in *Protestant Thought in the Twentieth Century: Whence and Whither?,* edited by Arnold S. Nash (New York: Macmillan, 1951), 18.

4. The story of this change deserves a complete intellectual and social history. Hints as to what it should contain are found in Alexandra Oleson and John Voss, eds., *The Organization of Knowledge in Modern America, 1860–1920* (Baltimore: Johns Hopkins University Press, 1979); Robert A. McCaughey, "The Transformation of American Academic Life: Harvard University 1821–1892," *Perspectives in American History* 8 (1974): 239–332; Burton J. Bledstein, *The Culture of Professionalism: The Middle Class and the Development of Higher Education in America* (New York: W. W. Norton, 1976); Mark A. Noll, "Christian Thinking and the Rise of the American University," *Christian Scholar's Review* 9 (1979): 3–16; and the sources cited in Chapter 2, note 3.

5. See James R. Moore, *The Post-Darwinian Controversies: A Study of the Protestant Struggle to Come to Terms with Darwin in Great Britain and America 1870–1900* (Cambridge: Cambridge University Press, 1979); Gary Scott Smith, *The Seeds of Secularization: Calvinism, Culture, and Pluralism in America 1870–1915* (Grand Rapids: Eerdmans, 1985), 93–111; and David N. Livingstone, *Darwin's Forgotten Disciples: The Encounter Between Evangelical Theology and Evolutionary Thought* (Grand Rapids: Eerdmans, 1987).

6. Owen W. Gates, "A General Index of the First Twenty Volumes," *Journal of Biblical Literature* 20 (1901): 175–81; Gates, "A General Index of Volumes XXI to XL," *Journal of Biblical Literature* 40 (1921): 185–93; yearly tables of contents, *Presbyterian Review* 1–10 (1880–1889); Joseph H. Dulles, "Index Volumes I to X," *Presbyterian and Reformed Review* 10 (1899): 727–98; "Index Volumes I–XXVII," *Princeton Theological Review* 27 (1929): 500–18. John Dewey's contribution to the *Presbyterian and Reformed Review* was a brief response to the query, "What is Animal Life?" vol. 1 (1890): 453–57.

7. See the prominence of moderate evangelicals like Charles Briggs, Francis Brown, F. B. Denio, Philip Schaff, William Arnold Stevens, and Milton S. Terry in Gates, "General Index," *Journal of Biblical Literature* 20 (1901): 175–81. Thomas Olbricht also charts the prominence of moderate views among early leaders of the SBL in the papers cited in Chapter 2, note 56.

8. Lefferts A. Loetscher, "C. A. Briggs in the Retrospect of Half a Century," *Theology Today 12* (April 1955): 27–42, quotation 41.
9. See George M. Marsden, *Fundamentalism and American Culture: The Shaping of Twentieth-Century Evangelicalism, 1870–1925* (New York: Oxford University Press, 1980), 43–123.
10. See, for example, Warfield, "The Gospel and the Second Coming" (1915) and "Antichrist" (1915), in *Selected Shorter Writings of Benjamin B. Warfield, Vol. I*, edited by John E. Meeter (Phillipsburg, NJ: Presbyterian and Reformed, 1970), 348–55, 356–62.
11. Marsden, *Fundamentalism and American Culture*, 141–84.
12. Figures are from the four-volume edition; see Chapter 3, epigraph note.
13. Dyson Hague, "The History of the Higher Criticism," in *The Fundamentals*, I, 37.
14. For perfunctory assertions, see William Caven, "The Testimony of Christ to the Old Testament," 225–26. In contrast is the more positive attitude of James Orr, "Holy Scripture and Modern Negations," 96: "By all means, let criticism have its rights. Let purely literary questions about the Bible receive full and fair discussion. Let the structure of books be impartially examined. If a reverent science has light to throw on the composition or authority or age of these books, let its voice be heard. . . . No fright, therefore, need be taken at the mere word, 'Criticism.' "
15. Reeve, "My Personal Experience with the Higher Criticism," 349.
16. George L. Robinson, "One Isaiah," 349; Joseph D. Wilson, "The Book of Daniel," 259; Dyson Hague, "The Doctrinal Value of the First Chapter of Genesis," 275. Similar views are found in Hague, "History of Higher Criticism," 40; Griffith Thomas, "Old Testament Criticism," 138; David Heagle, "The Tabernacle in the Wilderness," 155; James Orr, "The Early Narratives of Genesis," 233; Reeve, "Personal Experience," 348–49.
17. The assessment of the internal strength of *The Fundamentals* is more favorable in Ferenc Morton Szasz, *The Divided Mind of Protestant America* (University, AL: University of Alabama Press, 1982), 78–80, than in Marsden, *Fundamentalism and American Culture*, 118–22. For the fuller story of *The Fundamentals*, see Ernest R. Sandeen, *The Roots of Fundamentalism: British and American Millenarianism, 1800–1930* (Chicago: University of Chicago Press, 1970), 188–207.
18. Hague, "History of Higher Criticism," *The Fundamentals*, I, 40–41.
19. Ibid., 31. Johnson, "Fallacies of the Higher Criticism," 63; Anderson, "Christ and Criticism," 125–26.
20. Hague, "History of Higher Criticism," 12; Caven, "Testimony of Christ," 211–12.
21. F. Bettex, "The Bible and Modern Criticism," 76; Robinson, "One Isaiah," 242–45.
22. For example, Griffith Thomas, "Old Testament Criticism," 143–45; Heagle, "The Tabernacle in the Wilderness," 187.
23. Hague, "Doctrinal Value of the First Chapter of Genesis," 280.
24. Orr, "Early Narratives of Genesis," 237, 239, 240.
25. Orr, "Holy Scripture and Modern Negation," 109.
26. Orr, "Science and Christian Faith," 346.
27. Orr, "Early Narratives of Genesis," 233, 240; "Science and Christian Faith," 337.
28. Franklin Johnson, "Fallacies of Higher Criticism," 75, with a similar opinion in Griffith Thomas, "Old Testament Criticism," 133.

29. G. Osborn Troop, "Internal Evidence of the Fourth Gospel," 200.

30. Sandeen, *Roots of Fundamentalism*, 206–07.

31. William R. Hutchison, *The Modernist Impulse in American Protestantism* (Cambridge: Harvard University Press, 1976), 198–99.

32. Thomas S. Kuhn, *The Structure of Scientific Revolutions* (2d ed., Chicago: University of Chicago Press, 1970). For useful commentary, see also Gary Gutting, ed., *Paradigms and Revolutions: Applications and Appraisals of Thomas Kuhn's Philosophy of Science* (Notre Dame, IN: University of Notre Dame Press, 1980).

33. Wright, "Study of the Old Testament," 20.

34. Bowman, "Old Testament Research Between the Wars," in *The Study of the Bible Today and Tomorrow*, edited by Harold R. Willoughby (Chicago: University of Chicago Press, 1947), 12.

35. See Robert E. Clements, *One Hundred Years of Old Testament Interpretation* (Philadelphia: Westminster, 1976); Stephen Neil, *The Interpretation of the New Testament 1861–1961* (Oxford: Oxford University Press, 1964); Werner Georg Kümmel, *The New Testament: The History of the Investigation of its Problems* (Nashville: Abingdon, 1972); F. F. Bruce, "The History of New Testament Study," in *New Testament Interpretation: Essays on Principles and Methods*, edited by I. Howard Marshall (Grand Rapids: Eerdmans, 1977), 31–59; Amos N. Wilder, "New Testament Studies, 1920–1950: Reminiscences of a Changing Discipline," *The Journal of Religion 64* (October 1984): 432–51; and Robert M. Grant, "American New Testament Study, 1926–1956," *Journal of Biblical Literature 87* (1968): 42–50.

36. This is also the conclusion of a paper that was helpful in the preparation of this section, John G. Stackhouse, Jr., "Lost in Space: *The Fundamentals* and the Polarization of American Theology, 1910–1925" (seminar paper, University of Chicago, 1983).

37. Quoted in Norman H. Maring, "Baptists and Changing Views of the Bible, 1865–1918 (Part I)," *Foundations 1* (July 1958): 68; see also the companion piece in this fine series by Maring, "Baptists and Changing Views of the Bible, 1865–1918 (Part II), *Foundations 1* (October 1958): 30–61.

38. Quoted in Maring, "Baptists and Changing Views of the Bible (Part II)," 56.

39. Carl F. H. Henry, *Personal Idealism and Strong's Theology* (Wheaton, IL: Van Kampen, 1951); Grant Wacker, *Augustus H. Strong and the Dilemma of Historical Consciousness* (Macon, GA: Mercer University Press, 1985).

40. SBL membership lists are found in the *Journal of Biblical Literature 20* (1901): xv–xix, and 40 (1921): xi–xix. On Toy, see Joel Drinkard, Jr. and Page H. Kelley, "125 Years of Old Testament Study at Southern [Seminary]," *Review and Expositor 82* (Winter 1985): 7–19.

41. E. Glenn Hinson, "Southern Baptists and the Liberal Tradition in Biblical Interpretation, 1845–1945"; Claude L. Howe, Jr., "Southern Baptists and the Moderate Tradition in Biblical Interpretation, 1845–1945"; Richard D. Land, "Southern Baptists and the Fundamentalist Tradition in Biblical Interpretation, 1845–1945," *Baptist History and Heritage 19* (July 1984): 17, 25–26, 30. For a general account, see William E. Ellis, "*A Man of Books and a Man of the People": E. Y. Mullins and the Crisis of Moderate Southern Baptist Leadership* (Macon, GA: Mercer University Press, 1985).

42. Mullins, "The Testimony of Christian Experience," in *The Fundamentals*, IV, 319–22.

43. John H. Leith, ed., *Creeds of the Churches*, 3d ed. (Atlanta: John Knox, 1982), 345–46.

44. See John E. Meeter and Roger Nicole, *A Bibliography of Benjamin Breckinridge Warfield 1851–1921* (Nutley, NJ: Presbyterian and Reformed, 1974).
45. Warfield, "Inspiration," *The International Standard Bible Encyclopedia* (1915), from *The Works of Benjamin B. Warfield, Vol. I* (New York: Oxford University Press, 1929), 104.
46. John D. Davis, "Current Old Testament Discussions and Princeton Opinion," *Presbyterian and Reformed Review 13* (April 1902): 177–206, with quotations 188–89, 194–95.
47. Robert Dick Wilson, *A Scientific Investigation of the Old Testament* (Philadelphia: The Sunday School Times Co., 1926), 6–7, 11–12.
48. Edwin H. Rian, "Theological Conflicts of the 1920s and 1930s in the Presbyterian Church and on the Princeton Seminary Campus," *The Princeton Seminary Bulletin,* new ser., 5 (1984): 219.
49. Machen, *The Virgin Birth of Christ* (New York: Harper and Brothers, 1930), 381.
50. The extensive reviews of the two major books are discussed in Ned B. Stonehouse, *J. Gresham Machen: A Biographical Memoir* (Grand Rapids: Eerdmans, 1954), 328–34, 515.
51. During the period 1897–1899, for example, Vos contributed major essays to the *Presbyterian and Reformed Review* on the critical scholarship concerning Isaiah, Micah, Amos, and Hosea.
52. Richard B. Gaffin, Jr., "Introduction" to *Redemptive History and Biblical Interpretation: The Shorter Writings of Geerhardus Vos* (Phillipsburg, NJ: Presbyterian and Reformed, 1980), xv.
53. See the "Bibliography" in ibid., 547–59.
54. John W. Hart, "Princeton Theological Seminary: The Reorganization of 1929," *Journal of Presbyterian History 58* (Summer 1980): 124–40.
55. See Paolo E. Coletta, *William Jennings Bryan, Vol. III: Political Puritan 1915–1925* (Lincoln: University of Nebraska Press, 1969), 267.
56. For overviews from a critic and an advocate, see respectively Clarence B. Bass, *Backgrounds to Dispensationalism: Its Historical Genesis and Ecclesiastical Implications* (Grand Rapids: Eerdmans, 1960); and C. C. Ryrie, *Dispensationalism Today* (Chicago: Moody, 1965).
57. Sandeen, *Roots of Fundamentalism,* 222–24, 233–34.
58. As one example of this work, see the substantial one-volume work edited by British Plymouth Brethren and written exclusively by American and British Brethren, *A New Testament Commentary* (based on the Revised Standard Version), edited by G. C. D. Howley, F. F. Bruce, and H. L. Ellison (London: Pickering and Inglis, 1969).
59. James H. Brookes, *The Truth 5* (1879): 314, as quoted by Timothy P. Weber, "The Two-Edged Sword: The Fundamentalist Use of the Bible," in *The Bible in America: Essays in Cultural History* (New York: Oxford University Press, 1982), 110.
60. For old Princeton's impatience with dispensationalism, see B. B. Warfield, review of R. A. Torrey's *What the Bible Teaches,* in *Presbyterian and Reformed Review 10* (July 1899): 562–64; and more aggressively, O. T. Allis, *Prophecy and the Church: An Examination of the Claim of Dispensationalists That the Christian Church Is a Mystery Parenthesis Which Interrupts the Fulfillment to Israel of the Kingdom Prophecies of the Old Testament* (Philadelphia: Presbyterian and Reformed, 1945). For the dispensationalist-Princeton alliance, see Sandeen, *Roots of Fundamentalism,* 103–31; Marsden, *Fundamentalism and American Culture,*

109–18; and George W. Dollar, *A History of Fundamentalism in America* (Green-ville, SC: Bob Jones University Press, 1973), 173–83.

61. F. Lincoln, "Biographical Sketch," prefaced to Lewis Sperry Chafer, *Systematic Theology, Vol. VIII* (Dallas: Dallas Seminary Press, 1948), 5–6.

62. On the greater flexibility of modern dispensationalists, see Robert Saucey, "Contemporary Dispensational Thought," *TSF Bulletin* 7 (March–April 1984): 10–11; and Saucey, "Dispensationalism and the Salvation of the Kingdom," *TSF Bulletin* 7 (May–June 1984): 6–7.

63. See Joel A. Carpenter, "Fundamentalist Institutions and the Rise of Evangelical Protestantism, 1929–1942," *Church History* 49 (March 1980): 62–75.

64. Drinkard and Kelly, "Old Testament Study at Southern," 14.

4. AN ALTERNATIVE: GREAT BRITAIN, 1860–1937

Epigraph: James Orr, *Revelation and Inspiration* (New York: Charles Scribner's Sons, 1910), 175.

1. From Peter Toon, *Evangelical Theology 1833–1856: A Response to Tractarianism* (Atlanta: John Knox, 1979), 5.

2. J. C. Ryle, "Evangelical Religion," in *Knots Untied. Being Plain Statements on Disputed Points in Religion from the Standpoint of an Evangelical Churchman* (London: William Hunt, 1883), 4–6.

3. For general overview, see the scholarly treatments by Owen Chadwick, *The Victorian Church*, two vols. (2d ed., London: A. & C. Black, 1972); and a monograph that concentrates on the nineteenth century by Doreen Rosman, *Evangelicals and Culture* (Dover, NH: Croom Helm, 1984). More popular is David L. Edwards, *Christian England, Volume 3: From the 18th Century to the First World War* (Grand Rapids: Eerdmans, 1984); and Randle Manwaring, *From Controversy to Coexistence: Evangelicals in the Church of England 1914–1980* (Cambridge: Cambridge University Press, 1985).

4. This chapter depends heavily on the following sources for the general outline of events: Stephen Neill, *The Interpretation of the New Testament 1861–1961* (Oxford: Oxford University Press, 1964); Chadwick, "History and the Bible," in *The Victorian Church, Vol. II,* 40–111; H. D. McDonald, *Theories of Revelation, An Historical Study, 1860–1960,* bound with *Ideas of Revelation, An Historical Study, A.D. 1700 to A.D. 1860* (Grand Rapids: Baker, 1979 [orig. 1963]); Willis B. Glover, *Evangelical Nonconformity and Higher Criticism in the Nineteenth Century* (London: Independent Press, 1954); David F. Wright, "Soundings in the Doctrine of Scripture in British Evangelicalism in the First Half of the Twentieth Century," *Tyndale Bulletin 31* (1980): 87–106; F. F. Bruce, "The History of New Testament Study," in *New Testament Interpretation,* edited by I. Howard Marshall (Grand Rapids: Eerdmans, 1977), 21–59; and Thomas A. Langford, "Authority: Nonconformity and the Bible" and "Authority: Anglicanism, the Bible, and the Creeds," in *In Search of Foundations: English Theology 1900–1920* (Nashville: Abingdon, 1969), 88–142. In addition, two books which came to my attention late add significantly to the story, especially by noting the different paths to criticism in England, Germany, and Scotland. John Rogerson, *Old Testament Criticism in the Nineteenth Century: England and Germany* (Philadelphia: Fortress, 1984); and Richard A. Riesen, *Criticism and Faith in Late Victorian Scotland: A. B. Davidson, William Robertson Smith and George Adam Smith* (Lanham, MD: University Press of America, 1985). Although these books do not deal with America directly, they are nonetheless relevant, be-

cause American biblical scholars paid close attention to developments in
Germany and Scotland as well as in England.

5. Benjamin Jowett, "On the Interpretation of Scripture," in *Essays and Reviews*
(London: John W. Parker & Sons, 1860), 337, 338.

6. See Ieuan Ellis, *Seven Against Christ: A Study of "Essays and Reviews"* (Leiden:
E. J. Brill, 1980).

7. Neill, *Interpretation of the New Testament*, 31. Neill's own opinion, ibid., was that
although *Essays and Reviews* was neither a convincing book nor one which
Anglican clergymen should have written, it was nevertheless a mistake to
attempt its suppression: "The tide could not be turned back. It was quite
certain in 1860 that criticism had come to stay, and that henceforward the
Bible would be treated like any other book. No holds would be barred. The
Scriptures would be subject to ruthless examination. Unless they were able
on their own merits to stand up to the challenge, the cause might be held to
be lost in advance."

As an example of sentiment at the time, the high churchman E. B. Pusey
spent the last portion of his life defending traditional views on the book
of Daniel; see John Kenneth Mozley, *Some Tendencies in British Theology from
the Publication of "Lux Mundi" to the Present Day* (London: SPCK, 1951), 10–
13.

8. As Westcott, Light, and Hort; see Neill, *Interpretation of the New Testament*, 34
n2.

9. Glover, *Nonconformity and Higher Criticism*, 120.

10. The treatment of these three in Neill, *Interpretation of the New Testament*, 33–97,
is outstanding.

11. See Hort's letter to Lightfoot, May 1, 1860, in which he refuses to make "a
decided conviction of the absolute infallibility of the N.T. practically a *sine qua
non* for co-operation [on scholarly projects]." Although Hort was "most
anxious to find the N.T. infallible," and although he had "a strong sense of
the Divine purpose guiding all its parts," he could not "see how the exact
limits of such guidance can be ascertained except by unbiased *a posteriori*
criticism." Arthur Fenton Hort, *Life and Letters of Fenton John Anthony Hort*, two
vols. (London: Macmillan, 1896), I, 420.

12. Neill, *Interpretation of the New Testament*, 37.

13. Glover, *Nonconformity and Higher Criticism*, 18–27 and *passim*.

14. S. R. Driver, *An Introduction to the Literature of the Old Testament* (Gloucester,
MA: Peter Smith, 1972 [orig. 1897]), vii–x.

15. Charles Gore, "The Holy Spirit and Inspiration," in *Lux Mundi*, 5th ed.
(London: John Murray, 1890), 349, 347–48, 351, 355–56, 352. See also 354,
where Gore denies that inspiration by the Holy Spirit entailed "a miraculous
communication such as would make the recorder independent of the ordinary process of historical tradition." In addition, ibid., "there is nothing in
the doctrine of inspiration to prevent our recognizing a considerable idealiz-
ing element in the Old Testament history."

16. Ibid., 360–61.

17. Wright, "Soundings in the Doctrine of Scripture," 97. Confirmation for this
judgment is found in two works by Richard Riesen which examine the begin-
nings of criticism within the Scottish Free Church, a body known in the
second half of the nineteenth century for its orthodoxy: " 'Higher Criticism'
in the Free Church Fathers," *Records of the Scottish Church History Society* 20
(1979): 119–42; and *Criticism and Faith in Late Victorian Scotland*.

18. Alfred Cave, *The Inspiration of the Old Testament Inductively Considered* (2d ed., London: Congregational Union of England and Wales, 1888), 17.

19. For a negative view, see Glover, *Nonconformists and Higher Criticism*, 186, 190; more positive is H. D. McDonald, *Theories of Revelation*, 185.

20. On Sayce, see Barbara Zink MacHaffie, " 'Monument Facts and Higher Critical Fancies': Archaeology and the Popularization of Old Testament Criticism in Nineteenth-Century Britain," *Church History* 50 (September 1981): 316–28.

21. Both quoted in Glover, *Nonconformity and Higher Criticism*, 220.

22. Ibid., 244–45; McDonald, *Theories of Revelation*, 185.

23. R. D. Wilson, "The Aramaic of Daniel," in *Biblical and Theological Studies by the Members of the Faculty of Princeton Theological Seminary* (New York: Charles Scribner's Sons, 1912), 261–306.

24. This paragraph depends upon D. W. Bebbington, "The Persecution of George Jackson: A British Fundamentalist Controversy," in *Persecution and Toleration*, edited by W. J. Shiels, Studies in Church History 21 (Oxford: Oxford University Press, 1984), 421–33.

25. McDonald, *Theories of Revelation*, 208.

26. Ibid.; Wright, "Soundings in the Doctrine of Scripture," 95–96.

27. See Mozley, *Some Tendencies in British Theology*, 130–36; I. Howard Marshall, "James Denney," in *Creative Minds in Contemporary Theology*, edited by Philip Edgcumbe Hughes (Grand Rapids: Eerdmans, 1966), 203–38; and David F. Wells, "Introduction," to James F. Denney's 1895 book, *Studies in Theology* (Grand Rapids: Baker, 1976), v–xxvi.

28. Quoted in Wells, "Introduction" to Denney, *Studies in Theology*, xv.

29. Denney, *Studies in Theology*, 202, 204, 207, 209.

30. Quoted in Wells, "Introduction" to Denney, *Studies in Theology*, xxii.

31. Orr, *Revelation and Inspiration*, 147–54 on kenoticism; quotations from 154, 153, 215, 217, 198.

32. Neill, *Interpretation of the New Testament*, 95.

33. J. Russell Howden, *Evangelicalism* (London: Chas. J. Thynne & Jarvis, 1925), vi.

34. G. T. Manley, "The Inspiration and Authority of the Bible," in ibid., 136, 146–47.

35. This account follows Douglas Johnson, *Contending for the Faith: A History of the Evangelical Movement in the Universities and Colleges* (Leicester, Eng.: Inter-Varsity Press, 1979); and J. C. Pollock, *A Cambridge Movement* (London: John Murray, 1953).

36. Johnson, *Contending for the Faith*, 210.

37. For interesting reflections on this early period, see R. T. France, "The Tyndale Fellowship—Then and Now," *TSF Bulletin* (January/February 1982) 12–13; I. Howard Marshall, "F. F. Bruce as a Biblical Scholar," *Journal of the Christian Brethren Research Fellowship* 22 (1971): 5–12, distributed with *TSF Newsletter* (Spring 1975); and F. F. Bruce, *In Retrospect: Remembrance of Things Past* (Grand Rapids: Eerdmans, 1980), 110–11, 122–29, 173–74.

38. McDonald, *Theories of Revelation*, 208.

39. See Wright, "Soundings in the Doctrine of Scripture," 92–101.

40. A. J. Engel, *From Clergyman to Don: The Rise of the Academic Profession in Nineteenth-Century Oxford* (Oxford: Clarendon Press, 1983), 286, 294.

41. F. W. Dillistone, *C. H. Dodd: Interpreter of the New Testament* (Grand Rapids: Eerdmans, 1977), 48–49, 74–75; and for an evaluation of Dodd as relatively

conservative, F. F. Bruce, "C. H. Dodd," in *Creative Minds in Contemporary Theology*, 267.

42. C. H. Dodd, "Arthur Samuel Peake," *Dictionary of National Biography*, volume for 1922–1930, 657–58.

43. This general point is made also by Robert M. Grant, "American New Testament Study, 1926–1956," *Journal of Biblical Literature* 87 (1968): 48.

44. Hugh Hawkins, *Between Harvard and America: The Educational Leadership of Charles W. Eliot* (New York: Oxford University Press, 1972), 173–77.

45. F. F. Bruce has been the most prominent of these; for Bruce's own reflections on the subject, see his presidential address to the Society for New Testament Study, "The New Testament and Classical Study," *New Testament Studies* 22 (1975–1976): 229–42, especially 235–36.

46. For general background, see Wright, "Soundings in the Doctrine of Scripture"; and George Marsden, "Fundamentalism as an American Phenomenon, A Comparison with English Evangelicalism," *Church History 46* (June 1977): 215–32.

47. This paragraph follows McDonald, *Ideas of Revelation 1700–1860*, 266–88.

5. RETURN: 1935–1974

Epigraph: Arnold W. Hearn, "Fundamentalist Renascence," *Christian Century* (April 30, 1958): 528.

1. Gregory G. Bolich, *Karl Barth and Evangelicalism* (Downers Grove, IL: Inter-Varsity Press, 1980), 57–62, 66–73, 77–86; and Donald Dayton, "Karl Barth and Evangelicalism: The Varieties of a Sibling Rivalry," *TSF Bulletin* 8 (May–June 1985): 18–23.

2. Amos N. Wilder, "New Testament Studies, 1920–1950: Reminiscences of a Changing Discipline," *Journal of Religion 64* (October 1984): 444; a similar description that also singles out Cadbury's book is found in Robert M. Grant, "American New Testament Study, 1926–1956," *Journal of Biblical Literature 87* (1968): 46.

3. Nels F. S. Ferré, "Present Trends in Protestant Thought," *Religion in Life,* 17 (1948): 336.

4. See G. Ernest Wright, "The Study of the Old Testament: The Changing Mood in the Household of Wellhausen," in *Protestant Thought in the Twentieth Century, Whence and Whither?* edited by Arnold S. Nash (New York: Macmillan, 1951), 31 ff.

5. Grant, "American New Testament Study," 47.

6. Floyd Filson, "The Study of the New Testament: Through Historical Study to Biblical Theology," in *Protestant Thought in the Twentieth Century*, 64. Filson also spoke a word of appreciation for "such militant conservatives as J. G. Machen" who, while "not infallible on critical questions" and "not winsome in theological debate," were nonetheless "far truer to fact than much shallow theology which often marked the social gospel," 60. The same cautious notes could be heard from other mainline sources at the time, e.g., T. W. Manson, "The Failure of Liberalism to Interpret the Bible as the Word of God," in *The Interpretation of the Bible* (London: SPCK, 1944), 92–107; and several of the essays in *The Study of the Bible Today and Tomorrow*, edited by Harold R. Willoughby (Chicago: University of Chicago Press, 1947).

7. It is interesting to note that Willis B. Glover in 1954 used the term "neo-evangelicals" to describe the work of those linked in the parody, "Thou shalt

love the Lord thy Dodd with all thy Barth and thy Niebuhrs as thyself" Evangelical Nonconformity and Higher Criticism in the Nineteenth Century (London: Independent Press, 1954), 7.

8. The forthcoming book on Fuller Seminary by George M. Marsden contain full consideration of Ockenga.

9. "Billy Graham Recounts the Origin of Christianity Today," Christianity Toda (July 17, 1981): 26.

10. Joel A. Carpenter, "A Shelter in the Time of Storm: Fundamentalist Institu tions and the Rise of Evangelical Protestantism, 1929–1942," Church Histor 49 (March 1980): 68–69.

11. Wheaton College catalogues.

12. Kenneth Kantzer, "Documenting the Dramatic Shift in Seminaries from Lib eral to Conservative," Christianity Today (February 4, 1983): 10.

13. Rudolph L. Nelson, "Fundamentalism at Harvard: The Case of Edward Joh Carnell," Quarterly Review 2 (Summer 1982): 79–98.

14. The others were John Gerstner, Jack P. Lewis, and Lemoine Lewis, wh taught, respectively, at Pittsburgh Theological Seminary, the Harding Gradu ate School of Religion, and Abilene Christian University.

15. Roger Shinn, quoted in Nelson, "Fundamentalism at Harvard," 84.

16. More information on these volumes is found in Chapter 6.

17. James D. Bratt, Dutch Calvinism in Modern America: A History of a Conservati Subculture (Grand Rapids: Eerdmans, 1984), 59; this book is an exceptionall fine source for the whole denomination.

18. Eerdmans also published Bernard Ramm's Christian View of Science, man other books by Henry and Carnell, and volumes from several other "Harvar fundamentalists."

19. I. Howard Marshall, "F. F. Bruce as a Biblical Scholar," Journal of the Christia Brethren Research Fellowship 22 (1971): 12.

20. Ronald Inchley, "The Inter-Varsity Press," in Douglas Johnson, Contending fc the Faith: A History of the Evangelical Movement in the Universities and College (Leicester, Eng.: Inter-Varsity Press, 1979), 320.

21. See W. Ward Gasque, A History of the Criticism of the Acts of the Apostles (Gran Rapids: Eerdmans, 1975), 257–64.

22. Marshall, "F. F. Bruce as Biblical Scholar," 6.

23. Inchley, "The Inter-Varsity Press," in Johnson, Contending for the Faith, 32

24. Ibid.

25. From the "Constitution" to the Institute for Biblical Research.

26. Gasque, "Evangelical Theology: The British Example," Christianity Toda (August 10, 1973): 50.

27. For an overview, see "Index to Themelios Volumes 1–10," Themelios 10 (Apr 1985): 21–27.

28. See the excellent two-part study by Moises Silva, "Ned B. Stonehouse an Redaction Criticism," Westminster Theological Journal 40 (Fall 1977): 77–8 and (Spring 1978): 281–303.

29. Ned B. Stonehouse, The Witness of Matthew and Mark to Christ (Philadelphi The Presbyterian Guardian, 1944), xvi.

30. Ned B. Stonehouse, The Witness of Luke to Christ (Grand Rapids: Eerdman 1951), 5–6. The books cited in notes 29 and 30 have been published in helpful one-volume format as The Witness of the Synoptic Gospels to Christ (Gran Rapids: Baker, 1979).

31. Stonehouse, The Witness of Matthew and Mark, 83–84; The Witness of Luke, 14

32. Quoted in Silva, "Stonehouse and Redaction Criticism," 284.

33. Stonehouse, *The Witness to Luke*, 6.

34. See Silva, "Stonehouse and Redaction Criticism," 285–86, for a summary, and 281 n1 for the serious critical reaction.

35. For biographical information, see "Bruce M. Metzger: Curriculum Vitae and Bibliography," in *New Testament Textual Criticism: Its Significance for Exegesis: Essays in Honour of Bruce M. Metzger*, edited by Eldon Jay Epp and Gordon D. Fee (Oxford: Clarendon Press, 1981), xv–xxviii.

36. Bruce M. Metzger, "Literary Forgeries and Canonical Pseudepigrapha," *Journal of Biblical Literature* 91 (1972): 21–22.

37. Biographical information is from David A. Hubbard, "Everett F. Harrison: An Appreciation" and "A Bibliography of the Writings of E. F. Harrison," in *Scripture, Tradition, and Interpretation: Essays Presented to Everett F. Harrison by His Students and Colleagues in Honor of His Seventy-Fifth Birthday*, edited by W. Ward Gasque and William Sanford LaSor (Grand Rapids: Eerdmans, 1978), 1–5, 313–19.

38. Harrison, "The Phenomena of Scripture," in *Contemporary Evangelical Thought: Revelation and the Bible*, edited by Carl F. H. Henry (Grand Rapids: Baker, 1958), 238–239, 250.

39. For biographical information, see David A. Hubbard, "Biographical Sketch and Appreciation" and "Select Bibliography of George Eldon Ladd," in *Unity and Diversity in New Testament Theology: Essays in Honor of George E. Ladd*, edited by Robert A. Guelich (Grand Rapids: Eerdmans, 1978), xi–xv, 214–17.

40. George E. Ladd, *Crucial Questions About the Kingdom of God* (Grand Rapids: Eerdmans, 1952), 13, 59.

41. Reginald Fuller, review of Ladd's *Theology of the New Testament*, in *Anglican Theological Review* 58 (July 1976): 381, 384.

42. George E. Ladd, *The New Testament and Criticism* (Grand Rapids: Eerdmans, 1967), 215.

43. E. Earle Ellis, "The Authorship of the Pastorals," in *Paul and His Recent Interpreters* (Grand Rapids: Eerdmans, 1961), 49–57.

44. E. Earle Ellis, "Luke as Historian," *The New Century Bible Commentary: The Gospel of Luke* (Grand Rapids: Eerdmans, 1981; [orig. 1974]), 4–9.

45. Ladd, *New Testament and Criticism*, 125; Ladd's entire chapter on "Literary Criticism" fleshes out that conviction, 109–40.

46. G. Ch. Aalders, "The Historical Literature of the Old Testament," in *The New Bible Commentary* (Grand Rapids: Eerdmans, 1953), 34.

47. A. J. Macleod, "The Gospel According to John," in ibid., 866.

48. Quoted by H. D. McDonald, *Theories of Revelation: An Historical Study, 1800–1960* (Grand Rapids: Baker, 1979 [orig. 1963]), 209–10.

49. James Barr, *Fundamentalism* (Philadelphia: Westminster, 1978), 5. Similar views, expressed with various degrees of militance, are found in other recent writings by Barr—for example, "The Fundamentalist Understanding of Scripture," in *Conflicting Ways of Interpreting the Bible*, edited by Hans Küng and Jürgen Moltmann (New York: Seabury, 1980), 70–74; "The Problem of Fundamentalism Today," in Barr's *The Scope and Authority of the Bible* (Philadelphia: Westminster, 1980), 65–90; and *Beyond Fundamentalism: Biblical Foundations for Evangelical Christianity* (Philadelphia: Westminster, 1984).

50. See, for example, the able defense of modern textual study in D. A. Carson, *The King James Version Debate: A Plea for Realism* (Grand Rapids: Baker, 1979).

51. Another work from 1974 which also signaled an increasing scholarly maturity was the symposium entitled *New Dimensions in New Testament Studies*, edited by Richard N. Longenecker and Merrill C. Tenney (Grand Rapids: Zondervan, 1974). This work included papers given at the twenty-fifth annual meeting of the Evangelical Theological Society, held in December 1973, and included many essays of consequential scholarship.

52. J. I. Packer, *"Fundamentalism" and the Word of God* (Grand Rapids: Eerdmans, 1958), 41, 46, 32, 99.

53. Carl Henry, "American Evangelicals and Theological Dialogue," *Christianity Today* (January 15, 1965): 29.

54. Peter Craigie, "Narrowing the Scholar-Preacher Gap in Old Testament Studies," *Christianity Today* (March 4, 1983): 105.

55. The views held by professors at Westminster Theological Seminary illustrate this difference between New Testament and Old Testament scholarship. We have already noted the way in which Ned Stonehouse engaged modern theories of the New Testament. By contrast, his colleague E. J. Young (1907–1968) was very conservative on critical matters. Young's training took place at Stanford, Westminster, Leipzig, and Dropsie. His Old Testament work was often strong in exegesis (as in his three-volume commentary on Isaiah published by Eerdmans [1965, 1969, 1972]). But he allowed almost no place for modern conclusions about the Old Testament; see Young, *An Introduction to the Old Testament*, rev. ed., (Grand Rapids: Eerdmans, 1960); and *Studies in Isaiah* (Grand Rapids: Eerdmans, 1954), especially "The Study of Isaiah Since the Time of Joseph Addison Alexander," 9–101.

56. Ladd, *New Testament Criticism*, 11–12.

6. THE RECENT ACHIEVEMENT

Epigraph: Ernest W. Saunders, *Searching the Scriptures: A History of the Society of Biblical Literature, 1880–1980* (Chico, CA: Scholars Press, 1982), 84.

1. "Word Biblical Commentary in 52 Volumes: A Prospectus" (Waco, TX: Word, 1983).

2. *Factbook on Theological Education for the Academic Year 1984–1985*, edited by William L. Baumgaernter (Vandalia, OH: Association of Theological Schools in the United States and Canada, n.d.), 51–57.

3. Program of the 1982 annual meeting of the SBL. Of the 472 named participants on this program, I was able to identify 48 as evangelical from their institutional identifications or through personal knowledge.

4. For the *JBL*, at least 15 of the 192 authors in volumes 97 through 100 and 102 through 103 (1978–1981, 1983–1984) were from evangelical institutions or were known to me personally as evangelicals. Using the same criteria, I found 32 of 322 authors in *NTS* for volumes 23 through 30 (1977–1984) to be evangelicals.

5. Using the criteria of note 2, I found 3 of 212 authors in *Vetus Testamentum* for volumes 30 through 33 (1980–1983) to be evangelicals.

6. See Gerald A. Larue, "Another Chapter in the History of Bible Translation: The Attacks upon the Revised Standard Version," *Journal of Bible and Religion 31* (1963): 301–10.

7. For an overview, see Robert G. Bratcher, "The New International Version," in *The Word of God: A Guide to English Versions of the Bible*, edited by Lloyd R. Bailey (Atlanta: John Knox, 1982).

8. Interestingly, early reaction by evangelicals and conservative confessionalists to the NIV was not particularly favorable. See "The New International Version—Nothing New," *Concordia Theological Quarterly 43* (1979): 242–45; Willis P. DeBoer, review of the NIV in *Calvin Theological Journal 10* (April 1975): 66–78; William Sanford LaSor, "What Kind of Translation Is the New International?" and Leland Ryken, "The Literary Merit of the New International Version," *Christianity Today* (October 20, 1978): 78–80, 76–77. Legitimate strictures notwithstanding, the NIV is a remarkably clear, readable, and idiomatic translation. In spite of occasional lily-gilding to make doctrinal implications of certain passages unmistakeable (e.g., in John 2:11, "miraculous sign" for σημεῖον and questionable readings of a few passages pertinent to the issue of inerrancy (e.g., in Matthew 13:32, "the smallest of all your seeds" for ὅ μικρότερον μέν ἐστιν πάντων τῶν σπερμάτων), this version is certainly one of the most useful and responsible modern translations for American speakers of English.

9. Peter C. Craigie, "The *New International Version:* A Review Article," *Journal of the Evangelical Theological Society 21* (September 1978): 251–54, with quotation from 254.

10. Anthony A. Thiselton, *The Two Horizons: New Testament Hermeneutics and Philosophical Description* (Grand Rapids: Eerdmans, 1980); and J. I. Packer, "Infallible Scripture and the Role of Hermeneutics," in *Scripture and Truth,* edited by D. A. Carson and John D. Woodbridge (Grand Rapids: Zondervan, 1983), 325–56 and notes 412–19. But see also the perceptive essay and bibliography by Daniel P. Fuller of Fuller Seminary on "Interpretation, History Of," in *The International Standard Bible Encyclopedia,* edited by Geoffrey W. Bromiley, rev. ed. (Grand Rapids: Eerdmans, 1979), II, 863–74; and the contributions by Americans Roger Lundin and Clarence Walhout who, with Anthony Thiselton, have published *The Responsibility of Hermeneutics* (Grand Rapids: Eerdmans, 1985).

11. Recent examples do include American authors, but still arise from the British evangelical milieu—e.g., *Gospel Perspectives: Studies of History and Tradition in the Four Gospels,* edited by R. T. France and David Wenham (Sheffield, Eng.: JSOT Press, 1980); *New Testament Interpretation: Essays on Principles and Methods,* edited by I. H. Marshall (London: Paternoster, 1977); and *Essays on the Patriarchal Narratives,* edited by A. R. Millard and D. J. Wiseman (Leicester, Eng.: Inter-Varsity Press, 1983).

12. Institutions where Fee and the other scholars trained are enclosed in parentheses. It is possible to mention only respresentative works for these scholars, like Gordon Fee's *Papyrus Bodmer II* (University of Utah, 1968); "II Corinthians vi, 14–viii, 1 and Food Offered to Idols," *New Testament Studies,* 1977; and editor, *New Testament Textual Criticism* (Oxford: Oxford University Press, 1982).

13. Robert Mounce, *The Book of Revelation* (Grand Rapids: Eerdmans, 1977).

14. Robert Guelich, *The Sermon on the Mount* (Waco, TX: Word, 1982). Robert Stein, *The Method and Message of Jesus' Teaching* (Philadelphia: Westminster, 1978); *An Introduction to the Parables of Jesus* (Philadelphia: Westminster, 1981).

15. Richard Longenecker, *Paul: Apostle of Liberty* (New York: Harper & Row, 1968); *The Christology of Early Jewish Christianity* (Naperville, IL: Allenson, 1970); *Biblical Exegesis in the Apostolic Period* (Grand Rapids: Eerdmans, 1974); *The Acts of the Apostles: The Expositor's Bible Commentary, Vol. 9* (Grand Rapids: Zondervan, 1981).

16. D. A. Carson, *The King James Version Debate* (Grand Rapids: Baker, 1979); *Divine Sovereignty and Human Responsibility: Some Aspects of Johannine Theology Against a Jewish Background* (Atlanta: John Knox, 1980); "Christological Ambiguities in the Gospel of Matthew," in *Christ the Lord: Studies in Christology Presented to Donald Guthrie*, edited by H. H. Rowdon (Downers Grove, IL: InterVarsity Press, 1982); *Matthew: The Expositor's Bible Commentary*, Vol. 8 (Grand Rapids: Zondervan, 1984).

17. Peter C. Craigie, *The Book of Deuteronomy* (Grand Rapids: Eerdmans, 1976); *The Problem of War in the Old Testament* (Grand Rapids: Eerdmans, 1978); *Psalms 1–50* (Waco, TX: Word, 1983).

18. Walter Kaiser, *Toward an Old Testament Theology* (Grand Rapids: Zondervan 1978); *Toward an Old Testament Ethics* (Grand Rapids: Zondervan, 1983).

19. David Aune, *The Cultic Setting of Realized Eschatology in Early Christianity* (Leiden: Brill, 1972); *Prophecy in Early Christianity and the Ancient Mediterranean World* (Grand Rapids: Eerdmans, 1983).

20. Edward Yamauchi, *Gnostic Ethics and Mandaean Origins* (Cambridge: Harvard University Press, 1970); *Pre-Christian Gnosticism: A Survey of the Proposed Evidences* (Grand Rapids: Eerdmans, 1973).

21. Of the fifteen evangelicals who published in the *JBL*, 1978–1984 (cited in note 4), at least five or six are British or trained in Britain; at least twenty-four of the thirty-two evangelicals who published in *NTS*, 1977–1984 (cited note 4), are likewise British or British trained.

22. The experience of the most important American publisher of evangelical biblical scholarship bears out that impression. By 1985 the William B. Eerdmans Company had sold over 530,000 copies of books (commentaries, texts on Scripture, monographs on biblical themes) by the American Merrill Tenney and over 370,000 copies by his fellow countryman George Ladd. Yet by that date, the same firm had printed more than 550,000 books for each of four evangelical scholars from Britain or the Commonwealth. I am grateful to Mr Jon Pott and Mr. William Eerdmans, Jr., for permission to examine the firm's records. See also the Appendix for more information regarding academic influence on evangelical scholars.

23. For an account of the situation generally in the profession, see Dorothy Bass "Women's Studies and Biblical Studies in Historical Perspective," *Journal for the Study of the Old Testament* 22 (1982): 6–12.

7. THE STANDPOINTS OF EVANGELICAL SCHOLARSHIP

Epigraph: "The Chicago Statement on Biblical Inerrancy," *Journal of the Evangelical Theological Society* 21 (December 1978): 295.

1. Charles Hodge, *Systematic Theology* (Grand Rapids: Eerdmans, n.d. [orig. 1872–1873]), I, 188.

2. The statement of faith of Fuller Theological Seminary appears to be such an example. See the Fuller catalogue for 1985–1986, 9: "Scripture is an essential part and trustworthy record of [the] divine self-disclosure. All the books of the Old and New Testaments, given by divine inspiration, are the written word of God, the only infallible rule of faith and practice. They are to be interpreted according to their context and purpose and in reverent obedience to the Lord who speaks through them in living power."

3. I. Howard Marshall, *Biblical Inspiration* (Grand Rapids: Eerdmans, 1982) 63–65. For an evangelical response questioning the need for Marshall's con-

clusions about an error in this passage, see D. A. Carson, "Three Books on the Bible: A Critical Review," *Journal of the Evangelical Theological Society 26* (September 1983): 356–57.

4. R. T. France, "Evangelical Disagreements About the Bible," *Churchman 96* (1982): 226, 239 n1.

5. Rudolph Bultmann, *Kerygma and Myth* (New York: Harper & Row, 1961), 39, as quoted and discussed in Robert C. Roberts, *Rudolf Bultmann's Theology: A Critical Interpretation* (Grand Rapids: Eerdmans, 1976), 141.

6. Karl Marx, *Communist Manifesto* (New York: Penguin, 1967), 99.

7. Exceptions include, from an earlier period, James Orr, *The Ritschlian Theology and the Evangelical Faith*, 2d ed. (London: Hodder, 1898); and, in our own day, the work of such theologians and philosophers as Paul Helm, Carl Henry, Alvin Plantinga, Anthony Thiselton, Nicholas Wolterstorff, and members of the recently established Society of Christian Philosophers. For a description of the specific roles Scottish Common Sense Philosophy has played among evangelicals, see Mark A. Noll, "Common Sense Traditions and American Evangelical Thought," *American Quarterly 37* (Summer 1985): 216–38.

8. From a different angle of vision, this same point has been made by Robert W. Funk, "The Watershed of the American Biblical Tradition: The Chicago School, First Phase, 1892–1920," *Journal of Biblical Literature 95* (1976): 21.

9. "The Chicago Statement on Biblical Inerrancy," 290.

10. Examples of recent evangelical attention to this question include Carl F. H. Henry, *God, Revelation and Authority, Vol. III: God Who Speaks and Shows: Fifteen Theses, Part Two* (Waco, TX: Word, 1979), 249–487; Ronald H. Nash, *The Word of God and the Mind of Men* (Grand Rapids: Zondervan, 1982); Royce Gordon Gruenler, *New Approaches to Jesus and the Gospels: A Phenomenological Study of Synoptic Christology* (Grand Rapids: Baker, 1982); and a number of works by Anthony Thiselton, summarized and discussed by Brian J. Walsh, "Anthony Thiselton's Contribution to Biblical Hermeneutics," *Christian Scholar's Review 14* (1985): 224–35.

11. Evangelicals are the ones most responsible for the immense recent literature on the inerrancy of Scripture and related issues. For a list of some twenty-seven recent books on this subject—which represents only part of the recent outpouring—see Mark A. Noll, "Evangelicals and the Study of the Bible," in *Evangelicalism and Modern America*, edited by George Marsden (Grand Rapids: Eerdmans, 1984), 198–99 n39.

12. See the discussion, with reference to literature, in Ian Rennie, "Mixed Metaphors, Misunderstood Models, and Puzzling Paradigms: A Contemporary Effort to Correct Some Current Misunderstandings Regarding the Authority and Interpretation of the Bible, An Historical Response," paper presented at a conference on "Interpreting an Authoritative Scripture," Institute for Christian Studies, Toronto, June 1981; and John D. Woodbridge, *Biblical Authority: A Critique of the Rogers/McKim Proposal* (Grand Rapids: Zondervan, 1982), 212 n31, 228 n51.

13. J. I. Packer, *"Fundamentalism" and the Word of God* (Grand Rapids: Eerdmans, 1958), 95–96.

14. See Nathan O. Hatch, "Evangelicalism as a Democratic Movement," in *Evangelicalism and Modern America*, 71–82.

15. For a capable discussion of this background, see Harry S. Stout, "Word and Order in Colonial New England," in *The Bible in America: Essays in Cultural History* (New York; Oxford, 1982), 19–38.

16. See for the impact of revivalism, George M. Marsden, *Fundamentalism and American Culture* (New York: Oxford, 1980), 32–39 and *passim;* and for that of the American Revolution, Mark A. Noll, *Christians in the American Revolution* (Grand Rapids: Eerdmans, 1977), 163–75.

17. Quoted in H. D. McDonald, *Theories of Revelation: An Historical Study, 1860–1960* (Grand Rapids: Baker, 1979 [orig. 1963]), 204.

18. John Kennedy, *Old Testament Criticism and the Rights of the Unlearned* (London, 1897), 93.

19. David Wells, *The Person of Christ: A Biblical and Historical Analysis of the Incarnation* (Westchester, IL: Crossway, 1984), 35–36.

20. In this regard, evangelicals adopt a functionalist interpretation of recent higher education similar in form, though very different in content, to that advanced by scholars who conclude that the professionalization of American higher education was the product of economic, class, or other forms of social self-interest. See, for example, Burton J. Bledstein, *The Culture of Professionalism: The Middle Class and the Development of Higher Education in America* (New York: W. W. Norton, 1976); or David F. Noble, *American By Design: Science, Technology, and the Rise of Corporate Capitalism* (New York: Oxford, 1979 [orig. 1977]), 110–256.

21. See Chapter 8, pages 167–69, for further discussion of authorial intent.

22. In America, discussion of "the people of God" is complicated by the intersection of the biblical meaning of this concept and the American constitutional deference to "we the people."

23. Ethel Goss, "A Personal Viewpoint," *The Pentecostal Herald* (March 1950): 5.

24. Perry F. Rockwood, *Is the KJV God's Word for Today?* (Halifax, N.S.: The Peoples Gospel Hour, n.d.), 9, 11.

25. This diversity is one of the characteristics of evangelicals that James Barr has not perceived clearly, a point nicely made by Gabriel Fackre in a review of Barr's *Beyond Fundamentalism, The Christian Century* (May 15, 1985): 506–07.

26. Nigel M. de S. Cameron, "Inspiration and Criticism: The Nineteenth-Century Crisis," *Tyndale Bulletin 35* (1984): 155.

27. See Appendix for a fuller picture. The summation here does not include those who are members of both groups.

28. See Appendix for fuller data. In this summary, those who are members of both groups are counted with each body.

8. CONTEMPORARY UNCERTAINTIES

Epigraph: R. T. France, "Evangelical Disagreements About the Bible," *Churchman 96* (1982): 236–37.

1. Clark Pinnock, "The Inerrancy Debate Among the Evangelicals," *TSF Newsletter* (Summer 1976): 1.

2. Brief flurries of controversy, for example, surrounded the publication of works in which these matters received some consideration in the 1960s, e.g., Dewey M. Beegle, *The Inspiration of Scripture* (Philadelphia: Westminster, 1963); Daniel P. Fuller, "Benjamin B. Warfield's View of Faith and History: A Critique in Light of the New Testament," *Bulletin of the Evangelical Theological Society 11* (Spring 1968): 75–83.

3. Carl Armerding, *The Old Testament and Criticism* (Grand Rapids: Eerdmans, 1983).

4. Ibid., 5, 7, 13.

5. Representatives of such creative scholarship, in addition to the Old Testament scholars cited in Chapter 6, include the work of Meredith G. Kline, e.g., *Treaty of the Great King: The Covenant Structure of Deuteronomy* (Grand Rapids: Eerdmans, 1963).

6. Geoffrey Bromiley, "Evangelicals and Theological Creativity," *Themelios* 5 (September 1979): 49.

7. John R. W. Stott, *Between Two Worlds: The Art of Preaching in the Twentieth Century* (Grand Rapids: Eerdmans, 1982), 87.

8. Robert Johnston, *Evangelicals at an Impasse: Biblical Authority in Perspective* (Atlanta: John Knox, 1979), vii–viii.

9. Robert Gundry, *The Use of the Old Testament in St. Matthew's Gospel* (Leiden: Brill, 1967).

10. Robert Gundry, *Matthew: A Commentary on His Literary and Theological Art* (Grand Rapids: Eerdmans, 1981), 623.

11. Gundry, "A Theological Postscript," in ibid., 623–40.

12. D. A. Carson, "Gundry on Matthew: A Critical Review," *Trinity Journal*, new ser., 3 (1982): 77.

13. R. T. France and D. Wenham, eds., *Studies in Midrash and Historiography, Vol. III of Gospel Perspectives* (Sheffield: JSOT Press, 1983). Some of these criticisms are also echoed in Royce Gruenler, *New Approaches to Jesus and the Gospels: A Phenomenological and Exegetical Study of Synoptic Christology* (Grand Rapids: Baker, 1982), 245–51.

14. See the Appendix, especially the ranked lists of figures who have influenced modern evangelical scholars.

15. Leslie R. Keylock, "Evangelical Scholars Remove Gundry for His Views on Matthew," *Christianity Today* (February 3, 1984): 36–38. For a good summary of the Gundry case and related issues, see David L. Turner, "Evangelicals, Redaction Criticism, and Inerrancy: The Debate Continues," *Grace Theological Journal* 5 (1984): 37–45.

16. France, "Evangelical Disagreements about the Bible," 238.

17. For nuanced discussions of these distinctions, see D. A. Carson, "Redaction Criticism: On the Legitimacy and Illegitimacy of a Literary Tool," in *Scripture and Truth*, edited by Carson and John D. Woodbridge (Grand Rapids: Zondervan, 1983), 119–42; and "Redaction Criticism: Is It Worth the Risk?" a symposium discussion of the Christianity Today Institute, *Christianity Today* (October 18, 1985): insert 1–12.

18. I. Howard Marshall, review of Michaels's *Servant and Son*, *Evangelical Quarterly* 56 (January 1984), 50.

19. J. Ramsey Michaels, *Servant and Son: Jesus in Parable and Gospel* (Atlanta: John Knox, 1981), 33–34, 163–64, 273.

20. Gordon-Cowell catalogue for 1981–1982, 10, 21. As part of the general controversy surrounding the Michaels case, however, the Gordon-Conwell faculty did publish a lengthy statement, "The Mission of Gordon-Conwell Theological Seminary," which went a considerable distance toward resolving the ambiguities of the seminary's shorter basis of faith.

21. Marshall, Review of Michaels's *Servant and Son*, 50.

22. This last question presupposes that the larger evangelical convictions are themselves a product of more general biblical reflection. James Barr, in arguments set out in *Fundamentalism* (Philadelphia: Westminster, 1977) and *Beyond Fundamentalism: Biblical Foundations for Evangelical Christianity* (Philadelphia: Westminster, 1984), doubts that supposition. Barr's scruples

deserve full consideration. But that there is more congruence between evangelical views of Scripture and more general evangelical convictions is argued persuasively, with specific reference to Barr, by Clark Pinnock, *The Scripture Principle* (San Francisco: Harper & Row, 1984), 15–20 and *passim*.

23. James D. G. Dunn, "The Authority of Scripture According to Scripture," *Churchman* 96 (1982): 104–22 and 201–25, with summary at 118.

24. Ibid., 207, 210, 215–22.

25. See Roger Nicole, "The Inspiration and Authority of Scripture: J. D. G. Dunn versus B. B. Warfield," *Churchman* 97 (1983): 198–215, and 98 (1984): 7–27 and 198–208, with an exchange between Dunn and Nicole, 208–16.

26. Affirmations 13 and 14 in a statement concerning hermeneutics by the International Council on Biblical Inerrancy, as recorded in *Christianity Today* (December 17, 1982): 47.

27. Benjamin B. Warfield, "Inspiration and Criticism," in *The Works of Benjamin B. Warfield* (New York: Oxford, 1927), I, 420. The same sentiments are expressed at length in the essay written with A. A. Hodge, "Inspiration," *Presbyterian Review* 2 (1881): 245–46.

28. See the critical reviews of Abraham's *Divine Inspiration of Holy Scripture* by David Wells, *Christian Scholar's Review* 12 (1983): 356–58; and by D. A. Carson, *Journal of the Evangelical Theological Society* 26 (1983): 337–47. Also of interest is the largely favorable review of the same book by James Barr in *Journal of Theological Studies* 34 (April 1983): 370–76. Abraham also devoted special attention to a Wesleyan approach to these issues in an essay, "Inspiration in the Classical Wesleyan Tradition," in *A Celebration of Ministry: Essays in Honor of Frank Bateman Stanger*, edited by K. C. Kinghorn (Asbury, KY: Francis Asbury Pub. Co., 1982), 33–47.

29. Donald Hagner, "The Battle for Inerrancy: An Errant Trend Among the Inerrancists," *Reformed Journal* (April 1984): 22.

30. Benjamin B. Warfield, "Calvin's Doctrine of Creation," *Princeton Theological Review* 13 (1915), reprinted in *Works*, V, 287–349; and "The Divine and Human in the Bible," *Presbyterian Journal* (May 3, 1894), reprinted in *Selected Shorter Writings of Benjamin B. Warfield, Vol. II*, edited by John E. Meeter (Phillipsburg, NJ: Presbyterian and Reformed, 1973), 542–48.

31. Warfield, "Calvin's Doctrine of Creation."

32. The concept of *concursus* remains alive as a theological principle for some evangelicals, like J. I. Packer, but does not seem to be used self-consciously by biblical scholars in carrying out their work.

33. David Wright, review of James Barr's *Fundamentalism*, *Themelios* 3 (April 1978): 88.

34. Bernard Ramm, *After Fundamentalism: The Future of Evangelical Theology* (San Francisco: Harper & Row, 1983), 34.

35. See, for example, John Howard Yoder, *The Politics of Jesus: Vicit Agnus Noster* (Grand Rapids: Eerdmans, 1972); and Greg L. Bahnsen, *Theonomy in Christian Ethics*, rev. ed. (Phillipsburg, NJ: Presbyterian and Reformed, 1984). Theonomists hold that for a society to be properly administered, the law of God, especially as revealed in the Old Testament, deserves a nearly full implementation.

36. Evangelical literary scholars have made significant recent contributions to this task, as in Clarence Walhout, Roger Lundin, and Anthony C. Thiselton, *The Responsibility of Hermeneutics* (Grand Rapids: Eerdmans, 1985).

37. For a full explication of this assertion, see Nathan O. Hatch, "Evangelicalism

as a Democratic Movement," in *Evangelicalism and Modern America*, edited by George Marsden (Grand Rapids: Eerdmans, 1984), 71–82.

38. A different set of grids divide Christians holding to either of these views from members of other traditionally supernatural religions, like Jews, Muslims, or Mormons, who also divide among themselves on this issue.

39. E. A. Speiser, *The Anchor Bible: Genesis* (Garden City, NY: Doubleday, 1964), xx–xxi.

40. The phrase concerning Wellhausen echoes Barr, *Fundamentalism*, 145–49; the quotation is from a review of three volumes in the *Word Bible Commentary* by Herman C. Waetjen, *Christian Century* (January 18, 1984): 58.

41. Archie Nations has recently provided a helpful definition of "the historical-critical method," as "a set of assumptions thought to be operative in doing historical research; i.e. criticism must be freed from dogmatic presuppositions, maintain a high degree of objectivity, eschew ecclesiastical controls, and accept secular historians' notions of historical homogeneity, of cause and effect relationship and of the criticism of sources." Nations, "Historical Criticism and the Current Methodological Crisis," *Scottish Journal of Theology 36* (1983): 63.

42. Robert Funk, "The Watershed of the American Biblical Tradition: The Chicago School, First Phase, 1892–1920," *Journal of Biblical Literature 95* (1976): 21.

43. Peter C. Craigie, "The Role and Relevance of Biblical Research," *Journal for the Study of the Old Testament 18* (1980): 29.

44. On the other hand, one may question whether Barr is as free of unrecognized presuppositional influence as he claims; see on this and related matters, John F. Goldingay, "James Barr on Fundamentalism," *Churchman 91* (1977): 295–308.

45. Perhaps the most egregious example of such a critique in recent decades was Norman Perrin's review of George Ladd's *Jesus and the Kingdom: The Eschatology of Biblical Realism*, in *Interpretation 19* (April 1965): 228–31. While Perrin raised legitimate questions about Ladd's use of authorities, the review of this major book was, in general, offensively patronizing and naively triumphalist about contemporary (i.e., Perrin's) conclusions concerning the concept of the kingdom in the gospels. By contrast, F. H. Borsch's review of this same book in *Journal of Theological Studies 18* (1967): 195–97, was a fair examination of the volume's strengths and weaknesses that did not prejudge research on the basis of ideological presuppositions.

9. ASSESSMENT AND PROJECTION

Epigraph: Martin Marty, "America's Iconic Book," in *Humanizing America's Iconic Book: Society of Biblical Literature Centennial Addresses 1980* (Chico, CA: Scholars Press, 1982), 3.

1. Ibid., 1–23. Marty's essay is an excellent introduction to the possibilities in, and need for, study of the place of Scripture in American culture.

2. The figure of $150 million is from Richard N. Ostling, "Rivals to the King James Throne," *Time* (April 20, 1981): 62–63. See Chapter 1, note 2 for Gallup Poll results showing weaknesses in Bible knowledge by the "evangelical" public.

3. F. F. Bruce, *History of the Bible in English From the Earliest Versions* 3d ed. (New York: Oxford, 1978), 96.

4. A start has been made in telling this story by the six-volume series *The Bible in American Culture*, edited by Edwin S. Gaustad and Walter Harrelson (Philadelphia: Fortress, and Chico, CA: Scholars Press, 1983–1985). Individual volumes are *The Bible and Bibles in America*, edited by Ernest S. Frerichs; *The Bible and Popular Culture in America*, edited by Allene S. Phy; *The Bible and American Arts and Letters*, edited by Giles Gunn; *The Bible in American Law, Politics, and Rhetoric*, edited by James T. Johnson; *The Bible in American Education*, edited by David Barr and Nicholas Piediscalzi; and *The Bible and Social Reform*, edited by Ernest R. Sandeen. Also useful are the essays in *The Bible in America: Essays in Cultural History*, edited by Nathan O. Hatch and Mark A. Noll (New York: Oxford, 1982).

5. As Tables 2, 3, and 4 in Chapter 6 indicate, however, conservative Jewish universities (especially Brandeis and Dropsie) have provided doctoral certification for a large proportion of evangelical Old Testament scholars.

6. Paul Helm, "A Taproot of Radicalism," *Themelios* 11 (September 1985): 21.

7. Walter J. Ong, S.J., *American Catholic Crossroads* (Westport, CT: Greenwood, 1959), 109.

8. A fine example of such work is D. A. Carson, *Exegetical Fallacies* (Grand Rapids: Baker, 1984).

9. To indicate some of the factors concerning the use of the Bible by Protestant reformers, a vast and complicated subject, see as introductions, E. G. Rupp, "The Bible and the Age of the Reformation," in *The Church's Use of the Bible Past and Present*, edited by D. E. Nineham (London: SPCK, 1963), 73–87; Roland H. Bainton, "The Bible in the Reformation," in *The Cambridge History of the Bible, Vol. III: The West from the Reformation to the Present Day*, edited by S. L. Greenslade (Cambridge: Cambridge University Press, 1963), 1–37; A. Skevington Wood, *The Principles of Biblical Interpretation: As Enunciated by Irenaeus, Origen, Augustine, Luther, and Calvin* (Grand Rapids: Zondervan, 1967); Rupert E. Davies, *The Problem of Authority in the Continental Reformers* (London: Epworth, 1946); and Nathan O. Hatch, "*Sola Scriptura* and *Novus Ordo Seclorum*," in *The Bible in America*, 61–62.

10. John Lightfoot, *Horae Hebraicae et Talmudicae: or Hebrew and Talmudical Exercitations upon the Gospels of St. Matthew and St. Mark*, as quoted in Stephen Neill, *The Interpretation of the New Testament, 1861–1961* (Oxford: Oxford University Press, 1964), 293.

11. It is indicative of the world in which evangelical scholars live, as well as of the scope of their task, that the best-selling book in America during the whole decade of the 1970s, Hal Lindsey's *Late, Great Planet Earth*, was a work of questionable biblical exposition that blithely ignored most of the recent sturdy work by evangelicals, not to speak of nonevangelicals, on the nature of scriptural apocalyptic.

12. A. A. Hodge and Benjamin B. Warfield, "Inspiration," *Presbyterian Review* 2 (April 1881): 242.

13. F. J. A. Hort to B. F. Westcott, May 2, 1860, in Arthur Fenton Hort, *Life and Letters of Fenton John Anthony Hort*, two vols. (London: Macmillan, 1896), I, 422.

14. J. I. Packer, "Infallible Scripture and the Role of Hermeneutics," in *Scripture and Truth*, edited by D. A. Carson and John D. Woodbridge (Grand Rapids: Zondervan, 1983), 325.

10. AFTERWORD

1. I have tried to show how such conclusions derive from theological convictions in "Traditional Christianity and the Possibility of Historical Knowledge," *Christian Scholar's Review* 19 (June 1990): 388–406.

2. See, for example, the recent series on "Gospel Perspectives" from JSOT Press, Sheffield University, with six separate volumes: *Studies of History and Tradition in the Four Gospels I, Studies of History and Tradition in the Four Gospels II, Studies in Midrash and Historiography, The Rediscovery of Jesus' Eschatological Discourse, The Jesus Tradition Outside the Gospels,* and *The Miracles of Jesus.* A summary and expansion of the material in these books can be found in Craig Blomberg, *The Historical Reliability of the Gospels* (Downers Grove, IL: InterVarsity Press, 1987).

3. To cite recent publications from scholars singled out for special mention in *Between Faith and Criticism,* see, for example, Bruce M. Metzger, *The Canon of the New Testament: Its Origin, Development, and Significance* (New York: Oxford University Press, 1987); E. Earle Ellis, *Pauline Theology: Ministry and Society* (Grand Rapids: Eerdmans, 1989); Richard Longenecker, *Galatians,* Word Biblical Commentary (Waco, TX: Word, 1991); and Donald A. Carson, *The Gospel According to John* (Grand Rapids: Eerdmans, 1991).

4. For example, John Van Seters, *In Search of History* (New Haven: Yale University Press, 1983); and Giovanni Garbini, *History and Ideology in Ancient Israel* (New York: Crossroad, 1988).

5. A festschrift in honor of a notable evangelical student of the Old Testament that contains a healthy sampling of work from North American evangelicals is Lyle Eslingen and Glen Taylor, eds., *Ascribe to the Lord: Biblical and Other Studies in Memory of Peter C. Craigie* (Sheffield, Eng.: JSOT Press, 1988).

6. Wallace Alcorn, *New York Times Book Review,* Feb. 7, 1988, p. 35.

7. Marguerite Van Die, *An Evangelical Mind: Nathanael Burwash and the Methodist Tradition in Canada, 1839–1918* (Kingston, Ont.: McGill-Queen's University Press, 1989); Mark S. Massa, S.J., *Charles Augustus Briggs and the Crisis of Historical Criticism* (Minneapolis: Fortress, 1990); and Glen Scorgie, *A Call for Continuity: The Theological Contribution of James Orr* (Macon, GA: Mercer University Press, 1988).

8. Philip Barlow, *Mormons and the Bible: The Place of the Latter-day Saints in American Religion* (New York: Oxford University Press, 1991).

9. John L. Merrill, "The Bible and the American Temperance Movement: Text, Context, and Pretext," *Harvard Theological Review* 81 (1988): 145–70.

10. The series, edited by Edwin S. Gaustad and Walter Harrelson and co-published by Fortress Press and Scholars Press, includes *The Bible in American Education,* ed. D. L. Barr and N. Piediscalzi (1982); *The Bible and Social Reform,* ed. E. R. Sandeen (1982); *The Bible and American Arts and Letters,* ed. G. Gunn (1983); *The Bible and American Law, Politics, and Political Rhetoric,* ed. J. T. Johnson (1985); *The Bible and Popular Culture in America,* ed. E. S. Frerichs (1988). I have reviewed these six books as well as others in the SBL's Centennial Publications series, while also making preliminary comments about the ideological contests of biblical scholarship, in *Journal of Biblical Literature* 106 (1987): 493–509.

11. George M. Marsden, *Reforming Fundamentalism: Fuller Seminary and the New Evangelicalism* (Grand Rapids: Eerdmans, 1987); Rudolph L. Nelson, *The Making and Unmaking of an Evangelical Mind: The Case of Edward Carnell* (New York: Cambridge University Press, 1987).

12. See, for example, Donald Dayton, "Yet Another Layer of the Onion: Or Opening the Ecumenical Doors to Let the Riffraff in," *Ecumenical Review* 40 (Jan. 1988): 87–110; Leonard I. Sweet, "Wise as Serpents, Innocent as Doves: The New Evangelical Historiography," *Journal of the American Academy of Religion* 56 (Fall 1988): 397–416; Donald Dayton and Robert Johnston, eds., *The Variety of American Evangelicalism* (Knoxville: University of Tennessee Press; and Downers Grove, IL: InterVarsity Press, 1991); Douglas A. Sweeney, "The Essential Evangelicalism Dialectic: The Historiography of the Early Neo-Evangelical Movement and the Observer-Participant Dilemma," *Church History* 60 (Mar. 1991).

13. Randall Balmer, *Mine Eyes Have Seen the Glory: A Journey into the Evangelical Subculture in America* (New York: Oxford University Press, 1989); D. W. Bebbington, *Evangelicalism in Modern Britain: A History from the 1730s to the 1980s* (London: Unwin and Hyman, 1989); Mark Ellingsen, *The Evangelical Movement: Growth, Impact, Controversy, Dialog* (Minneapolis: Augsburg, 1988); Nathan O. Hatch, *The Democratization of American Christianity* (New Haven: Yale University Press, 1989); David N. Livingstone, *Darwin's Forgotten Defenders: The Encounter Between Evangelical Theology and Evolutionary Thought* (Grand Rapids: Eerdmans, 1987); G. A. Rawlyk, ed., *The Canadian Protestant Experience 1760 to 1990* (Burlington, Ont.: Welch, 1991).

14. See, for example, Fr. William G. Most, *Free from All Error: Authorship, Inerrancy, Historicity of Scripture, Church Teaching, and Modern Scripture Scholars* (Libertyville, IL: Prow Books/Franciscan Marytown, 1985); and the discussion from many theological angles reported in Richard J. Neuhaus, ed., *Biblical Interpretation in Crisis: The Ratzinger Conference on Bible and Church*, vol. 9 of the Encounter Series (Grand Rapids: Eerdmans, 1989).

15. "Fundamentalist" and "moderate" are polemical terms that cannot be taken at face value. For a fine recent overview, see Nancy T. Ammerman, *Baptist Battles: Social Change and Religious Conflict in the Southern Baptist Convention* (New Brunswick: Rutgers University Press, 1990). For books addressing specifically the question of Scripture among Southern Baptists, see *The Proceedings of the Conference on Biblical Inerrancy 1987* (Nashville: Broadman, 1987); and Robison B. James, ed., *The Unfettered Word: Southern Baptists Confront the Authority-Inerrancy Question* (Waco, TX: Word, 1987).

16. There is now an immense literature on this subject. Among the overviews are Harvie Conn, "Evangelical Feminism: Bibliographical Reflection on the Contemporary State of the 'Union,'" *Westminster Theological Journal* 46 (Spring 1984): 104–24; and John G. Stackhouse, "Women in Public Ministry in Twentieth-Century Canadian Evangelicalism: Five Models," *Studies in Religion/Sciences Religieuses* 17 (1988): 471–85. As a sample of recent exegesis supporting traditional views, see the essays in John Piper and Wayne A. Grudem, eds., *Recovering Biblical Manhood and Womanhood: A Response to*

Evangelical Feminism (Westchester, IL: Crossway, 1991). For examples of the opposite conclusions, see Gloris Neufeld Redekop, "Let the Women Learn: I Timothy 2:8–15 Reconsidered," *Studies in Religion/Sciences Religieuses* 19 (Spring 1990): 235–45; and Gordon D. Fee, "Issues in Evangelical Hermeneutics, Part III: The Great Watershed—Intentionality and Particularity/Eternality: I Timothy 2:8–15 as a Test Case," *Crux* 26 (Dec. 1990): 31–37. An interesting case study on how a confessionally evangelical denomination, the Christian Reformed Church, shifted its exegetical conclusions away from traditional answers is *Women in Office* (Grand Rapids: CRC Publications, 1990).

17. I use "predispose" instead of "pre-determine" since exegesis by its nature involves a process of exploration in which the overturning of pre-understandings is possible.

18. For a recent perceptive survey of that politicization, see John R. Searle, "The Storm over the University," *New York Review of Books*, Dec. 6, 1990, pp. 34–42. For how politicization affects the place of religion, see George M. Marsden, "The Soul of the American University," *First Things*, Jan. 1991, pp. 34–47.

19. George Steiner, "The Good Book," *New Yorker*, Jan. 11, 1988, pp. 94–98; and Donald Davie, "Reading and Believing," *New Republic*, Oct. 27, 1987, pp. 28–33.

20. David Brion Davis, "Review Essay," *Religion and American Culture* 1 (1991): 119–27, especially 127.

Bibliography

This bibliography is limited to sources that list or describe evangelical works on Scripture, and to secondary accounts that place in context the historical development of evangelical biblical scholarship. For the most part, works on the doctrine of inspiration, studies of theological themes pertinent to the subject, and books and articles on the Scriptures themselves—though all are relevant to the subject—have had to be set aside to keep the following within manageable proportions. In the first section, almost all of the guides discuss pertinent material from other points on the theological compass along with evangelical literature. This first section also includes a few texts that contain outstanding bibliographies.

BIBLIOGRAPHICAL

Allison, Joseph D. *The Bible Study Resource Guide.* Nashville: Thomas Nelson, 1982.

Aune, David E. *Jesus and the Synoptic Gospels.* TSF-IBR Bibliographic Study Guides. Madison, WI: Theological Students Fellowship, 1980.

Barber, Cyril J. *The Minister's Library.* Grand Rapids: Baker, 1974, and periodic updates.

A Bibliography of Bible Study for Theological Students. 2d ed. Princeton: Princeton Theological Seminary, 1960.

Billy Graham Center (Archives), Wheaton College, Wheaton, IL. Papers from the annual meetings of the Evangelical Theological Society.

Branson, Mark Lau. "Evangelicals in Biblical Studies: A Survey of Basic Books." *TSF Bulletin* 5 (March/April 1982): S-1-2.

————. *The Reader's Guide to the Best Evangelical Books.* San Francisco: Harper & Row, 1982.

Bush, Frederic William, David Allan Hubbard, and William Sanford LaSor. *Old Testament Survey: The Message, Form, and Background of the Old Testament.* Grand Rapids: Eerdmans, 1981.

Christianity Today. Annual reviews of biblical literature, in a February issue 1957–1972, in a March issue 1973–1981.

Essential Books for Christian Ministry. Forth Worth: Southwestern Baptist Theological Seminary, 1972.

France, R. T., ed. *A Bibliographic Guide to New Testament Research.* 3d ed. Sheffield, Eng.: JSOT Press, 1979.

Goldingay, John. *Old Testament Commentary Survey,* with additions and editing by Mark Branson and Robert Hubbard. 2d ed. Madison, WI: Theological Students Fellowship, 1981.

Guthrie, Donald. *New Testament Introduction.* Rev. ed. Downers Grove, IL: InterVarsity Press, 1981.

Hemer, C. J. *"Tyndale Bulletin:* Index to Volumes 1–30." Leicester, Eng.: Inter-Varsity Press, n.d.

McKim, Donald K. "The Authority and Role of Scripture: A Selected Bibliography." *TSF Bulletin* 5 (May/June 1982): S-1-2.

Martin, Ralph P. *New Testament Books for Pastors and Teachers.* Philadelphia: Westminster, 1984.

Osborne, Grant, ed. *An Annotated Bibliography on the Bible and the Church.* Deerfield, IL: Trinity Evangelical Divinity School, 1982.

———. "TSF Research—Bibliography: Redaction Criticism." Madison, WI: Theological Students Fellowship, 1977.

Scholer, David E. *A Basic Bibliographic Guide for New Testament Exegesis.* 2d ed. Grand Rapids: Eerdmans, 1973.

Smith, Wilbur M. *A Treasury of Books for Bible Study.* Natick, MA: W. A. Wilde, 1960.

Thiselton, A. C. *New Testament Commentary Series,* revised by D. A. Carson. Madison, WI: Theological Students Fellowship, 1977.

HISTORICAL

Armerding, Carl. *The Old Testament and Criticism.* Grand Rapids: Eerdmans, 1983.

Bailey, Warner M. "William Robertson Smith." *Journal of Presbyterian History 51* (1973): 285–308.

Balmer, Randall H. "The Princetonians and Scripture: A Reconsideration." *Westminster Theological Journal 44* (Spring 1982): 352–65.

Barr, David, and Nicholas Piediscalzi, eds. *The Bible in American Education.* Philadelphia: Fortress, 1982.

Barr, James. *Fundamentalism.* Philadelphia: Westminster, 1977.

———. *Beyond Fundamentalism: Biblical Foundations for Evangelical Christianity.* Philadelphia: Westminster, 1984.

———. "The Fundamentalist Understanding of Scripture." In *Conflicting Ways of Interpreting the Bible,* edited by Hans Küng and Jürgen Moltmann. New York: Seabury, 1980.

Bebbington, D. W. "The Persecution of George Jackson: A British Fundamentalist Controversy." *Persecution and Toleration,* Studies in Church History 21, edited by W. J. Shiels. Oxford: Oxford University Press, 1984.

Bowman, Raymond A. "Old Testament Research Between the Great Wars." In Willoughby, *The Study of the Bible.*

Bozeman, Theodore Dwight. *Protestants in an Age of Science: The Baconian Ideal and Antebellum American Religious Thought.* Chapel Hill: University of North Carolina Press, 1977.

Bratcher, Robert G. "The New International Version." *The Word of God: A Guide to English Versions of the Bible,* edited by Lloyd R. Bailey. Atlanta: John Knox, 1982.

Brown, Ira W. "The Higher Criticism Comes to America." *Journal of the Prebyterian Historical Society 38* (December 1960): 193–212.

Brown, Jerry Wayne. *The Rise of Biblical Criticism in America, 1800–1870.* Middletown, CT: Wesleyan University Press, 1969.

Bruce, F. F. *History of the Bible in English from the Earliest Versions.* 3d ed. New York: Oxford, 1975.

————. "The History of New Testament Study." In *New Testament Interpretation: Essays on Principles and Methods,* edited by I. Howard Marshall. Grand Rapids: Eerdmans, 1977.

————. *In Retrospect: Remembrance of Things Past.* Grand Rapids: Eerdmans, 1980.

Cameron, Nigel M. de S. "Inspiration and Criticism: The Nineteenth-Century Crisis." *Tyndale Bulletin 35* (1984): 129–59.

Carpenter, Joel A. "Fundamentalist Institutions and the Rise of Evangelical Protestantism." *Church History 49* (March 1980): 62–75.

Chadwick, Owen. *The Victorian Church.* 2d ed. London: A. & C. Black, 1972.

Clements, Ronald E. *One Hundred Years of Old Testament Interpretation.* Philadelphia: Westminster, 1976.

Craigie, Peter. "The Role and Relevance of Biblical Research." *Journal for the Study of the Old Testament 18* (1980): 19–31.

Drinkard, Joel Jr., and Page H. Kelley. "125 Years of Old Testament Study at Southern [Baptist Seminary]." *Review and Expositor 82* (Winter 1985): 7–19.

Dugmore, C. W., ed. *The Interpretation of the Bible.* London: SPCK, 1944.

Dunn, J. D. G. "The Authority of Scripture According to Scripture." *Churchman 96* (1982): 104–22, 201–25.

Ellis, Ieuan. *Seven Against Christ: A Study of "Essays and Reviews."* Leiden: E. J. Brill, 1980.

Ferichs, Ernest S., ed. *The Bible and Bibles in America.* Philadelphia: Fortress, forthcoming.

Filson, Floyd V. "The Study of the New Testament: Through Historical Study to Biblical Theology." In Nash, *Protestant Thought in the Twentieth Century.*

France, R. T. "Evangelical Disagreements About the Bible." *Churchman 96* (1982): 226–40.

————. "The Tyndale Fellowship—Then and Now." *TSF Bulletin 5* (January/February 1982): 12–13.

Fuller, Daniel P. "Interpretation, History Of." *The International Standard Bible Encyclopedia,* edited by Geoffrey W. Bromiley. Rev. ed. Grand Rapids: Eerdmans, 1979– .

Funk, Robert W. "The Watershed of American Biblical Tradition: The Chicago School, First Phase, 1892–1920." *Journal of Biblical Literature 95* (1976): 4–22.

Gaffin, Richard. "Introduction." *Redemptive History and Biblical Interpretation: The Shorter Writings of Geerhardus Vos.* Phillipsburg, NJ: Presbyterian and Reformed, 1980.

Gasque, W. Ward. "Evangelical Theology; The British Example." *Christianity Today* (August 10, 1973): 49–50.

———. *A History of the Criticism of the Acts of the Apostles.* Grand Rapids: Eerdmans, 1975,

———. "Nineteenth-Century Roots of Contemporary New Testament Criticism." In *Scripture, Tradition, and Interpretation,* edited by Gasque and William Sanford LaSor. Grand Rapids: Eerdmans, 1978.

Glover, Willis B. *Evangelical Nonconformists and Higher Criticism in the Nineteenth Century.* London: Independent Press, 1954.

Goldingay, John F. "James Barr on Fundamentalism." *Churchman 91* (1977): 295–308.

Grant, Robert M. "American New Testament Study, 1926–1956." *Journal of Biblical literature 87* (1968): 42–50.

———. *A Short History of the Interpretation of the Bible.* Rev. ed. New York: Macmillan, 1963.

Greenslade, S. L., ed. *The Cambridge History of the Bible, Vol. III: The West from the Reformation to the Present Day.* Cambridge: Cambridge University Press, 1963.

Gunn, Giles, ed. *The Bible in American Arts and Letters.* Philadelphia: Fortress, 1983.

Hagner, Donald A. "What is Distinctive About 'Evangelical' Scholarship?" *TSF Bulletin 7* (January/February 1984): 5–7.

Hatch, Nathan O. and Mark A. Noll, eds. *The Bible in America: Essays in Cultural History.* New York: Oxford, 1982.

Hatch, Nathan O. "Evangelicalism as a Democratic Movement." In Marsden, *Evangelicalism and Modern America.*

———. "*Sola Scriptura* and *Novus Ordo Seclorum.*" In Hatch, *The Bible in America.*

Hayes, John H. and Frederick C. Prussner. *Old Testament Theology: Its History and Development.* London: SCM Press, 1985.

Helm, Paul. "A Taproot of Radicalism." *Themelios 11* (September 1985): 18–22.

Henry, Carl F. H. "American Evangelicals and Theological Dialogue." *Christianity Today* (January 15, 1965): 27–29.

Hinson, E. Glenn. "Southern Baptists and the Liberal Tradition in Biblical Interpretation, 1845–1945." *Baptist History and Heritage 19* (July 1984): 16–20.

Howe, Claude L., Jr. "Southern Baptists and the Moderate Tradition in Biblical Interpretation, 1845–1945." *Baptist History and Heritage 19* (July 1984): 21–28.

Hutchison, William R. *The Modernist Impulse in American Protestantism.* Cambridge: Harvard University Press, 1976.

"The Issue of Biblical Authority Brings a Scholar's [J. Ramsey Michaels] Resignation." *Christianity Today* (July 15, 1983): 35–38.

Johnson, Douglas. *Contending for the Faith: A History of the Evangelical Movement in the Universities and Colleges.* Leicester, Eng.: Inter-Varsity Press, 1979.

Johnson, James T., ed. *The Bible in American Law, Politics, and Rhetoric.* Philadelphia: Fortress, 1985.

Johnston, Robert K. *Evangelicals at an Impasse: Biblical Authority in Perspective.* Atlanta: John Knox, 1979.

———, ed. *The Use of the Bible in Theology: Evangelical Options.* Atlanta: John Knox, 1985.

Jones, J. Estill. "The New Testament and Southern [Baptist Seminary]." *Review and Expositor 82* (Winter 1985): 21–29.

Kannengiesser, Charles, ed. *Bible de tous les temps, Vol. VIII: Le monde contemporain et la Bible.* Paris: Beauchesne, 1985.

Keylock, Leslie R. "Evangelical Scholars Remove Gundry for His Views on Matthew." *Christianity Today* (February 3, 1984): 36–38.

Kümmel, Werner Georg. *The New Testament: A History of the Investigation of Its Problems.* Nashville, Abingdon, 1972.

Ladd, George Eldon. *The New Testament and Criticism.* Grand Rapids: Eerdmans, 1967.

Lampe, G. W. H. "The Bible Since the Rise of Critical Study." In *The Church's Use of the Bible Past and Present,* edited by D. E. Nineham. London: SPCK, 1963.

Land, Richard D. "Southern Baptists and the Fundamentalist Tradition in Biblical Interpretation, 1845–1945." *Baptist History and Heritage 19* (July 1984): 29–32.

Langford, Thomas A. *In Search of Foundations: English Theology 1900–1920.* Nashville: Abingdon, 1969.

Larue, Gerald G. "Another Chapter in the History of Bible Translations: The Attacks Upon the Revised Standard Version." *Journal of Bible and Religion 31* (1963): 301–10.

Lightfoot, R. H. "The Critical Approach to the Bible in the Nineteenth Century." In Dugmore, *The Interpretation of the Bible.*

Livingstone, David N. *Darwin's Forgotten Defenders: The Encounter Between Evangelical Theology and Evolutionary Thought.* Grand Rapids: Eerdmans, 1986.

Loetscher, Lefferts A. *The Broadening Church: A Study of Theological Issues in the Presbyterian Church since 1869.* Philadelphia: University of Pennsylvania Press, 1957.

———. "C. A. Briggs in the Retrospect of Half a Century." *Theology Today 12* (April 1955): 27–42.

Lundin, Roger. "Our Hermeneutical Inheritance." In *The Responsibility of Hermeneutics,* by Lundin, Clarence Walhout, and Anthony C. Thiselton. Grand Rapids: Eerdmans, 1985.

McDonald, H. D. *Theories of Revelation: An Historical Study 1700–1960.* Grand Rapids: Baker, 1979. Incorporating *Ideas of Revelation, An Historical Study, A. D. 1700 to A. D. 1860* (1959) and *Theories of Revelation, An Historical Study, 1860–1960* (1963).

MacHaffie, Barbara Zink. " 'Monument Facts and Higher Critical Fancies': Archaeology and the Popularization of Old Testament Criticism in Nineteenth-Century Britain." *Church History 50* (September 1981): 316–28.

Manson, T. W. "The Failure of Liberalism to Interpret the Bible as the Word of God." In Dugmore, *The Interpretation of the Bible.*

Manwaring, Randle. *From Controversy to Coexistence: Evangelicals in the Church of England 1914–1980.* Cambridge: Cambridge University Press, 1985.

Maring, Norman H. "Baptists and Changing Views of the Bible, 1865–1918." *Foundations 1* (July 1958): 52–75, and (October 1958): 30–61.

Marsden, George M. "The Collapse of American Evangelical Academia." In *Faith and Rationality: Reason and Belief in God,* edited by Alvin Plantinga and Nicholas Wolterstorff. Notre Dame: University of Notre Dame Press, 1983.

———. "The Evangelical Denomination." In Marsden, *Evangelicals and Modern America.*

———. "Everyone One's Own Interpreter? The Bible, Science, and Authority in Mid-Nineteenth-Century America." In Hatch, *The Bible in America.*

———. *Fundamentalism and American Culture: The Shaping of Twentieth-Century Evangelicalism 1870–1925.* New York: Oxford, 1980.

———. "Fundamentalism as an American Phenomenon: A Comparison with English Evangelicalism." *Church History 46* (June 1977): 215–32.

———, ed. *Evangelicalism and Modern America.* Grand Rapids: Eerdmans, 1984.

Marshall, I. Howard. "F. F. Bruce as a Biblical Scholar." *Journal of the Christian Brethren Research Fellowship 22* (1971): 5–12.

Marty, Martin. "America's Iconic Book." In *Humanizing America's Iconic Book: Society of Biblical Literature Centennial Addresses 1980,* edited by Gene M. Tucker and Douglas A. Knight. Chico, CA: Scholars Press, 1982.

Mozley, John Kenneth. *Some Tendencies in British Theology from the Publication of "Lux Mundi" to the Present Day.* London: SPCK, 1951.

Nash, Arnold S., ed. *Protestant Thought in the Twentieth Century: Whence and Whither?* New York: Macmillan, 1951.

Nations, Archie. "Historical Criticism and the Current Methodological Crisis." *Scottish Journal of Theology 36* (1983): 59–71.

Neil, W. "The Criticism and Theological Use of the Bible 1700–1950." In Greenslade, *The Cambridge History of the Bible.*

Neill, Stephen. *The Interpretation of the New Testament 1861–1961*. Oxford: Oxford University Press, 1964.

Nelson, Ronald. "Higher Criticism and the Westminster Confession: The Case of William Robertson Smith." *Christian Scholar's Review 8* (1978): 199–216.

Nelson, Rudolph L. "Fundamentalism at Harvard: The Case of Edward John Carnell." *Quarterly Review 2* (Summer 1982): 79–98.

Nicole, Roger. "The Inspiration and Authority of Scripture: J. D. G. Dunn versus B. B. Warfield." *Churchman 97* (1983): 198–215, and 98 (1984): 7–27, 198–216.

Noll, Mark A. "Common Sense Traditions and American Evangelical Thought." *American Quarterly 37* (Summer 1985): 216–38.

———. "Evangelicals and the Study of the Bible." In Marsden, *Evangelicalism and Modern America.*

Olbricht, Thomas (Abilene Christian University). "The Society of Biblical Literature: The Founding Fathers"; "The First Ten Years of the *Journal of Biblical Literature:* An Analysis of Content"; "Biblical Primitivism in American Biblical Scholarship, 1630–1870." Unpublished papers.

Parvis, Merrill. "New Testament Criticism in the World-Wars Period." In Willoughby, *The Study of the Bible.*

Phy, Allene S., ed. *The Bible and Popular Culture in America.* Philadelphia: Fortress, 1985.

Pollock, J. C. *A Cambridge Movement* [Cambridge Inter-Collegiate Christian Union and Inter-Varsity Christian Fellowship]. London: John Murray, 1953.

Ramm, Bernard. *After Fundamentalism: The Future of Evangelical Theology.* San Francisco: Harper & Row, 1983.

"Redaction Criticism: Is It Worth the Risk?" A symposium discussion of the Christianity Today Institute, *Christianity Today* (October 18, 1985): insert 1–12.

Reid, J. K. S. *The Authority of Scripture: A Study of the Reformation and Post-Reformation Understanding of the Bible.* New York: Harper and Brothers, n.d.

Rennie, Ian. "Mixed Metaphors, Misunderstood Models, and Puzzling Paradigms: A Contemporary Effort to Correct Some Current Misunderstandings Regarding the Authority and Interpretation of the Bible, An Historical Response." Paper at conference on "Interpreting an Authoritative Scirpture," Institute for Christian Studies, Toronto, June 1981.

Richardson, Alan. "The Rise of Modern Biblical Scholarship and Recent Discussion of the Authority of the Bible." In Greenslade, *The Cambridge History of the Bible.*

Riesen, Richard A. *Criticism and Faith in Late Victorian Scotland: A. B. Davidson, William Robertson Smith and George Adam Smith.* Lanham, MD: University Press of America, 1985.

———. " 'Higher Criticism' in the Free Church Fathers." *Records of the Scottish Church History Society* 20 (1973): 119–42.

Roberts, Robert C. *Rudolf Bultmann's Theology: A Critical Interpretation.* Grand Rapids: Eerdmans, 1976.

Rogers, Jack B. and Donald K. McKim. *The Authority and Interpretation of the Bible: An Historical Approach.* San Francisco: Harper & Row, 1979.

Rogerson, John. *Old Testament Criticism in the Nineteenth Century: England and Germany.* Philadelphia: Fortress, 1984.

Rosman, Doreen. *Evangelicals and Culture.* Dover, NH: Croom Helm, 1984.

Rowley, H. H., ed. *The Old Testament and Modern Study: A Generation of Discovery and Research.* Oxford: Clarendon, 1951.

Rylaarsdam, J. Coert. "Introduction: The Chicago School—and After." In *Transitions in Biblical Scholarship,* edited by Rylaarsdam. Chicago: University of Chicago Press, 1968.

Sandeen, Ernest R. *The Roots of Fundamentalism: British and American Millenarianism, 1800–1930.* Chicago: University of Chicago Press, 1970.

———, ed. *The Bible and Social Reform.* Philadelphia: Fortress, 1982.

Saunders, Ernest W. *Searching the Scriptures: A History of the Society of Biblical Literature, 1880–1980.* Chicago, CA: Scholars Press, 1982.

Silva, Moises. "Ned B. Stonehouse and Redaction Criticism." *Westminster Theological Journal 40* (Fall 1977): 77–88, and (Spring 1978): 281–303.

Stackhouse, John G., Jr. "Lost in Space: *The Fundamentals* and the Polarization of American Theology, 1910–1925." Seminar paper, University of Chicago, 1983.

Stonehouse, Ned B. *J. Gresham Machen: A Biographical Memoir.* Grand Rapids: Eerdmans, 1954.

Szasz, Ferenc Morton. *The Divided Mind of Protestant America, 1880–1930.* University, AL: University of Alabama Press, 1982.

Turner, David L. "Evangelicals, Redaction Criticism, and the Current Inerrancy Crisis." *Grace Theological Journal 4* (1983): 263–88.

———. "Evangelicals, Redaction Criticism, and Inerrancy: The Debate Continues." *Grace Theological Journal 5* (1984): 37–45.

Wacker, Grant. *Augustus H. Strong and the Dilemma of Historical Consciousness.* Macon, GA: Mercer University Press, 1985.

———. "The Demise of Biblical Civilization." In Hatch, *The Bible in America.*

Walsh, Brian J. "Anthony Thiselton's Contribution to Biblical Hermeneutics." *Christian Scholar's Review 14* (1985): 224–35.

Wells, David F. "An American Evangelical Theology: The Painful Transition from *Theoria* to *Praxis.* " In Marsden, *Evangelicalism and Modern America.*

Weber, Timothy P. "The Two-Edged Sword: The Fundamentalist Use of the Bible." In Hatch, *The Bible in America.*

Wenham, Gordon. "History and the Old Testament." In *History, Critism and Faith,* edited by Colin Brown. Downers Grove, IL: InterVarsity Press, 1976.

Wilder, Amos N. "New Testament Studies, 1920–1950: Reminiscences of a Changing Discipline." *The Journal of Religion 64* (October 1984): 432–51.

Willoughby, Harold R. *The Study of the Bible Today and Tomorrow.* Chicago: University of Chicago Press, 1947.

Woodbridge, John D. *Biblical Authority: A Critique of the Rogers-McKimn Proposal.* Grand Rapids: Zondervan, 1982.

———. "Evangelicals and the Bible." In *The Gospel in America: Themes in the Story of America's Evangelicals,* by Woodbridge, Mark A. Noll, and Nathan O. Hatch. Grand Rapids: Zondervan, 1979.

Woodbridge, John D., and Randall H. Balmer. "The Princetonians and Biblical Authority: An Assessment of the Ernest Sandeen Proposal." In *Scripture and Truth,* edited by Woodbridge and D. A. Carson. Grand Rapids: Zondervan, 1983.

Wright, David F. "Soundings in the Doctrine of Scripture in British Evangelicalism in the First Half of the Twentieth Century." *Tyndale Bulletin 31* (1980): 87–106.

Wright, G. Ernest. "The Study of the Old Testament: The Changing Mood in the House of Wellhausen." See Nash, *Protestant Thought in the Twentieth Century.*

Index